One Family's Journey through Time

1845 - Present

By R. G. (Jerry) Tidwell

Published by:
Bluewater Publications
1812 CR 111
Killen, Alabama 35645
www.BluewaterPublications.com

Dedication

This book is not only dedicated to **Virgiline Tidwell Hale**, a cousin and long time friend, who most graciously shared her stories, treasured photographs and recipes with me, it is also dedicated to other family members that I knew and loved dearly while growing up and whose stories I have tried to tell. They willingly gave me the guidance, love, nurturing and correction that a young inquisitive boy needs while growing up.

It is also dedicated to my lovely wife of 39 years, **Lana Alsman Tidwell.**

Lana Alsman Tidwell at home about 1995

Lana has stuck by me all of these years and has taken all of my antics pretty much in stride. She never lets me forget any of my mistakes and heaven knows there have been plenty.

I have not told all of my stories in this book because I don't want to be locked up either in an insane asylum or in jail!

Acknowledgments

I wish to offer my most sincere appreciation to the people who helped and encouraged me in this effort.

First of all, the members of the Scottsboro Advanced Writers group who are all friends and writing associates. They acted as a sounding board for some of my stories. I wish to most specifically thank the following:

Ann Chambless the leader of our group who was most encouraging to me every step of the way and helped in editing. She offered me many suggestions which I appreciated and tried to act on.

Cathy Palmer who helped me clean up my hillbilly English and also helped in editing.

Ilena Holder who offered me encouragement and also helped in editing.

Last but not least, I offer my thanks to **Doxie Oliver Tidwell** (Uncle Doc) for instilling his love of woodworking with simple hand tools and gardening to me at an early age. I started to develop my roots and learned many of the traits from "Uncle Doc" that have shaped my thoughts, decisions and actions for much of my life and still do today. I also wish to thank his daughter, **Virgiline Tidwell Hale,** who most generously offered her stories, recipes and shared her treasured photographs. I have included a lot of them.

Also my sister **Ann Crittenden** who jogged my memory about some of the details of the stories that I had forgotten and helped me do some of the research.

Cover Acknowledgment

The Reid Sisters

Left to Right: Maud Reid Young, Beulah Reid Moomaw, Alice Genova Reid Tidwell, and Maggie Earline Reid Tidwell. Taken mid '50s.

Two of the Reid sisters, Grandmother Alice and Aunt Mag play a pivotal role in this book.

Their grandfather, Christopher Columbus Everett Reid, in his Confederate uniform is on the cover. It is the oldest photograph that exists in the family. It was an old tintype that was one of Aunt Mag's treasures. She let me borrow it so that I could have Jim Eiford copy it. Virgiline Tidwell Hale currently has it.

Their father, John Wesley Reid, was C.C.E. Reid's son.

John Wesley was a very colorful person as was his father. The Reid family will be the subject of another work.

The Reid family is summarized in Part Two as "The Reid Connection."

Preface

The setting of this book is Northern Alabama. The story could have taken place anywhere with the trail of immigrants from Pennsylvania down through the Appalachians into Virginia, North Carolina, Tennessee, South Carolina and Georgia. All of our ancestors from that time shared pretty much the same struggles to survive and many of the same type of experiences. These stories could have happened anywhere in northern Mississippi, Alabama, Georgia, and all across Tennessee, Virginia, the Carolinas and all across the Appalachian Mountains. One only has to change the names of the characters of this story to those of his ancestors to make much of this book relevant to their family's journey through time all across frontier America.

Research on the Tidwell family has been an active project for various members of the family for a number of years. General William A. Tidwell did a lot of work on the family during and after World War II, tracing them back in England and to Virginia and across America to Warren County, Tennessee. Family members David and Joyce Grigsby have traced our particular ancestors back from North Alabama to Warren County, TN. Reuben Tidwell was an only child and was born in Westmoreland County, Virginia. He moved to Warren County Tennessee along with several children that were also born in Virginia. He had several sons and daughters, among them was Robert Tidwell. Robert was the father of Richard T. Tidwell and John Dee Tidwell as well as several other children. All of the early family members were very prolific and had numerous children. It was mind boggling for me when I realized while doing research for this book just how many branches of our family there actually are. We are now spread all across the United States.

There are those who have traced and entered the family lineage on Ancestry.com and familysearch.org back to Warren of Tideswell, born 1238 and died 1299 in England.

I don't know about all of this as it happened centuries before I came along. I have limited what is reported in this book to what I actually know from growing up in the area, associating with the old timers and the stories they told me about their parents.

This book is truly a journey through time for our family. It starts in 1845 with the birth of our family patriarch, Richard T. Tidwell. There are photographs and stories covering members from six generations. It also touches on Richard T. Tidwell's younger brother John Dee Tidwell's family.

The purpose of my starting this work was to preserve some of these memories and family stories before they get lost in the deep endless black bog of time. They can never be fully reconstructed once the older generation dies or their memory starts to fade. I started one generation earlier than the people I knew and lived around while growing up. I have recorded some of the stories they relayed to me about Richard T. and John Dee Tidwell.

There are photographs in the Family Memorial section of the grave markers for all names marked with an asterisk (*).

Table of Contents

Part One

Although we can trace our ancestors back in time
Sometimes pretty far
We can determine where they came from, something about their station in life,
Things they had to do to survive, how they lived
And in many cases something about their failures and accomplishments
We still cannot use this as a map or plan for our own life
We have to live that ourselves in our own way
Only faith, hard work, dedication, determination and perseverance
Can influence our outcome
We must all take time out occasionally to smell the roses
Or our own life will turn out uneventful

The author

1

Memories and Tidwell Family Stories

Introduction

Becky

There I was, laying at least twenty feet from the gravel road, flat of my back in a freshly plowed rocky field with stars swirling before my eyes. The pain from each stone beneath me and pressing into my body was very intense. I noticed that the seams of both legs of my prized almost outgrown tight fitting blue jeans were split from my knees to my thighs when I tried to sit up. Becky's hoof beats on the gravel road as she headed back to the barn reminded me of what I was doing there, all sprawled out on my back in that rocky field with split jeans and seeing stars before my eyes.

This was not my first encounter with a frisky horse but was my last. I have never mounted another horse since that time. I sold Becky shortly afterwards!

Why was my family so enamored with horses and other livestock? The answer did not become clear to me for fifty years or so afterward and only then when I was writing this book.

The Race Horse

My first encounter with a frisky horse happened when I was a senior in high school. One of Finney Gray's brothers, that could sell ice to Eskimos, had a beautiful large black mare that he claimed was the best saddle horse ever to hit the Brush Creek area. This horse was certainly the most beautiful one that I had ever seen. Its hair seemed to glow and glisten in the sunlight.

Needless to say, I was delighted when dad traded for this horse.

Dad wanted me to ride it one Saturday shortly after he brought it home. Never mind that this was supposed to be a high stepping saddle horse and we had no saddle, I could take it around the circular bottom behind the old log house bareback. I just had to trot it around a little bit so that dad could see how it moved. I had never seen dad ride a horse and never did. He just encouraged my brothers and me to ride the horses that he brought home!

Dad caught this horse and put a bridle on it. We then led it out into the bottom and I started to pet it and calm it down a little bit. The horse looked the circular bottom over and I slid up on its back. The horse sat there for a little while with me urging it on before it started to move. It did not trot in a high stepping manner at all. It broke into a full run around the circular field. I watched the blackberry briars and brambles flash by and dug my knees in as tightly as I could. I was not riding this horse Indian style at this point, I was just trying to hold on and keep from being thrown into the blackberry briars. I just knew that I would be cut into shreds if I landed in them.

I thought this horse was running as fast as it could but I was wrong. It turned up the steam and really starting going fast when we reached what would have been the backstretch of a racetrack. That was the fastest running horse I have ever seen. The faster it ran, the tighter I dug my knees in and the harder I just tried to hold on!

I was still on the horse's back when we got back to where we started and the horse decided that our ride was over. It wheeled and I suddenly found myself going in our original direction while the horse just stopped to watch me as I sailed into a brush pile. I bounced around in the brush pile for a little bit and finally came to rest with the back of my head on a large log. Fortunately the large log was rotten and just crumbled under my head.

Dad came running over and asked if I was alright. I didn't know but started to get up and dust myself off. The horse was still watching and it gave a loud and long whinny, sort of like a horse laugh.

It became evident to all of us that dad had not bought a high stepping saddle horse; he had bought a racehorse.

I was so beat up that I could hardly walk at school the next week. I would just painfully hobble around ever so slowly when I had to move between classes. Some of my friends asked me why I was walking so funny but none of them believed me when I tried to tell them what had happened.

I was walking almost normally by the end of the week!

None of us ever tried to ride this horse again. Dad finally sold it to a gentleman who owned the company that made *Sweet Sue* canned chickens. There was a picture of this man's daughter, "Sweet Sue" riding a horse that looked just like our horse on the labels of his canned chickens. Dad just repeated the line that Finney Gray's brother had given him and never told the man that he was perhaps buying a racehorse.

We were very glad the horse was gone. Dad made a little money off of the trade. I always wondered about "Sweet Sue's" surprise the first time she tried to ride the horse.

Back to Becky

Dad was always going to the mule barn in Saint Joseph, Tennessee, to buy scraggly horse colts that the owner had gotten from somewhere by the truckload. He was the local mule and horse trader and always seemed to have a steady supply of these scraggly colts. Dad would always feed them well and get my younger brothers and their friends to groom the colts and break them in to ride a little bit. I was in college by then and did not participate much in this endeavor. Dad would then sell the colts for a profit and go back to the mule barn to buy some more.

I went with dad on one of his buying trips. The owner had a beautiful chestnut filly that he said was a thoroughbred. He told me he would get me the registration papers on her and took me around behind the barn and taught me the fine art of horse trading. Never trust anything that a horse seller tells you about a horse. He is flat out lying between his teeth just to make a sale!

We agreed on what was more than a fair price for a registered horse colt, $125.00. I was to pick up the registration papers from him in about two weeks.

I went back the first time and the owner told me that the papers had not arrived yet.

I went back the second time and he had changed his story. He said this time that he had never said he could produce the papers, he had just said that the horse could be registered. He would not back down from his story even after a heated argument. There were no witnesses since the deal had been struck out behind the barn!

I named the filly Becky after one of my first college sweethearts.

I began to groom Becky and get her used to me. We still did not have a saddle but she broke easily to being ridden bareback.

She was really too young to train but I did not know it at the time. I rode her around the barnyard for a while and then decided to take her out on the gravel road up by our house. She did not want to leave the barn and would start to turn around in the road in circles until I could finally coax her to go a little bit further.

We finally got to where she was comfortable in going up to Uncle Doc's house before she refused to budge any further.

I was finally able to get her to ride about a mile and a half from the barn without difficulty.

On this particular morning she would not go any farther up the road than the freshly plowed field. Dad had put up an electric fence around the field to keep out any stray livestock.

Becky started doing her circling movements again and got closer and closer to the electric fence. She finally brushed against the electric fence and exploded. This was why I was 20 or more feet from the gravel road in the rocky plowed field with split blue jeans, stars before my eyes, and Becky hoofing it hastily toward the barn!

I had closed the gate to the barnyard as we left. I don't know if Becky jumped the gate to get back in or not but she must have. She was in the barnyard when I got back and the gate was still closed. She was agitated but I was finally able to catch her and remove the bridle.

I was getting too busy in college to continue with Becky's training. Anyway the original Becky was no longer my sweetheart. I sold *Becky the Second* for my original $125.00 and this ended my career as a horseman.

It became evident to me while writing this book that our family having to rely so heavily on livestock to survive had engrained this love of livestock in all of us. We depended on chickens for eggs and meat, cows for milk, butter and meat, horses and mules to ride and pull our plows and other farm equipment and pigs for our beloved cured smoked pork.

This dependence and love of livestock still resonates through much of our family as it did in Richard T. Tidwell's time. This dependence and love must have existed since the first Europeans came to America and had to have existed in the old countries as well.

My Early Family Memories

The following are memories and stories of family members that I witnessed and heard while growing up on Brush Creek in Lauderdale County, Alabama.

The purpose of this exercise is to document some of the stories, conversations and interactions that I had while growing up. My sister Ann and I are the oldest people left in the family with some of this knowledge. Ann is eighteen months younger than I am and she does not remember some of this material. I knew these people. Later family members never got the opportunity to know them or hear their stories. Some of my brothers are up to twenty years younger than I am.

There are a lot of questions that I now wish that I had asked and pressed for answers from these old timers but never did. Their answers are now buried with them in either the Tidwell or the Cox Cemeteries near where they lived.

This work starts with Richard T. Tidwell, our family patriarch. It details his children, except the four daughters from his first marriage. I never knew any of these daughters with the exception of Bama Hale, but some of their descendants visited from time to time. I think they wanted to keep in contact with the old family home place.

Everything in the South seems to date from the Civil War. Richard T. fought in this uprising as is documented later. Nathan Jerry, my grandfather, was born 29 years after the Civil War and Grandmother Alice was born 33 years after it was over. They learned how to farm, keep house and do the things for survival from their ancestors and they in turn had learned from theirs.

Many of my memories while growing up are based on the old log house and the everyday things we had to do to survive. Many of the old items that we used daily possibly date to Richard T's time. I know that an old grain cradle that I have does, as well as an old spigot for use with a wooden barrel. I am sure that many of the things we did such as soap making, cooking, washing clothes and the way we preserved meat date back pretty much to colonial times.

I was born in June of 1942, seventy-seven years after the end of the Civil War. I left the area in July of 1966. I have never returned except for visits. These memories encompass a span of twenty-four or so years while I was growing up.

As stated earlier, our family patriarch was Richard T. Tidwell. I never did know what the initial *T* stood for. He fought in the Civil War on the Confederate side according to family lore. I later heard that he was in something like the home guard. I often wondered if he was not in one of the groups that are described in *"The Bugger Saga"* which was still in print in paperback not many years ago. I have owned several copies of this work but have loaned them to various family members and didn't know if I still had one. I was finally able to find a copy after a long search of all of the boxes of family data that I have. It describes the turbulent times in the area during this period of time up into the early 20th century. It was written by Dr. Maurice Pruitt, M.D. who used the name Wade Pruitt and the copy I finally found was published by P-Vine Press. It can be ordered from Mrs. Polly C. Warren, Route 7, Box 264, Columbia, Tennessee, 38401. The phone number is listed as 615-388-1965. It is well worth reading. This book describes people and things that happened in the Shoals area during these awful times. I am sure that the same or similar happenings occurred in north Mississippi, Alabama, Georgia and southern Tennessee during this time.

Richard T. Tidwell settled on a small farm situated on Brush Creek in Lauderdale County, Alabama, shortly after the Civil War. He and his brother, John Dee Tidwell, both settled there. Richard built his house near the creek in what bottom land there was while John Dee built his house on the hill above. Brush Creek ran through both properties. The area, except for the low land along the creek, is hilly and not very suitable for farming.

But they did farm the hillsides and scratched out a living for themselves and their families.

Richard T. got his water from springs along the creek. There were three springs on the hill west of the house that were on his property while there were three more springs on the hill east of his house but were not on his property. John Dee had to dig a well for his water. His well house was still standing until recently while Richard's spring house fell during a thunderstorm in the late '40s. Both were sided with elaborate lattice work. The lattice siding was later whitewashed. I remember that the spring that Richard T. used as the primary source for water came out of a hill about two and one-half to three feet up into the side. It had been dammed up with a small concrete dam and had about a one inch pipe coming out of it to deliver water. A lot of water from this spring and a nearby spring ran through the spring house. The spring house had a concrete floor and there were recesses in the floor to put milk jars in to keep them cold and/or other items as well. Someone in the years before my time had planted ivy around the spring. It covered the hill around the spring for some way up the hillside.

I remember as a child accompanying grandmother Alice, Aunt Jane and my mother to the spring to gather buckets of water. We had to walk across a foot log to get across the creek. The foot log was actually a springy, bouncy, two by twelve. It is a wonder that none of us ever fell off of the foot log into the creek. The bottom of this shallow creek was solid flint rock. We could have broken bones if we had fallen.

The bucket we used for drinking water was made of red cedar and was held together with metal straps of some kind. We all drank from a dipper that was kept in the bucket. The cedar bucket was made entirely of the heart of red cedar. It gave the water a very pleasant taste as it sat there waiting for all of us to drink from it.

There were numerous clumps of wild spearmint growing along the creek. The leaves made a very pleasing summer drink when crushed and mixed in cold spring water with some sugar added. The old timers called it "horse mint."

There were several clumps of what we called spider lilies on the east side of the creek by the foot log. They were especially pretty when they bloomed. I have never seen lilies like them since. They are long gone along with everything else.

6

Uncle Doc and Aunt Mag were our nearest neighbors. They had a well near their house for their water and another well in a well house about one hundred feet away. They used this second well to keep things cold. They would lower their milk or whatever into the well by means of a bucket. Uncle Doc was Doxie Oliver, one of John Dee's sons, and Aunt Mag was our Grandmother Alice's youngest sister, Maggie Earline. Dad always called her Aunt Lindy, for what reason I do not know.

Dad and I were visiting Richard T.'s grave years later. It was on the high point of the hill west of the old house. The graveyard had been overgrown but Dad and his cousins William Tidwell and Ollie Tidwell, with my financial assistance, had cleaned it up and put a chain link fence around it. Most of the old farm was visible from up there. After surveying the barren fields that were largely covered with sage grass and scrubby blackberry briars I asked Dad, "How did anyone ever make a living off of this place?"

Dad's reply was, "Nobody ever made a living here, son, they only survived."

Nobody knew where either Richard T. or John Dee came from, at least nobody on Richard T's side of the family. I asked this question to all of the old timers who knew him while he was alive and they simply said they didn't know. They either had something to hide or it was not important enough to them to discuss with their family. Perhaps it took so much energy out of them scratching out a living from those hillsides that they didn't have enough energy left to discuss such matters. Perhaps they were very private. To a young boy growing up this led to all sorts of possibilities for his imagination. They lived just a short distance from the Tennessee state line. Were they horse thieves, gun runners, or were they hiding due to their activities during the Civil War? They certainly picked a good place to hide out if that was what they were doing. This area was very remote even when I was growing up some eighty to ninety years later. I didn't realize until much later that John Dee was much too young to be in the Civil War. Anyway, this was food for all sorts of fantasies for a young inquisitive boy with a very vivid imagination.

I never discovered the truth until I started doing research for this book. The truth is not as exciting as some of my fantasies were while growing up.

Research on the Tidwell family has been an active project for various members of the family for a number of years. Brigadier General William A. Tidwell did a lot of work on the family during and after World War II tracing them back in England and to Virginia and across America to Warren County, Tennessee. Family members David and Joyce Grigsby have traced our particular ancestors back from North Alabama to Warren County, Tennessee. Reuben Tidwell was an only child and was born in Westmoreland County, Virginia. He moved to Warren County Tennessee along with several children that were also born in Virginia. He had several sons and daughters. Among them was Robert Tidwell. Robert was the father of Richard T. Tidwell and John Dee Tidwell as well as several other children. All of the early family members were very prolific and had numerous children. It was mind boggling for me when I realized while doing research for this book just how many branches of our family there actually are. We are now spread all across the United States.

The last time that I looked there were those who had traced and entered the family lineage on familysearch.org back to William Tideswell (born 1230) of Tideswell, Derbyshire England. His father is now listed as Warenus Tideswell born about 1208 of Tideswell, Derbyshire England.

I don't know about all of this as it happened centuries before I came along.

Except for a brief summary of the very early Tidwells in England and America as well as Reuben Tidwell's family, I have limited what is reported in this book to what I actually know from growing up in the area, associating with the old timers and the stories they told me about their parents. I offer a longer summary from Reuben Tidwell's family since many of the old timers that I knew while growing up may have known some of these people or at least had heard stories of them. They just never talked about them.

Early Tidwells in England and America.

This summary deals somewhat with internet research but primarily offers comments from Brigadier General William Albert Tidwell that he generated from doing genealogical research the hard way. Through hard work in locating original documents.

General William A. Tidwell published several books on mostly military subjects. Some of them are still listed for sale on Amazon.com. I think they are all out of print and what Amazon.com offers are mostly limited copies of new books and some used copies.

Virginia Military Institute has a collection of miscellaneous papers and memorabilia from Brigadier General W. A. Tidwell. I will type it as it is listed in their listing of *"Letters, Diaries, and Manuscript Guide. VMI Faculty and Alumni Papers."*

"Tidwell W. A., papers (MS # 0426)
Miscellaneous papers (seventeen items) of Brigadier General William Albert Tidwell Jr., USA. (1918 - 1999). Tidwell was a graduate of the Virginia Military Class of 1939. During his military career he worked primarily as an Intelligence officer and was assigned to the Central Intelligence Agency in the 1950's and 1960's. The collection includes four routine letters (1965 - 1968) from General William Westmoreland to Tidwell; Tidwell's Legion of Merit citation and certificate awarded for his service as Chief of Reconnaissance and Photographic Intelligence Division in Viet Nam, 1964 and 1965; other certificates and citations; 3 photographs. BG Tidwell died in June of 1999."

The author is privileged to have copies of two partial manuscripts from BG Tidwell detailing his research on the Tidwell Family.

The first one came to me by my first cousin Marti Tidwell Randall of West Camp, NY, and I don't know where she obtained it. She is recovering from two strokes just now and I don't know when or if she will ever be able to tell me. It is a partial copy of a 1955 article published by W. A. Tidwell in possibly the Virginia Genealogist.

In this article he details the movement of the early Tidwells in Virginia, their land transactions and their dealings with their neighbors. He even offers a copy of a will written by Robert

Tidwell dated as follows. The will is typed and the spelling, grammar and punctuation is preserved and is the same as General Tidwell typed it, apparently preserving that used in the original will.

"In the name of God Amen, I Robert Tidwell of Cople Parish in Westmoreland County in the Colony of Virginia, being weak of body but sound of perfect sence and memory (blessed be God for it) do make ordain and declare this to be my last will & testament in manner and form following hereby revoking and making void all former Wills and testaments by me made , dated by me at my house in the parish and County afore said this twenty seventh day of September in the year of our Lord Christ One Thousand seven hundred and fifty seven, and in the thirty first of the reign of Our sovereign Lord George the second of great Britain France and Ireland King Defender of the ----." I must be missing the next page as the sentence was not finished. The next page goes into the distribution of his goods to various people. He bequeaths his lands, slaves, horses, cattle, sheep and other livestock to various people. He even made special disposition for several slaves, which the will names as a girl called Frank, Judith, George, Lucy, Jack, Jean, and the wench called "Plumber's Judy." Other slaves he did not name but listed who would get certain numbers. He even left about forty-six pounds (that is in my house) to his son William (Carr Tidwell) and his heirs forever to purchase a "good young negro fellow." The will specified that funds be used from his crops if "that sum should not be sufficient to purchase a good young Negro fellow, my will and desire is that there shall be money raised out of my crops the sum that shall be wanting in making that purchase." He even willed furniture and clothing such as my fustian coat, thicken waistcoat, bear skin coat, camblet waistcoat, two pair of cloth breeches, hats, shoes, stockings and one fine shirt."

William Carr Tidwell's will was probated on March 9, 1774. His only child, Reuben Tidwell inherited most of his father's estate. In 1786, Reuben's personal property included five horses, thirty cattle, nine grown slaves and eleven slave children. This was well above the average number of slaves owned in the county.

Due to hard times hitting the area, Reuben sold off some of his slaves and finally on February 12, 1812, Reuben sold his entire property on Machodoc Creek This is the last report of the Tidwell family in Virginia.

According to the census of 1810, Reuben Tidwell had two sons and three daughters but their names were not given. Tennessee was being settled at that time and there is a record of a land grant to Reuben Tidwell in Warren County, Tennessee in 1824. There is also a record of service performed by Mark Tidwell in the Tennessee Militia during the war of 1812 and Mark appears to be Reuben Tidwell's eldest son.

The second manuscript came to me by my first cousin Marti Tidwell Randall and was sent to her on February 1, 1988, by Jewell Donato of 44 A Weaver Street, Greenwich, CT 06830. This was a copy of a letter written by General W. A. Tidwell on January 23, 1990, to someone he addressed it to as Dear Cousin. He was still researching and trying to trace various members of the family at that time. He said that "after puzzling for about twenty years, the obvious thought finally occurred to me" and he elaborates upon that point. He elaborates on twenty-eight different bits of information and facts which he called scenarios. He was searching for Presley Tidwell and also makes mention of Richard 1 Tidwell, Richard 2 Tidwell and Richard 3 Tidwell. It is seven pages long and gives short summaries and details of his work on the Tidwell family to that date. General Tidwell was living at 3701 Blackthorn Court, Chevy Chase, Maryland at that time.

It is unknown to the author if General W. A. Tidwell ever published any of his genealogical work except for that mentioned in the first manuscript that I have. Remember that he died in June of 1999, a little over nine years after this letter was written.

I have used excerpts from both documents in the following.

The author will start with the earliest Tidwell Immigrant from England as listed on familysearch.org. The names and lineage agree closely with what General W. A. Tidwell had determined from his research. The only difference detected is the name of William Carr Tidwell's wife. General Tidwell could not determine it for certain from searching available old records. He surmised that William Carr Tidwell could have married his brother John's widow Anne Barbara Tidwell. The family tree on familysearch.org lists William Carr Tidwell's wife as Anne Barbary Muse. Could Muse have been her maiden name or the surname of her first husband? If so she was married three times according to General Tidwell.

The internet lineage, along with some pertinent comments from the manuscripts that I have from him, are as follows:

1. The first of our lineage in America was **Richard 1 Tidwell** born about 1636 Alton Parish, Denstone, Staff, England, died 1689 at Cople Parish, immigrated from England to Virginia as an indentured servant. He was the son of Robert (Tideswall) Tiddeswall born 1601 Alton Parish, Denstone, Staff, England and died after 1635 in England. His mother was Marie Marsh born Ellastone Parish, Staff, England and she died after 1639. They were married in Denstone, Staff, England on 28 January, 1633.

Richard 1 Tidwell's contract was bought by a man with the last name of Nelms who lived at the head of the Great Wicomico River in Northumberland County. Richard 1 Tidwell was brought at about age eighteen to the Wicomico in 1656 where his contract was bought by Nelms. Richard 1 Tidwell must have established a reputation for reliability and Nelms put him to work on his other property on the Yeocomico River where he would be working with almost no supervision. He may have continued working there on a wage or share basis after his indenture expired in 1661.

On May 9, 1674 Richard 1 Tidwell married Anna Barnett, age seventeen or younger. Presumably they met at the Yeocomico Church, which was two miles north of Richard 1 Tidwell and was the nearest church to Farnham Creek at that time. Anna was born in 1657 at Farnham Creek, Richmond, Virginia, died 1699, Westmoreland, Virginia.

2. The second in our lineage in America was **Robert Tidwell**, son of Richard 1 Tidwell and Anna Barnett, and the author of the previously mentioned will. Robert Tidwell was born 1690, in Cople Parish, Westmoreland, Virginia and died 29 July, 1761 in Cople Parish, Westmoreland, Virginia. He married in 1718 Hanna (Ann) Carr in Westmoreland, Virginia. Hanna was born about 1692 in Cople Parish, Westmoreland, Virginia and died 28 July 1761 in Cople Parish, Westmoreland, Virginia.

Hanna Carr was the daughter of William Carr, a prosperous planter of Westmoreland, Virginia.

3. The third in our lineage in America was **William Carr Tidwell**, the eldest son of Robert Tidwell and Hanna Carr Tidwell.

William Carr Tidwell was born about 1720 in Tidwell, Westmoreland, Virginia and died 29 March 1774 in Cople Parish, Westmoreland, Virginia.

He married about 1758 Anne Barbary Muse (Anne Barbara Tidwell?). Anne was born about 1723 in Tidwell, Westmoreland, Virginia and died 28 March 1786 in Cople Parish Westmoreland, Virginia.

I quote a little more freely from the article by General W. A. Tidwell about William Carr Tidwell as follows: "The house occupied by William Carr Tidwell, and probably built by him, survived until 1947 when it burned. It was a four room, two story house with a chimney at each end and a gently sloping roof. One fireplace was about eight feet long. According to local tradition, this house was known as the "Manor House." It was the central part of a group of plantation buildings such as kitchen, smoke house, laundry, etc., whose foundations are still buried nearby although the buildings themselves disappeared years ago. The house was not a mansion like Stratford or Naomi but was a neat and prosperous establishment.

William Carr Tidwell was a gentleman planter, neighbor to the Washingtons, Lees, Turbervilles and Carters. His property on Machodoc Creek eventually encompassed 373 acres and became the site for a small village that is still known as Tidwells', Virginia. The survival of the name and locality suggests that the place must have had some local prominence.

William Carr Tidwell would have been about forty when his father died. His son Reuben Tidwell was born in 1766 or 1767. In other words, he was probably married sometime between 1760 and 1765 and had only one child. He died in 1774 and although he left considerable property there is no record of a Mrs. Tidwell who can be identified as his widow except for a brief entry in the accounting rendered by the executors of his estate. The only Tidwell widow living during the period that appears in the records was Anne Barbara Tidwell, Widow of John Tidwell. Could it be that William Carr Tidwell married his brother's widow and became her third husband? If that were the case she would have been about forty when Reuben was born, accounting perhaps for the failure of William Carr Tidwell to have more than one child."

Reuben Tidwell's Family

This summary deals with primarily internet research but offers a few comments from Brigadier General William Albert Tidwell. Again, remember that Internet Research is only as accurate as the efforts by others who have researched and entered the information. Discrepancies can and will be found. This is very tedious work and it is easy for one to track down a person of the same name but will turn out to be the wrong person in the end. I had this problem tracking down Edward Tidwell. It turned out that I was tracking two different Edward's and had to eliminate one of them when the facts that I found did not match the facts that I knew about the Edward that I was trying to locate.

I use familysearch.org for a macro search to get the broad picture and then use Ancestry.com for a micro search to refine various areas that need finer resolution. I have used the historical documents offered there as well as various family trees. Among them are the Rogers Family Tree, Samuel L. Davis Family Tree, Morrow Family Tree, Rodgers Family Tree, Tidwell Family Tree, Sheehan Family Tree, and others as reference. This is to tie in information from my various researches that none of them have completely covered. Perhaps they can use some of this information to add to their family trees.

The author had taken most of the following three paragraphs about Reuben Tidwell from General W. A. Tidwell's two manuscripts.

4. The fourth in or lineage in America was **Reuben Tidwell**, the only child and son of William Carr Tidwell and Anne Barbary Muse (Anne Barbara Tidwell?). Reuben Tidwell was born 1767 in Westmoreland, Virginia and died in 1835 in Warren County, Tennessee. Reuben Tidwell married on 2 December 1788 Mary Winfred Coles of Northumberland, Virginia, then a girl of fifteen, in Machodoc Neck, Northumberland, Virginia. Reuben Tidwell was twenty-one years old at this time. This would have meant that Mary Winfred Coles was born about 1773 in Virginia. Her death date and place is unknown.

Reuben Tidwell owned slaves in Virginia as did most of his ancestors. He also owned slaves in Tennessee as did his son Mark. Some of the Reids from the section on them later in the book also owned slaves, one or two reportedly owned very many. While most people in the southeastern United States including Tennessee and Georgia did not own slaves at that time there was nothing illegal about it and it was accepted. I am not proud of this and I have some very good friends who are African Americans. We must not judge the old timers by our standards. People lived differently back then, had different ideas, standards and reacted to the environment they lived in.

The number of children that Mary Winfred Coles and Reuben Tidwell had is very confusing. The census records from 1810, 1820 and 1830 did not contain any names except the head of the household. They had a form that was filled out by the census taker during the census that had columns for the various household members from different age groups and numbers listed for both males and females, as well as separate column for slaves. General W. A. Tidwell had the same problem getting the names of the children from the 1810 U. S. Census for Reuben Tidwell's family. I have also had this problem even for the 1820 and 1830 census. David and Joyce Grigsby also must have faced this problem in their research as well but they listed some of the names of the children of Reuben Tidwell and Mary Winfred Cole as "Mark, Richard, John and our Robert."

From my internet research Mary Winfred Coles and Reuben Tidwell's children are given but not completely in a few family trees and are listed as I found them in the family trees below:
1. Mark Tidwell born 1790 in Virginia. Probably Westmoreland since Reuben Tidwell did not sell his Machodoc Creek property until February 12, 1812.
2. Mary Tidwell born 1792 in Virginia. Probably Westmoreland since Reuben Tidwell did not sell his Machodoc Creek property until February 12, 1812.
3. Edward Tidwell born about 1794. Probably Westmoreland since Reuben Tidwell did not sell his Machodoc Creek property until February 12, 1812.
4. Frances Tidwell born 1797. Probably Westmoreland since Reuben Tidwell did not sell his Machodoc Creek property until February 12, 1812.

5. Robert Tidwell born 1798. Probably Westmoreland since Reuben Tidwell did not sell his Machodoc Creek property until February 12, 1812. I could find no birth record on familysearch.org for this Robert Tidwell. Could the Robert listed above actually have been Richard since they were both born the same year?
6. Richard Tidwell born 1798. Probably Westmoreland since Reuben Tidwell did not sell his Machodoc Creek property until February 12, 1812.
7. John Tidwell born 1802. Probably Westmoreland since Reuben Tidwell did not sell his Machodoc Creek property until February 12, 1812.
8. Betty E. Tidwell born 1810. Probably Westmoreland since Reuben Tidwell did not sell his Machodoc Creek property until February 12, 1812.
9. Robert Tidwell 1814 - 1870. Born in Virginia but I don't know where.

I have eliminated those I could not find any information on from other sources. My final listing is given below. Some of this information is still very confusing and the accuracy of some of it is questionable. I had no accurate documentation or family stories to rely on in most instances. Only what I could find on the internet and this is by no means complete.

1. **Mark Tidwell** - Mark Tidwell is the oldest child of Reuben Tidwell and Mary Winfred Coles (Cole). He was born 1790 in Westmoreland, Virginia. I also found an entry for him on familysearch.org born about 1805 to Reuben Tidwell and Mary Winfred Cole. I also found a record of his marriage on the same website to one Frances Boyd on 11 October 1812 in South Carolina. There was a listing on Ancestry.com for his children and their names and places of birth as well as a marriage in 1815 in Warren, Tennessee. The name of his spouse was not listed. The children's names are as follows:

A. John Tidwell born 1810 in Virginia.
B. Betty Tidwell born 1811 in Warren, Tennessee.
C. Richard Tidwell born 1812 in Warren, Tennessee.
D. Rebecca Tidwell born 1814 in Warren, Tennessee.
E. Joseph Tidwell born 1815 in Warren, Tennessee.
F. Thomas Tidwell born 1817 in Warren, Tennessee.

The dates of the birth of Mark Tidwell's children indicates that Mark Tidwell was in Warren County, Tennessee, before Reuben Tidwell sold his property in 1812 in Virginia and moved sometime later to Warren County, Tennessee with the rest of his family.

2. **Mary Tidwell** - There was a birth record on familysearch.org for Mary Tidwell born 1792 in Westmoreland Virginia and whose parents were Reuben Tidwell and Mary (Winfred) Cole. I also picked up an 1860 census record of a Mary Tidwell living in Warren County, Tennessee. Her age was given as sixty-five and her occupation was housekeeper. Could this be the same Mary? Probably not but the birth dates match pretty closely.

3. **Frances Tidwell** - There was a birth record on familysearch.org for Frances Tidwell born 1797 in Westmoreland, Virginia, and whose parents were Reuben Tidwell and Mary (Winfred) Cole. I also picked up an 1870 census record on Ancestry.com for a Frances Tidwell living at District 9, Maury County, Tennessee. Her Post office was given as Columbia. Her age was given as 77. Could this be the same Frances? Probably not but the year of birth match fairly closely. If so, members of her household were given as:

A. Emilina Tidwell age 27.
B. John B, Tidwell age 10.
C. George Tidwell age 8.

4. **Edward Tidwell** - 1794 - There was a birth record on familysearch.org for Edward Tidwell born 1794 in Westmoreland, Virginia, and whose parents were Reuben Tidwell and Mary (Winfred) Cole. Edward Tidwell married in Tennessee 1825 Nancy Brown born 1800 in North Carolina, died about 1858. I also picked up an 1850 U. S. census record on Ancestry.com for an Edward Tidwell living at District 34, Madison, Alabama. Household members were:

A. Edward Tidwell age 56.
B. Nancy Tidwell age 50.
C. Rebecca Tidwell age 20.
D. Martha Tidwell age 18.
E. Nancy Tidwell age 14.
F. Reubin Tidwell age 12.
G. Jno Tidwell age 10.

5. **John Tidwell** - I have no doubt that Reuben Tidwell and Mary Winfred Cole had a son named John Tidwell. He was supposedly born in 1802. I could not find any record of his birth in either Virginia or Tennessee. There was a John Tidwell age ten and born in Virginia living with Mark Tidwell on a record that I found about Mark's family. Could this be the "elusive" John?

6. **Richard Tidwell** - There was a birth record on familysearch.org for Richard Tidwell born 1808 in Westmoreland, Virginia, and whose parents were Reuben Tidwell and Mary (Winfred) Cole. From 1860 U. S. Census records that I picked up on Ancestry.com, Richard Tidwell was living at District 2, Lauderdale, Alabama, at that time.

Edward Tidwell and his family were living at District 2, Lauderdale, Alabama, apparently with his brother Richard Tidwell, during the 1860 U. S. census as well. Family members were given as:

A. Richard Tidwell age 52.
B. Edward Tidwell age 64.
C. R. E. Lawson age 14.
D. Rebecca Tidwell age 30.
E. Martha McCord age 28.
F. Tam Tidwell age 24.
G. Reuben Tidwell age 21.
H. John Tidwell age 20.
I. Rebecca Fulcher age 6.
J. Ann McCord age 3.
K. James Edwards age 2.

7. **Betty Elizabeth Tidwell** - I also had problems tracking down Betty Tidwell. I searched familysearch.org and could find no birth record in Virginia and had all but given up looking. I

tried Tennessee as a last resort. BINGO! I found a record of her birth in about 1810 in Tennessee and her parents were listed as Reuben Tidwell and Mary (Winfred) Cole.

I also found a record of her on Ancestry.com but they had her birth listed as Virginia.

8. **Joseph Tidwell** - I found birth Record of Joseph Tidwell on familysearch.org. He was born about 1815 in Westmoreland, Virginia and his parents were Reuben Tidwell and Mary (Winfred) Cole. I could find no other information about him.

9. Last but not least, **Robert (Dick) Tidwell** - Robert Tidwell, Edward Tidwell and Richard Tidwell, all sons of Reuben Tidwell and Mary Winfred Cole, all lived in Lauderdale County Alabama at one time or the other. I knew while growing up in Lauderdale County that there were three different and distinct Tidwell Families living in the Shoals Area. I counted Richard T. Tidwell and John Dee Tidwell's families as one extended family. Two of the Tidwell families lived in Lauderdale County and the other one lived in Colbert County across the Tennessee River. I thought at the time that we all three must be related someway but none of us knew just how.

I now think that we can all trace our lineage back to Reuben Tidwell and Mary Winfred Cole through Robert, Edward or Richard Tidwell.

Robert (Dick) Tidwell Family

There are a lot of loose ends to be tied up by the descendants of Robert Tidwell and Martha McBride Brown. I encourage all of the descendants of their children to write their stories and tie up these loose ends before these stories are lost. The only two that I have told their stories are Richard T. Tidwell and John Dee Tidwell. I am not sure that I have adequately covered John Dee's story but some of his family members have. I encourage them to publish their work.

I am sure that Angela Broyles of Bluewater Publications will be most happy to assist in the publication of your work.

There were two Robert Tidwell's listed as the son of Reuben Tidwell and Mary Winfred Cole. The first one was born in 1798 in Westmoreland, Virginia. The second one was born in 1814 in Westmoreland, Virginia, and is the direct ancestor of our clan. He died in 1870 in Lauderdale County, Alabama.

Our Robert (Dick) Tidwell was a blacksmith by occupation.

Robert married Martha McBride Brown in Warren County, Tennessee about 1836. She was born in Tennessee in 1817.

The 1850 U. S. Census lists the family living at Division 2 East of the Military Road, Lauderdale, Alabama. Family members listed were:

1. Robert Tidwell Age 35.
2. Martha Tidwell age 35.

3. Elizabeth Tidwell age 12.
4. Samuel Tidwell age 10.
5. Leroy Tidwell age 8.
6. Richmond Tidwell age 7.
7. Sousan Tidwell age 6.
8. Thomas Tidwell age 4.
9. Sarah Tidwell age 0.

The 1860 U.S. Census the family living at District 2, Lauderdale, Alabama. Family Members listed were:

1. Robert Tidwell age 46.
2. Martha Tidwell age 40.
3. Samuel Tidwell age 21.
4. Leroy Tidwell age 18.
5. Susan M. Tidwell age 14.
6. Richard Tidwell age 16.
7. Thomas Tidwell age 13.
8. Sallie Tidwell age 10.
9. Emma Tidwell age 7.
10. John Tidwell age 5.

Elizabeth had moved on by 1860 and Robert died in 1870.

I have researched each of the children from this marriage and my results are as follows:

1. **Elizabeth Tidwell** - I could find nothing more about Elizabeth Tidwell.

2. **Samuel Tidwell** - Samuel was born in 1840 in Tennessee, probably in Warren County. He died in 1885 in Alabama. His residence in the 1850 and 1860 U. S. Census was at home with his parents. In the 1870 U. S. Census his residence was Township 13, Walker, Alabama. His residence in the 1880 Census was Claysville, Marshall, Alabama. He died in 1885.

He married Jane, last name unknown, in 1842.

The children listed for this marriage were:

Thomas Tidwell born 1858.
Sarah Tidwell born 1862.
Martha A. Tidwell 1861 - 1933.
Mary Ellen Tidwell born 1905.

3. **Leroy Tidwell** - Born 1842 in Tennessee, probably in Warren County. He was living at home with his parents during the 1850 census in Lauderdale County, Alabama. Nothing more could be found about him.

4. **Susan M. Tidwell** - Also listed as Susan T. Tidwell in the Tidwell family tree, was born in Tennessee, probably Warren County in 1846. She was living at home with her parents in

Lauderdale County, Alabama during the 1850 and 1860 U. S. Census. She married William J. White on October 3, 1865 in Lauderdale County, Alabama. William J. White was born in 1840. Nothing else was found about this couple.

5. **Richard (T.) Tidwell** born April 1 1845 in Madison County, Alabama near Triana. Died October 4, 1917 at home in Lauderdale County, Alabama. His story is told in the body of this book.

6. **Thomas Tidwell** - Thomas Tidwell was born in May of 1847 in Lauderdale County Alabama. He died on June 13, 1918. Place of death is unknown.

He married Nancy A. (last name unknown) in 1870 in Lauderdale County Alabama.

His place of residence listed in the 1870 U. S. Census was Township 13, Walker, Alabama and his place of residence in the 1880 U. S. Census was Beat 1 Walker, Alabama. No other information could be found about this couple.

7. **Sallie Tidwell** - Sallie (Sarah) Tidwell was born in 1850 Lauderdale County Alabama. According to the 1850 U. S. Census, when her age was listed as 0, her parents resided at Division 2 East of the Military Road, Lauderdale, Alabama. She married on 24 May 1875 in Lauderdale County, Alabama, Issac Price, born about 1850. No other information was found about this couple.

8. **Emma Tidwell** - Emma Tidwell was born about 1852 in Alabama. Probably at District 2, Lauderdale, Alabama. Her parents were listed as living there during the 1860 U. S. Census when she was listed as being seven years of age.

The 1870 U. S. Census lists her living at Township 5 Range 4, Limestone, Alabama. Household members were listed as:

Isaah Tidwell Age 27.
Emma Tidwell Age 18.
Martha Tidwell Age 7.

Nothing else was found listed for Emma Tidwell.

9 **John Tidwell** - John Dee Tidwell - was born on May 1, 1856 in Lauderdale County, Alabama. He died on May 20, 1918 in Lauderdale County Alabama. His story is told in the body of this book.

The purpose of this exercise is to document some of the stories, conversations and interactions that I had while growing up. My sister Ann and I are the oldest people left in our immediate family with some of this knowledge. Ann is 18 months younger than I am and she does not remember some of this material. I knew these people. Later family members never got the opportunity to know them or hear their stories. Some of my brothers are up to twenty years younger than I am.

There are a lot of questions that I now wish that I had asked and pressed for answers from these old timers but never did. Their answers are now buried with them and their ancestors in either the Tidwell or the Cox Cemeteries near where they lived.

This work starts with Richard T. Tidwell, our family patriarch. It details his children and their families. It also included information for his brother John Dee Tidwell's family as well.

A cousin of mine and his wife, David and Joyce Grigsby, traced the family back from Alabama to Warren County, Tennessee. I have copies of some of their work.

I have referenced David and Joyce Grigsby's work as well as that by Joanne Tidwell Forsythe in some of the following sections. I will attempt to limit my writing to what I actually saw, heard and experienced while growing up on Brush Creek.

Remember that all farming back in Richard T's time and later had to be done with horses and mules. This was true up until the late '50s at which time my dad, Richard Almon Tidwell, bought the first tractor on the property. This was a small Farmall Cub garden tractor. This old tractor was even more temperamental than a mule. It ran when it wanted to and would just die in the middle of a field. I ran the battery down many times trying to get it restarted and then had to use the hand crank. I would twist that hand crank until I had blisters on my right hand. This tractor still would not start. I would finally get it started in its own good time. Tractors also took gas to run. Even though gas only cost thirty cents a gallon or less back then, it still cost more money than the grass and small amount of corn that a mule ate. We used mules for gardening up until the late '50s and early '60s. The old home place was grown up by then and there was no farming of any significance being done, only big gardens.

Dad was an electrician. He had a friend who sold used bulldozers and heavy equipment. This friend was trying to use junk and surplus equipment to outfit a barge on Shoals Creek in Happy Hollow as a dredge. I think this guy intended to take the barge to Florida and try to hire it out. Dad agreed to wire everything on this barge up to where it would work and in return dad's friend agreed to use his bulldozers to clear off the small trees and brush that had taken the old family farm over. Dad then built a new barn, fenced the place and ran cattle on it until grandmother Alice sold the place to Ferrell Allen. I understand that Ferrell now has the place up for sale but I doubt that any family members either want it or can afford Ferrell's asking price. Apparently he has very few bargains on anything that he sells!

Practical methods of photography did not become commonplace in America until shortly before the Civil War. The first photograph of any family member was a tintype of Christopher Columbus Everett Reid in his confederate uniform and is used on the cover. Aunt Mag had this photograph and I had it copied and have used it in some of my earlier work. All other photographs in this work date from after that time.

2

Richard T. Tidwell*

Every family needs someone who stands out from the rest of the group to look up to. Richard T. filled this role for our family.

Until recently, when members of the family did research work into our family history, no one claimed to know where Richard T. or John Dee came from. Family members did not talk about it if they knew. I find it hard to believe that neither one of them ever revealed their histories to family members but it may have happened that way. Remember they lived in a different time and had different ideas about life than we have today. Times were hard back then and they had to be tough to survive. They may have been too busy scratching out a living on those rough hillsides to talk much about their past.

Some of the first section about Richard T. references research done by cousin David and his wife Joyce Grigsby. David is a distant cousin on John Dee's side of the family. I have added clarification from my own research.

Richard T. Tidwell was born on April 1, 1845, in Madison County, Alabama, near Triana. David and Joyce refer to him as Dick in their work. It was only later that I remembered hearing Uncle Doc and dad refer to him as Dick as well. He served in the Civil War as a private in the 4th Alabama Cavalry, Company F. The 4th Alabama Cavalry was known as Roddey's Cavalry. Dick joined this unit in August of 1863, at the age of eighteen, as a private in Florence, Alabama. Company F was also referred to as the "Rebel Troopers" according to Bryan Summerhill of Florence, Alabama.

Richard T. must have gone by the name of Dick as a young man. I ask my writing mentor and friend, Ann Chambliss, to help me research Richard T's Civil War enlistment date. She subscribes to the website, Ancestry.com. Neither of us could find any reference to a Richard Tidwell in the 4th Alabama Cavalry. Ann did find reference to Dick Tidwell in work published on the internet by Scott K. Williams, who quoted work done by Bryan Summerhill, of Florence.

The first list gives the roster of Company F. Dick Tidwell is listed as a private.

The second list is the roster of General P. D. Roddey's Escort Alabama Calvary. I quote Scott K. Williams, "While some of these men may have served in the 4th Alabama Cavalry and other units, they were distinguished enough to become General Roddey's escort cavalry or "Headquarters guards." Many of these men came from the northwest Alabama region, others from elsewhere."

D. R. Tidwell is on this roster.

This is most certainly Richard T. who went by the name of Dick back then.

From research that I have conducted on the internet, the 4th Alabama Cavalry was formed in April 1862, in Tuscumbia, Alabama under Colonel Philip Dale Roddey. The 4th was sent to middle Tennessee where it wintered and was sent to the Tennessee Valley in the spring of 1863. A lot of information can be picked up by running a Google search on this unit. The authors are not identified in some of this information. I will not retype this information because it would take pages and pages. It is readily available on the internet for those who are interested. I will only summarize parts of it.

Something that I did enjoy reading about was an incident that happened during the battle of Bear Creek in the spring of 1863. There the 4th Alabama Cavalry unit under the command of Roddey made lots of noise and fired their pistols at night to confuse the much larger Federal unit under the command of Dodge. This commotion made Dodge's mule mounts panic and they stampeded. Four hundred mules drowned or got away. This bought valuable time for the confederates under General Forrest and ultimately caused Dodge to have to pull back. He retreated to Corinth, Mississippi. This ended Straight's rear guard and line of supply and left him vulnerable for his chase across North Alabama and capture in Rome, Georgia.

The 4th Alabama Cavalry was a very storied unit and had a distinguished record. It was publicly commended in April, 1863, by General Braxton Bragg, for good discipline, etc. Colonel Roddey was later promoted to brigadier general on August 3, 1863.

From Richard B. Davis' website, "In his scouting and raiding operations, which were mostly in northern Alabama, Lawrence County Alabama tailor, sheriff, and river man Philip D. Roddey proved highly successful and rose to the command of a Confederate cavalry division. He served as Bragg's personal escort at the Battle of Shiloh and then led forces in northern Alabama where he raised several regiments, the most famous of which is the 4th Alabama Cavalry (Roddey's Regiment). Sometimes operating with larger forces in Georgia, Tennessee and Mississippi, he usually operated independently in his home region."

From another page on Richard B. Davis' website, he lists over a hundred different engagements and actions of the 4th Alabama Cavalry. Among the listings are operations, skirmishes, expeditions, actions, major battles, campaigns, and sieges. They range across Tennessee, Mississippi, Alabama, and into Georgia. Richard Davis also states that they spent most of their time in northern Alabama with certain units being detached and serving elsewhere.

He lists major full scale battles as Chickamauga and Tishomingo Creek (Brices Crossroads). In his lists are a raid at Chattanooga with Wheeler and Roddey, and the siege of Atlanta. His entire website is well worth reviewing.

From work by Marc Barker in "Interesting Confederate Units" as reported on the internet, "At the end of the war, the larger part of the 4th Alabama Cavalry was captured at Selma Alabama, and the remnant lay down their arms at Pond Spring." In further internet research, I learned that Pond Spring is the home of general Joseph Wheeler near Town Creek, Alabama.

Dick Tidwell could not have participated in the Bear Creek engagement since this happened in the spring of 1863 and he did not join until that August. This story does make interesting reading though.

What follows was reported by David and Joyce Grigsby and is quoted in large part from a September 15, 1991 *Times Daily* edition of the *"The Journal of Muscle Shoals History Bicentennial; Nathan Bedford Forrest And His Critter Company"* written by Andrew N Lytle, pp. 151 - 175. This accurately describes this early action of the 4th Alabama Cavalry.

The 4th Alabama Cavalry was formed in Tuscumbia, Alabama in October of 1862. The 4th Alabama Cavalry fought the Yankees at Bear Creek starting a running battle, which kept them occupied until Nathan Bedford Forrest could go to Colonel Philip D. Roddey's aide. Due to the railroads and the Tennessee River, the Shoals area was important to the Confederate effort.

On April 27th, 1863 the battle of Town Creek began and Colonel Roddey's men again played an important part. These boys were sometimes called "Roddey's Raiders." This battle preceded Forrest's run against Colonel Abel D. Streight across north Alabama, with Roddey and his men in his midst, ending with Streight's capture along with his mule brigade in Rome, Georgia. This running engagement against all odds by Forrest's men helped boost morale in north Alabama and Roddey's men played their part in all of this.

Dick served until May, 1865 and was paroled at Pond Springs, Alabama.

This pretty well matches family stories of how the end of the war came for Dick. I remember Grandpa Nathan and dad talking about Dick having to walk home barefooted from Selma at the end of the war. He may have walked home from Pond Spring instead. Pond Spring was closer. Anyway, it was a long walk for a barefooted young man of the ripe old age of twenty.

North Alabama was utterly destroyed by the Civil War. It is hard to believe just how thorough the devastation was. I have cut and pasted a description from Scott Williams' website. It is graphic. I hope Scott doesn't mind.

Historical Tidbits of North Alabama
(During the War Between the States)
If anyone has information to contribute to this page, please contact Scott Willliams
I will be adding tidbits continually to this page.

Domestic Terrorism by US Army on Southern Civilians (Men, Women and Children Held as Hostages)
Gen. Sherman ordered Gen. Wm. Sooy Smith to burn both towns of Florence and Tuscumbia, and deport it's inhabitants North of the Ohio River, if Gen. Forrest moved his forces into Tennessee.
"Send notice to Florence [Alabam] that if Forrest invades Tennessee from that direction, the town will be burned, and if it occurs you will remove the inhabitants north of the Ohio River, and burn the town and Tuscumbia, also"
---Gen. Wm. T. Sherman (Official Records Serial No. 75, p. 462)

> *"The Government of the United States has in North Alabama any and all rights they may choose to enforce in war, to take their lives, their homes, their lands, their everything... because war does exist there, and war is simply power unrestrained by constitution or compact...Next year their lands will be taken; for in war we can take them, and rightfully too; and in another year they may beg in vain for their lives." "...To the ...persistent secessionists, why, death is mercy, and the quicker he or she is disposed of the better."*
> *---Gen. W. T. Sherman (Union Army)*

Col. Roddey and Tuscumbia Citizens Give Kind Treatment to Yankee Prisoner

During Union General Dodge's invasion of Franklin County during the "Battle of Leighton",

Capt. Levi Utt, a Kansas Jayhawker of the 7th Kansas Cavalry was severely wounded. A shell had tore his left leg at the ankle. When General Dodge's army retreated, Capt. Utt had to be left behind at a Tuscumbia hotel and suffer the consequences at the hands of the enemy. Instead, Utt received kindness from Mrs. Inman, landlady of the hotel and "pretty girls" of town brought him strawberries and cream." Col. Roddey "saw to it the man was left undisturbed; and when Utt was strong enough to travel, Roddey paroled him and sent him to the Union lines at Corinth with an escort to protect him from guerillas." Capt. Utt later showed his appreciation to the girls of Tuscumbia, by getting approval from Gen. Dodge, "to grant several of passes through the lines at Corinth so that they could buy "the various articles dear to the female heart" which were no longer obtainable in the Confederacy." Unfortunately this small kind act did not matter too much as Gen. Dodge's route from Town Creek to Tuscumbia left a path of destruction and hundreds of residents homeless, thanks to the pillage committed by his command.

Confederate and Unionist Families of Franklin County Suffered Alike

Union troops coming from Town Creek to Tuscumbia were reported to have "burned all the corn and most of the houses. We found the country beyond Tuscumbia about the best and richest I ever saw and left it nothing but a wilderness with nothing scarcely but the chimneys left to show where once had been the habitations of man." This was after the Tenth Missouri, Seventh Kansas, Fifteenth Illinois and First Alabama Cavalry "did themselves credit" with "excellent" fighting, driving "the enemy, no matter what their forces."

"By the end of the war, all of the...population that could get away had 'refugeed' farther south."... "Roddey 'the Defender of North Alabama' and the other Confederate commanders did their best to hold down such terrorists (pro-Yankee Unionist) and to check Federal depredations, but their forces were generally too small to be of much avail" in the long run. By the end of the war, "Tuscumbia was all but destroyed."

> *"The United States has the right, and...the ...power, to penetrate to every part of the national domain... We will remove and destroy every obstacle--if need be, take every life, every acre of land, every particle of property, everything that to us seems proper;...we will not cease until the end is attained... If the people of the South oppose, they do so at their peril."*
> *---Gen. W.T. Sherman*

Other Locations Across North Alabama

Florence, Alabama (Lauderdale Co) and Huntsville (Madison Co.)

"At Florence, Colonel Cornyn's 10th Missouri Cavalry, assisted by gunboats, burned an estimated two million dollar's worth of property in 1863. In fact, most of the towns of the Great Bend (Tennessee River) were destroyed...either by shellfire or by deliberate burnings." Even Huntsville, a Federal Headquarters of Gen. Ormsby Mitchel, had it's shops and rolling stock of the railroad destroyed. This financially ruined many Madison County residents for years to come.

Guntersville, Alabama (Marshall Co.)

"With the exception of half a dozen dwellings, which were spared because they sheltered the sick or wounded...the village had disappeared. Nothing but tumbledown walls and a mass of brick debris was left of our home. The nearest shelter which could be obtained was in a log house on Sand Mountain, five miles from town, and in this my parents found temporary abode. We were not wholly unprepared for the scene of desolation about us. As we came west on the train nothing but lonesome-looking chimneys remained of the villages and farmhouses. They were suggestive of tombstones in a graveyard. Bridgeport, Stevenson, Bellefonte, Scottsboro, Larkinsville, Woodville, Paint Rock---in fact, every town in northern Alabama to and including Decatur (except Huntsville, which, being used as headquarters, had been spared)--had been wiped out by the war policy of starvation by fire. Farmhouses, gins, fences, and cattle were gone. From a hilltop in the farming district a few miles from New Market, I counted the chimneys of six different houses which had been destroyed."---John Wyeth (Confederate soldier returning home)

Dick returned from the war and married his first wife, Rebecca McGee on January 4, 1869. The date is from David and Joyce Grigsby.

This must have been a trying time for the young couple. After they settled on Brush Creek they had to clear much of the land and cut the timbers to build their house. Such an endeavor must have brought them very close together. They had five children and four of them lived to adulthood. All of the surviving children were female. I never knew any of them except for Bama Hale who was Grandfather Nathan's half sister.

They built a log house or large cabin for their family. I have included a picture of this house. This was quite an impressive house for the time and area. It served as home and the focal point for our branch of the family for over a hundred years. It consisted of two large rooms with a dog trot as it was called between them. The dog trot was just a wide open area under roof. There was an upstairs over the entire structure and it was roofed originally with wooden shingles. The house was constructed of hand hewn logs. It must have been fifty feet or longer across the front. Two extra long hand hewn logs formed the top sill for the front porch. They were notched in the middle and held together with wooden pegs. The foundation for this log house was, as most houses were from that time and area, simply piles of rocks at the corners and other strategic locations.

There was a shallow cellar under the west room that must have originally served as a root cellar. It had dirt walls with a large shelf that was not dug as deep as the rest of it. The dirt floor was a muddy mess in wet weather.

Heat originally was from two fireplaces, one at each end of the house in each downstairs room. The upstairs had two windows. One of them, the one on the east side, had a window in it. The one on the west side had a homemade sliding wooden shutter to keep out the elements.

All of the original doors were handmade. They had cross braces in them to make them sturdy. The door to the east downstairs room, or *far room* as we called it, had a handmade iron latch. There was a hole in the door where a string or small rope could be poked out during the day and pulled back inside at night.

Richard T. later added a bedroom to the north side of the large west downstairs room. This bedroom addition was long gone before I could remember. I was the last child born in this house in June of 1942 in the "*far room*." Mother was attended by a traveling country doctor from Cow Pens which was about six or seven miles away. All of the Tidwell children were born in the old house up until that time. All of the children after me were born at the Eliza Coffee Memorial Hospital in Florence, Alabama.

There were several family stories about Richard T. that I still remember. Richard T. was long gone and he and his deceased immediate family members were buried in the family cemetery on top of the hill west of the house before I came along. There had not been a burial there for years before I could remember and there has not been one since.

Richard T. was apparently quite an astute business man for his time. He acquired several tracts of land which he farmed, traded and took timber from as he needed. He had extensive holdings at one time. Family stories told that he owned a continuous tract of land from his original farm west to what was eventually prime lakefront property on Shoals Creek after Wilson Dam was built. This land was not in the family at that time.

One of the stories of his land dealings that dad related to me was that Richard T. sold a piece of property but cut all of the timber off of it before the new owner could take it over. Dad told of a trial held down the road at a house that is still standing. They convicted Richard T. and sentenced him to hang. Richard T. asked the judge if his understanding that a condemned man had one last wish was correct. The judge agreed. Richard T. apparently looked each jury member in the eye and told the judge, in more colorful language than I will use here, that he requested that the jury members pay him what they owed him in full before he was hung. The jury reconsidered and released him at that point according to dad's story. The intended "Hanging Tree" still stands.

Dad also said that Richard T. was an accomplished blacksmith and had a shop on the property. Everyone had to be self sufficient back then so this can be well understood. All traces of the blacksmith shop were gone before I could remember. The only structures still standing as I grew up were the spring house before it fell, the log house, original barn, smoke house and a one car garage that Grandpa Nathan had built for his shiny, new Plymouth.

The old barn was about to fall down in the early '60s and dad wanted it torn down so he could build a new one where it stood. The old barn was impressive for its time and had a lattice front for ventilation of the hay loft. I have included a picture of it. Richard T., three of his four sons with their mules and some pigs are in the photograph. The barn originally had four stalls, a corn crib and what was probably a tack room at one time. There is a separate structure to the left in the photograph that was probably a corn crib.

It took me about three or four days to clean the old barn out and tear it down. There were some old saddles, one of them a woman's side saddle, and some men's saddles and general saddle horse harness that I am sure dated to shortly after the Civil War if not to the Civil War. There was an old tall cherry headboard and some other old furniture in it. This stuff would bring a fortune today.

I put it all outside and protected it as well as I could with limited resources. Unfortunately it rained before we could get the new barn built and the old stuff stored back inside. This stuff was so old that it just fell apart once it got wet.

The barn's top sills were joined by notching them and were held in place with wooden pegs. This was better carpentry than what we replaced it with.

The only thing that was saved from the old barn was the rusty tin roof. Dad wanted to save it for something. I don't know if he ever used it.

The only family member with a blacksmith shop was Uncle Doc when I grew up. I can still remember the sound of Uncle Doc pounding metal to shape on his anvil when I was little. The sound could be heard all over the creek bottom. Sometimes I would go watch him, and if I was lucky, he would let me turn the handle of the air pump for the forge. Sparks would fly! He used coke for his forge. I don't know what Richard T. used. The building for Uncle Doc's blacksmith shop is still standing but family members and an auction after his death scattered his tools.

Another story that dad related to me was that Richard T. had a special corn crib on the east side of his main barn. Richard T. had an ample supply of corn there. It was not uncommon for neighbors to run out of corn in the winter to feed their animals or to make corn meal for their own cornbread. Richard T. would supply his neighbors with all of the corn they needed with the stipulation that they pay him 2 bushels at the next harvest for every one they took. This is an excellent return even for today. It would now probably be called gouging or something worse!

All that Uncle Doc would say about Richard T. was that he liked his whiskey and women. Unfortunately, many of his male descendants inherited this trait as well.

Richard T. was married three times and had two families. The first marriage produced four daughters and the second marriage produced four sons. I know of very little about the daughters and never had contact with any of them but one, Bama Hale. She used to visit when I was small.

25

$\underline{3}$

Richard T. Tidwell's First Family

At first I had very little to go on in reconstructing Richard T. Tidwell's first family. I have included all of the steps and confusing information that one has to dig out, sift through and try to understand in his effort to reconstruct a family where almost all of the family members who had this information have taken it to their graves with them.

I had the following names from the 1880 Census listed on familysearch.org to begin with.

Rebecker Tidwell, wife, age 38
Derrinda N. Tidwell, daughter, age 10
Mattie B. Tidwell, daughter age 9
Florence A. Tidwell, daughter, age 5
Fannie Tidwell, age 3
William T. Tidwell, son, age 1

I was later able to obtain from Ollie Tidwell a note where Uncle Albert had written down the half heirs of Richard T. Tidwell and listed only their husband's initials. I have included Uncle Albert's note in its entirety in the Family Memorial section. Family sources told the story of him having to reconstruct his family history in order to join Social Security since he did not have a birth certificate.

In recent conversations with Virgiline Tidwell Hale, she knew the given names of three of the daughters and their married names. She also knew where they were buried.

I was able to use all of this family information with searches on ancestry.com and visits to the cemeteries to piece together the following. I took the dates on the tombstones as being factual if there was any discrepancy in information.

Photographs appear in the Family Memorial section of the grave markers for the names marked with an asterisk (*).

Derendia Naomi Oma (Omie) Tidwell *, born November 14, 1868 in Lauderdale County, Alabama, died January 14, 1926 in Killen Alabama**,** Married in Lauderdale County, Alabama:

1. January 6, 1888 **Andrew Peck*** born December 1, 1857 Lauderdale County, died December 13, 1890. No children listed for this marriage.

2. December 17, 1893 **John Samuel Peck*** born September 13, 1861 Lauderdale County, died November 15, 1939. All three spouses are buried in the Peck Cemetery, Killen, Alabama, as are all of the children with the exception of Percy D. Peck.

There were 11 children from the marriage to John Samuel Peck.

Percy D. Peck 1892 - ? No information was available until I ran an internet search on Ancestry.com. Percy is listed as being age seven and living at home with his parents in the 1900 census. He was living in Memphis, Shelby County, Tennessee when he registered for the WWI draft in 1917 - 1918. He was living at home in Killen, Alabama, with his wife Jewel and three and a half year old child Edna Earl Peck in the 1920 census. Uncle Albert listed him as address unknown, somewhere in Texas in the note he wrote prior to 1951. The trail ended here.

Granville Alison Peck* September 28,1893 - May 22,1977. Buried in Peck cemetery, Killen, Alabama, next to wife Lucy Ann born October 7, 1900 died August 15, 1959.

Dalma Bama Susan Peck* May 31,1896 - July 27,1971. Buried in Peck cemetery next to her husband Dolph W. Peck born April 13, 1894, died November 29, 1974.

Bessie M. Peck* March 26, 1898 - March 5, 1980. Buried next to her husband George A. Martindale born September 25,1891, died June 23, 1971.

Lucian Peck* 1899 - 1904. Buried in Peck cemetery.

Hiarm Peck* 1902 - 1904. Buried in Peck cemetery.

Lucille Lucy Peck* July 21, 1905 - April 8,1986. Buried in the Peck cemetery next to her husband Earl L. Covington born September 19, 1898, died August 9, 1952.

Frederick Fred T. Peck* July 31, 1907 - October 26, 1926. Buried in Peck cemetery.

Albert Peck* February 10,1909 - August 28, 1989. Buried in Peck cemetery next to his wife Hautie born March 24, 1909, died June 3, 1982.

Walter Waltie Lee Peck* March 11, 1911 - May 18, 1978. Buried in Peck cemetery.

Emma Mattie Peck Covington* April 15, 1913 - April 17, 1973.

After researching the Peck family I vaguely remember Grandmother Alice repeating something that Omie had said about two pecks making a bushel. It was one short of a dozen children in this case.

Mattie B Tidwell*, born January 29,1871 in Lauderdale County, Alabama, died January 30, 1941. Married July 25, 1897, **Andrew Lee Phillips*** born January 13, 1855 in Lauderdale County, Alabama, died November 13, 1938. Buried in the old Lexington cemetery, Lexington, Alabama, as are all of their children that grave markers could be located. Ora was apparently the oldest child of Mattie B and A. L. Phillips. He had several children by a previous marriage. I had difficulty researching this branch of the family. I could not pick up anything on the internet until Virgiline Tidwell Hale remembered A. L. Phillips' given name was Andrew. I have had to reconstruct what I have from the 1910 - 1930 census records, Virgiline Tidwell Hale's memory, Ancestry.com and a visit to the Lexington cemetery. It was like trying to peel an onion one layer at a time. Some of the children's given names are different from one census to the next. I know from the census records and subtracting their ages from the year of the census approximately what year the children were born. I use this information, Virgiline's memory and tying this to the information on the grave markers as the final authority in conflicting information. Mostly, I rely the grave marker data tied with the approximate date of birth.

Mattie B. and A. L. Phillips apparently had eight children and raised seven to adulthood.

From the 1910 census the children listed in the household are listed as
Lutie Phillips age 21. Born about 1889
Lillie Phillips age 19. Born about 1891
Hart Phillips age 17. Born about 1893. All three of these children were born before Mattie B.'s marriage in 1897.

Other children listed that could have been Mattie B's were:

Ora Phillips age 11. Born about 1899
Ruby Phillips age 9. Born about 1901
Thomas Phillips age 8. Born about 1902
Almond Philips age 6. Born about 1904
Mary Phillips age 3. Born about 1907
Paul Phillips age 1. Born about 1909

From the 1920 census the following children are listed for this household.

Ora had disappeared. Presumably she had married Dr. Taylor by that time.
Rydey A. Phillips age 19. Born about 1901. Probably the given name of Ruby listed above.
Ausson E. Phillips. Born about 1904. Probably the given name of Almond listed above.
Mary E. Phillips age 13. Born about 1907
Richard P. Phillips age 10. Born about 1910. This is probably Paul listed above.
Mattie I. Phillips age 6. Born about 1914
Rebecca Phillips age 3. Born about 1917

Thomas Phillips had disappeared. He had probably died between 1910 and 1920. He is listed in Ancestry.com as being born Andrew Thomas Phillips on September 2, 1901 in Lexington, Alabama. I could find no other information for him.

The following children are listed for this household in the 1930 census.

N. Pawel Phillips age 21. Born about 1909. Probably Paul listed previously?
Mary Phillips age 23. Born about 1907
Isabel Phillips age 16. Born about 1914. This is probably Mattie I.'s middle name.
Rebecca Phillips age 13. Born about 1917
Ruby A. Clements age 29. Born about 1901. Ruby's married name?

Virgiline Tidwell Hale remembers six of their names.

Ora Phillips - Married Dr. Taylor, a pharmacist in Lexington, Alabama. No Children. I remember Ora visiting the old log home place when I was growing up. She was always dressed up and looked most feminine. She was, I thought, the most beautiful woman that I had ever seen. Ora died in the late 1970's and the location of her burial is not known. The information for her that I was able to find in Ancestry.com lists her full name as Ora Caldonia Phillips born May 11, 1898 in Lexington, Alabama.
Pete Phillips* - He is listed on his grave marker in the old Lexington cemetery as Paul R. "Pete" Phillips born November 30, 1908, died November 11, 1996 and is buried next to his wife Beulah Mabe born March 7, 1915, died February 23, 1995.
Edward A. "Polly" Phillips* - born November 21, 1903, died April 20, 1978.
Mary Phillips - Died in Florida by Virgiline Tidwell Hale's memory. Ancestry.com lists her full name as Mary Elizabeth Phillips born May 15, 1906 in Lexington, Alabama. She died about 1993 in Mobile, Alabama and her husband was H. L. Worral.

Martha Isabel Phillips* - Born May 22, 1913, died February 22, 2000. She is buried in the old Lexington Cemetery next to her husband Carmichael White born June 12, 1909, died December 1, 2006. and they lived on Alabama 101 near Lexington. He inherited Ora Taylor's property as she had no children according to Virgiline.

Becky Phillips* - 1916 - 1939. She is buried in the old Lexington cemetery with her husband. She married **Horace Paul Houf** 1914 - 1939 who was a Second Lieutenant in the U. S. Marine reserve and died in a plane crash. According to Virgiline a hole was dug on top of Rebecca's grave for his ashes.

<u>**Florence Alabama (Bama) Hale***</u> - born August 22, 1881, in Lauderdale County. Died March 17 1957 in Killen. Married about 1894 **William A. (Bill) Hale*** born April 15,1874, in Murry County, Tennessee. Died April 5 1957 in Florence, Alabama. They are buried next to each other in the old Killen, Alabama cemetery.

One child from this marriage.

Malcolm Hale born about 1895. Virgiline thinks he lived in Texas.

<u>**Fannie Tidwell**</u> born 1877, died about 1960. Married December 22, 1896 T. W. Brewer born about 1877, died about 1960.

I think that Fannie and T. W. Brewer must have moved from the area some time after they were married. I never heard any stories about Fannie or her family while growing up. Virgiline Tidwell Hale does not know anything about her either and never remembers hearing her name mentioned.

The information I have collected was picked up on the internet and I have been unable as yet to find out where they lived.

Four children from this marriage. All lived in Colorado according to Uncle Albert's note.

Willie Brewer born about 1900, died about 1980.
Kathleen Brewer born about 1902, died about 1988.
Thomas Brewer born about 1904, died about 1990. Pueblo, Colorado by Uncle Albert.
Elizabeth Brewer born about 1905, died about 1990. Pueblo, Colorado by Uncle Albert.

<u>**William T. Tidwell**</u> born 1879 in Lauderdale county, died ? William is found on the 1880 census but I can find no mention of him afterward.

Could his have been one of the first burials in the old Tidwell cemetery on the top of the hill west of the old log home place? There were three tombstones in this cemetery and several graves only marked by a pile of rocks. The tombstones were for Richard T. Tidwell, Nannie Tidwell wife number two and Lucinda Tidwell wife number three.

It is not known where Rebecca McGee Tidwell, wife number one is buried but I think she is probably buried in the Tidwell cemetery as well, but without a tombstone.

Original **Andrew Lee Phillips** house where he and **Mattie B. Tidwell Phillips** raised all of their children in Lexington, Alabama. It has been remodeled and updated in recent years.

4

Richard T. Tidwell's Sons

Richard T. married his second wife, Nancy Erwin by one account and Nancy Urban by another. She was most certainly Nancy C. Erbin listed in familysearch.org and Ancestry.com. Her father was Henry Erbin born 1832 in Prussia. Her mother was Mary A. Erbin born 1828 in Kentucky. Nancy C. was born in 1861 and was nineteen at the time of the 1880 census. The only other child was listed as James J. Erbin born 1860 and was twenty at the time. The Erbin family were listed as farmers and were in the same general area as Richard T., namely Township 2, Beat 6, Lauderdale, Alabama.

Could this be where Uncle Albert got his middle name Henry?

They had four sons, Edward, Albert, Jesse and Nathan, who was my grandfather. Education for children was rare back then and children were needed on the farm if schools were available. I don't know anything about the schooling of Richard T. or of any of his children. Except for family living nearby, they lived in a very remote area. I think most of Richard T. sons tried their hand at farming back then, as did most country people.

Richard T's sons were a very fractious lot. None of them had anything much but they were very protective of what little they had.

For example, there was an old kraut knife dating from Richard T's time at the old home place. Uncle Albert thought it should belong to him for some reason. He borrowed it once and didn't return it. This started a war of words between his family and ours. He finally did return it but it caused hard feelings for a long time.

The kraut knife was a simple homemade affair. It was basically a flat board with a hole cut in the middle. Three blades were set at an angle in the hole which cut the cabbage head into shreds when it was worked against it. The shredded cabbage then fell out the bottom into a stone churn and was then mixed with salt water and allowed to ferment until it could then be placed into canning jars. It had guide boards on the edge to hold the cabbage head in place. Not much to get into a fight about. This is but one example of several.

Richard T. Tidwell's home place. Left to right: **Albert,** unknown, unknown, thought to be the 3rd wife's daughter, **Jesse, Nathan, Richard T. Tidwell** and 3rd wife, **Lucinda,** the former **Mrs. L. C. Denison.**

This photograph was taken sometime between the 1910 census and Richard T's death in 1917.

Please note the lathing boards on the left top of this photograph that the shingles were nailed to. These same lathing boards were used when the original shingles were replaced with a "tin" roof.

Left to right: **Richard T. Tidwell, Albert, Nathan** and **Jesse** with their mules and some pigs. Note the old barn in the background. This is the one that I tore down years later.

This photograph was also taken sometime between the 1910 census and Richard T's death in 1917.

Richard Edward Tidwell*

Born November 11, 1887 in Lauderdale County, Died May 8, 1966. Buried in Cox cemetery near Killen, Alabama.

Married Lizzie Owen* born December 15, 1890 in Lauderdale county, died November 17, 1983 in Killen, Alabama. Buried Cox cemetery near Killen.

I had very little contact with Edward, or Uncle Ed as we called him, except for visits. He lived close to the old family log house for a while, as did the rest of the surviving sons, but moved frequently into a number of rental places. He lived for a while south of the old family log house, in the house where Richard T's trial was supposedly held, as did Uncle Albert later. Uncle Ed and his family lived in our house for the eighteen months we lived near Paducah, Kentucky, in 1952 and '53 while dad was working on the construction of TVA's Shawnee Steam Plant. I remember Uncle Ed and his family later living off of the Bridge Road near Killen, Alabama, and they had an old refrigerator with the large circular coil on top. I remember this well as I had never seen one before. I also remember his being the caretaker and living at the Boy Scout camp on Shoals Creek for awhile. He and his wife, Lizzie, had two daughters and a son.

Robert Tidwell, born 1914 in Lauderdale County.

Annie Mae Tidwell Wallace, born 1916 in Lauderdale County.

Lou Edna Tidwell*, born November 26, 1920, died August 24, 1974 in Lauderdale County. Buried in Cox cemetery near Killen, Alabama.

Uncle Ed worked for a number of years at the Coca-Cola bottling plant in Florence. He would always bring dad some old advertising materials that were no longer used. He brought some thermometers shaped like coke bottles that dad used to feed his chickens from. He brought some old metal billboards that dad used to cover the outside of a hay storage barn. The printed side was put inside so that it did not look like a patchwork quilt from the outside. Some bits and pieces of the printed advertising were still visible the last time that I looked inside this shed. I even used a piece of one of these metal signs to patch a hole in the floorboard of my 1953 Ford. People now collect this old stuff and it would be worth a small fortune if we had kept it.

Albert Henry Tidwell*

Born April 17, 1889, died March 31, 1965.

Married Cleavie Lee Haygood* born April 17, 1891, died September 25, 1939.

Both are buried in the Cox cemetery near Killen, Alabama.

Uncle Albert was the second oldest son. He married Clevie Haygood and they had seven sons and daughters.

Selma C. Tidwell Wallace born May 27, 1913.

Vernon A. Tidwell* born May 4, 1915 in Lauderdale county, Alabama, died February 1, 1995. Buried in Cox cemetery near Killen, Alabama.

Jesse F. Tidwell, born 1917 in Lauderdale county, Alabama.

Ethel Tidwell, born April 18, 1918.

William Lloyd Tidwell* born July 19, 1920 in Lauderdale county, died March 6, 2006. Buried in the Cox cemetery near Killen, Alabama.

Edgar James Tidwell born September 4, 1924.

Ollie Ernest Tidwell born July 17, 1928 in Lauderdale County.

Dad always called Albert Uncle Putt for some unknown reason.

Uncle Albert bought the Cox farm about a mile north of the old home place at one time but lost it during hard times well before my time. He then later rented the house immediately to the south of the old home place where Uncle Ed had lived and he lived there a number of years. I remember Uncle Albert paying fifteen dollars per month rent for this place.

Uncle Albert made his living doing carpentry and masonry work.

One of my first memories of Uncle Albert was his helping dad build our 4 room concrete block house in the late '40s between Grandpa and Grandma's house and Uncle Doc and Aunt Mag's house. Uncle Albert's finishing touch to the house was putting his initials in the wet stucco on the west side of the house with his finger. His initials can still be seen in the upper left of the pantry that was added during a remodeling several years later.

Years later, Uncle Albert was laying the foundation for the new Harrison Chapel Methodist Church. At some point, the residents of the Brush Creek Area decided they needed a church. Richard T. Tidwell donated 1 acre of land for the original church and a fellow with the last name of Harrison donated the lumber to build the building. It was a high vaulted frame building with a tin roof next to a creek that ran into Brush Creek about a quarter mile downstream. My earliest recollection of this church was that it had several kerosene lamps attached to the walls with brackets for light during night services. Heat was supplied by a large coal stove in the center of the church and it had the longest stovepipe running up to the high vaulted ceiling that I have ever seen!

There was no outhouse so all of the conveniences were outside, behind trees, or otherwise out of sight. I was too young to remember just how all of this was worked out.

The pews were homemade of one by four inch pine boards with cracks between them. The bases for the pews had some curvature to them but the benches were still hard! Cooling during the summer was by all of the windows being opened and everyone had hand fans supplied by a local funeral home with their advertising on the back of the fans and some bible picture on the front. I still remember some ample local women getting carried away with the preaching, fanning themselves vigorously with sweat running down their faces, and shouting AMEN as the preacher made his point. I remember when dad and some other members wired it up for electricity and the kerosene lamps were retired. I also remember when a thunderstorm rolled through one summer night and a limb was knocked loose from a large water oak tree next to the church This limb did not come straight down and hit the ground like limbs are supposed to do. It instead came down straight as an arrow and went through the tin roof of the church and the pine boards on the inside and penetrated into the roof BIG TIME! I don't remember how the local men got the limb out but I remember that neither the roof nor the vaulted ceiling were ever the same again!

Back to Uncle Albert.

The congregation decided it was time to build a new church shortly after the limb incident. The first step was to build some Sunday school rooms. This was a concrete block free standing building set next to the creek. It had four Sunday school rooms in a row. Folding doors were used as room dividers so the entire building could be opened up and used as one big room.

I don't remember but I am sure that Uncle Albert did most of the concrete block laying.

The congregation decided to build a new sanctuary about two years after the Sunday school rooms were completed. I was sixteen at the time. Uncle Albert had two grandsons about my age and all three of us were helping him lay the foundation for the new church. We would mix mortar, under his close supervision, and carry the mortar and concrete blocks to him as he needed them. The new church took off from the Sunday school rooms and went east toward the road in front.

Anyway, Uncle Albert was laying the second course of blocks on the north side of the building when two of his sons came by with a six pack or two of Schlitz beer. Uncle Albert quenched his thirst with two beers and promptly deposited the empty cans in the holes of the concrete block he was working on. The Methodist congregation took a dim view of beer drinking or drinking of any kind back then and probably still does. Anyway, the new church has two empty Schlitz cans in the foundation with Uncle Albert's fingerprints all over them. They are about a third way up from the Sunday school rooms on the north side of the building!

Jesse F. Tidwell*

Born February 20, 1891, died July 9, 1939. Buried in the Cox cemetery near Killen, Alabama.

Jesse Tidwell never married, however he did serve in the Army. He died in Texas, according to Grandmother Alice. I never knew the details. Grandmother related stories to me at various times that led me to believe that everyone considered him to be a colorful figure. Perhaps that was because he was in the Army and had been to places and seen things that they never would or that Grandma Alice thought he was a ladies' man and had affairs on his visits home. She even named names! Perhaps it was because he brought his pistol home with him on leave like grandmother claimed he did when the old home place was auctioned off after Richard T's death. Grandmother always thought it was to protect her and grandfather as they tried to buy the old home place. I don't know.

Jesse is buried in the Cox cemetery nearby with all of his brothers.

Nathan Jerry Tidwell*

Nathan Jerry Tidwell was born December 20, 1894 in Lauderdale County, and died July 19, 1954, at home from complications due to strokes. He is buried at the Cox Cemetery near Killen, Alabama.

Nathan married Alice Genova Reid (born December 20, 1898, in Lawrence County Alabama) on October 28, 1917 in Florence, Alabama. She died the age of 82 on April 27, 1981 at the Eliza Coffee Hospital in Florence, Alabama, due to the complications from a stroke. She is buried at the Cox Cemetery near Killen, Alabama next to her husband.

Nathan was the youngest son. Grandmother always called him N.J. when she called him to meals. They had four children, three boys, Walter Glen, Richard Almon, Owen Reid, and one daughter, Reba Jane. Owen died in childhood of a ruptured appendix.

Grandpa Nathan and Grandma Alice bought Richard T's old log house and original property at auction after he died. They had to borrow the money from Bama Hale and her husband to do so. I have a copy of the mortgage. Family rumor had it that Richard T. had a lot of gold coins when he died. Some thought he had buried them someplace and they were never found. Others thought Grandma and Grandpa found them and used them to make a down payment on the old family home place. Grandmother Alice would never comment either way. Again, this was just a family rumor.

The house was covered with a rusty tin roof from my first memories. It had this same roof on it when it was sold. The tin roof had several small holes in it and it leaked when it rained. I can still remember everybody putting pots and pans in the floor to catch the water from the leaks while I was a young boy growing up. The tin roof made things so hot in the summer that the only thing the upstairs rooms could be used for was storage by the time I can remember.

People came around later every year trying to get everyone to let them spray a sealant on their old rusty tin roofs. Grandma and Grandpa had this done several times. This eliminated the leaks, or at least slowed them down, for a year or two.

Grandpa got some doors from TVA and boxed in the dog trot and made a small sitting room out of it before dad and mom built their house. These doors had glass on top and a wooden panel on the bottom. This made a small sitting room that Aunt Jane and Finney used during their courting years. He then finished a bedroom for Aunt Jane. This room had been started when they added the kitchen and dining room to the south side of the house years earlier but it had never been finished until that time.

I was born in their house in 1942 and we lived with Grandma and Grandpa while dad served in World War II and afterward while dad was getting established after the war. I don't remember exactly when it was, probably around 1949 or 1950, but Grandpa Nathan and Grandma Alice gave dad and mom one acre of land and loaned them $750, according to family stories, to build their original four room concrete block house. I can well understand Grandma and Grandpa wanting their house back to themselves after raising three kids myself.

I remember dad wiring the old house for electricity after we built our house and we were already living in it when the electricity was finally turned on.

After we finally got electricity, Dad, Walter and cousin William put up a concrete block spring house over a spring just north of the original one that been relied on for water. They installed a well pump. Cousin William dug a long ditch from the spring house to the old log house and Dad and Uncle Walter ran a copper line from the pump to the house and installed a used sink for Grandmother in the kitchen. Uncle Walter was a plumber. Grandmother later bought a used hot water heater and dad and I installed it for her. An electric range, refrigerator and deep freezer were later added along with a clothes washer and dryer. I can remember when we boxed in the back porch and converted one end of it into an indoor bathroom for Grandmother. I remember having to help Raleigh Barnett dig a septic system for the new bathroom. The dirt along the entire creek bottom was only about 2 ½ feet deep. There is nothing but solid flint rock under the dirt. Raleigh had to drill holes in the flint rock with a hammer and star drill and dynamite the rock away so that the septic system could be installed. We then lined the hole that he had blasted with concrete blocks to form the septic tank. A wire was run from the dynamite caps to his son Jimmy's car and we used the car battery to set off the dynamite. We found Bermuda grass runners in flint rock cracks 6 feet underground while we were digging!

Times were still tough but they were getting better!

Nathan was a farmer early on and served in World War I as a private in France. He later worked for TVA but was not working much when I could remember due to a physical disability with a hernia. He did not want to have surgery to correct it. This limited what he could do.

My memories of Grandpa Nathan are limited.

I remember Grandpa catching chickens every Sunday morning to have for Sunday dinner (lunch). He would sprinkle corn on the ground for the chickens to eat and snare a chicken's leg with a long bamboo fishing pole that had a bent piece of wire on the end while they were distracted by the corn. He would catch 2 chickens if the Methodist preacher was coming for dinner and wring the chicken's necks. I would then help him scald the chickens in hot water so that we could remove the feathers, and singe the pin feathers off. I would then watch him finish cleaning the chickens. He would take them inside and Grandma Alice would fry them. The preacher and his family would usually come home from church with us for diner. I have never seen anybody clean the meat off of a chicken breast all the way down to the rib bones like those Methodist preachers could. I had to wait until the grownups were finished for my lunch and hope there was some chicken left!

Dad, Grandpa and I would usually sit on the front porch while the chicken cooking was going on and polish our shoes before church. Grandpa would then put on his Sunday suit of clothes and Grandma, Mother and Aunt Jane would get ready for church as well. We would then all usually walk the mile or so to church. I can still remember Grandpa's "Sunday Go To Meeting" shoes squeaking every time he took a step. We had to walk the entire distance over dirt roads and all of our freshly polished shoes were dirty when we got there. Grandmother was a Sunday School teacher.

Grandpa's favorite aftershave lotion was Old Spice. It was also Dad's favorite when I was growing up. I have used Old Spice most of my adult life. My oldest grandson, the only one old enough to shave, also uses it now. Strange! Must be in the genes.

Grandpa also chewed plug tobacco. After much thought, I remember the brand was Bloodhound. It had a picture of a flop eared bloodhound on the front wrapper. He used, what was to me back then, a big pocket knife to cut his chew off of the plug. Grandma gave me the knife he used to cut his tobacco after he died and it still had some tobacco stuck to the blade. I took this knife to Indiana with me. I showed it to Dad once after I moved back to Alabama and he told me the story of this knife. It was a Remington that dad had bought for Grandpa at a hardware store in Florence. I gave it back to Dad because it had more meaning for him than it did for me. This knife was not in Dad's personal possessions after he passed away. I don't know what happened to it.

Once Grandpa forgot to feed or slop the hogs until after he had put his Sunday suit on. I went with him to the barn where the hog pen was. The hogs were particularly hungry since it was late and they tried to fight to be the first one to the trough. They thoroughly **splattered** Grandpa with the hog slop which was always smelly. Hog slop generally consisted of dirty dish water, garden scraps and left over food from the day before, Grandpa would always mix a little ground corn with it. Grandpa kept his composure but gave the hogs a good talking to. He said something like "You dang blasted devils, I don't care if you never get another bite to eat." He didn't jump up and down and swear like a lot of people might, me included if it happened to me today.

Another memory was the time he killed a copperhead snake and brought it up to our house for us to see, draped over his briar blade. One of my brothers currently has this briar blade and it probably dates all the way back to Richard T. It is identical to the one that the "Grim Reaper" is always depicted carrying.

Grandpa had two hound pups about this time and they would not mind him. He would get on them and sometimes switch them. They would always run to our house yelping every step of the way.

Grandpa never wanted either Ann or me to play with the stuff stored in the attic. He told us stories of "Raw Eyes and Bloody Bones" that lived up there. This kept us properly scared and we didn't spend much time upstairs without grownups after that. There was a lot of neat stuff stored there. I was particularly intrigued by the old spinning wheel and some old iron shoe lasts. These came in different sizes and were used as the forms to hand make shoes. Shoemaking by hand was a long lost art by the time that I came along, as well as the use of spinning wheels. The feather beds were also stored up there in the summer months.

You have never lived unless you have slept in a feather bed. They were made of striped bed ticking filled with hand grown and plucked duck and goose down. Grandmother would always take them down from the attic after it had started to get cold in the fall. She would shake them up to fluff up the feathers and put them on top of the normal cotton mattress that we used. She would have to shake them up again each morning when she made the beds. There is nothing like getting into bed in an unheated room and sinking down into that soft warm feather bed. It was like floating on a cloud I always imagined. On a cold fall or winter morning, there was nothing like waking up in that warm feather bed snuggled warmly under the handmade quilts that the neighbor ladies would make every summer. Grandmother had the quilt frame and all of the quilting parties would take place at her house. Those parties went on almost every day for weeks at a time until they had all made their quilts.

Grandmother would hang the feather beds on the clothesline outside along with the heavy winter quilts to "air out" every spring and then retire them back to the attic where they would spend the summer.

We were all dirt poor back then but we did have our luxuries. Most notably our feather beds!

There was still a portion of an old rail fence on the hillside west of Grandpa's old house while I was growing up. It was only four or five rails high. People were always getting a stomach ailment of one kind or another because of lack of refrigeration. We also had an outhouse that we had to use and nothing was as sanitary as it is today. Sometime when Grandpa's stomach would be rumbling and grumbling he would make a comment such as "If my belly doesn't settle down, I will be squirting over a ten rail fence soon!" I had never seen a ten rail fence but I could imagine that it was big and high and require quite an effort if Grandpa did what he said he thought he could! I could relate to what he was talking about since I had had the "squirts" a number of times.

Another memory of Grandpa was the time he bought a snazzy, fairly new, shiny black Plymouth coupe. Grandpa had always had to drive old beat up rusty Ford coupes before that. He drove his old Ford to town one Saturday and came back in his shiny new car. The entire family was flabbergasted and did not understand. Grandpa then built a garage for his new car. The family later made excuses for his buying this car as signs of his later problems with strokes. I think that Grandpa just wanted it!

Grandpa Nathan had a series of strokes when I was a young boy and I don't remember too much about him after that. I remember them having to prop him up in a chair on the front porch so he could get some fresh air after he got so bad. I can remember his death and funeral in 1954. This was the first time that I had ever been this close to somebody that had died.

Our family had outgrown our four room concrete block house by this time. Ann and I had shared a bedroom until we moved to Kentucky. We rented a three bedroom house up there. This was the first time that I had ever had my own bedroom. I would not have another bedroom to myself until I moved to Indiana in 1966.

Dad and mom decided that I had to sleep in their room after we moved back. They put my bed in the corner of the room. This greatly reduced their marital privacy. After Grandpa died, dad decided that it was not right for Grandma and Aunt Jane to have to stay alone by themselves at night. I started sleeping down there and continued to do so for several years. I not only slept down there but spent most of my time there as well. I enjoyed Grandma's good cooking and all of the attention they lavished upon me. Grandmother put my bed in the corner of the west room which was her combination living room and bedroom, next to the warm coal heater.

Grandmother always made certain that I had a good breakfast. Breakfast at home had been pretty much of an afterthought at that time. Grandma got up early and made me sausage or bacon and eggs if I wanted them. She always made the most delicious dish that I had ever tasted up until that time. That was always a big bowl of fresh made oatmeal. This would not be instant oatmeal, there was nothing like that back then. She would dip whatever she wanted to cook out of a cylindrical cardboard Quaker Oats container that had a paper top. She would simmer this on the stove for the appropriate amount of time and serve it with sugar and lots of butter that she had churned herself. Sometimes we would use brown sugar and sometime white. I was particularly fond of brown sugar. It gave the oatmeal a special taste, I thought.

I was visiting grandmother for one of the last times while she was in the hospital trying to recover from her stroke. She was getting better and wanted me to take her home. They knew that they could not let her go and that didn't make her very happy. They served her oatmeal for breakfast that morning and she was fussing and didn't want to eat it. I picked up the spoon and started feeding her. She didn't want to be fed but I told her "Grandma, you fed me oatmeal when I needed it and I can feed it to you now!"

She died shortly after that.

I will cover how Grandmother Alice churned milk, then made butter and buttermilk later. She always had extra butter to sell and someone was always wanting to buy any extra that she had.

I began to fatten up and look healthy for the first time in my life.

Over time, I became closer to them than I was my own family. I was one of them. There was always a fight of one sort of another going on between Mom and Dad anyway. I didn't miss any of that screaming and yelling.

Aunt Jane married Finney Gray later but I continued to eat most of my meals with them and slept there every night. Finney and I were always close as well. I felt much closer to him at that time, and for a good portion of my life, than I did my own dad.

Dad and Mom finally had enough money to remodel and expand our original four room house. They made a three bedroom house out of it and added an indoor bathroom. I started the process of moving back home. I didn't want to but I had to.

My being so close to Grandmother Alice caused Mother no end of frustration. She always accused Grandmother Alice of trying to steal me away from her. I didn't consider it stealing, Mother had given me away as I considered it. I realize now that Mother had simply done the best that she could with what she had at the time.

Mother and I grew closer after I started to college. I had to depend on her more and more after I started working. Every minute of every day had to be scheduled so that I could accomplish what I was trying to do. My daily schedules changed slightly from semester to semester but remained basically the same. I could not have accomplished my Herculean task if she were not there to cook my meals on time, keep my clothes clean, prepare my lunch for work and do all of the basic things I could not have done on my own.

Mother became frazzled by the things that had to be done on time especially every Monday and Tuesday when I was on the four to twelve shift. I would come home from college and just have time to change into my work clothes, eat lunch, and head out for work. The entire family loved Great Northern Beans and she would usually try to have them ready for lunch at least one of those days. When she was particularly rushed for time she would prepare them in a pressure cooker and I don't even know if she would soak them before. She just plopped them in the old pressure cooker and they would be done to perfection in no time.

These streamlined beans tasted good and went down easily. I sometimes had two helpings. Those were the gassiest beans ever known to mankind unfortunately!

My job was to keep track of a very large group of thirty furnaces and take samples and run a quality control check on the molten aluminum at the appropriate time. The string of furnaces was a little over a quarter mile long. Sometimes those beans would start paying off unexpectedly and, honest to God, I would pass gas for the entire quarter mile. I didn't know anything about the Guinness book of world records at that time but I do believe that I could have set a world record for that category with two helpings of those beans!

I didn't realize how deep Mother's resentment had become with my close relationship with Grandmother Alice until my daughters came along. Lana named the first two but had run out of names by the time the third one came along. We both liked the name Cynthia so I named her Cynthia Alice, after my grandmother. Mother came unhinged and thought that I should name my daughter after her. I told Mother that if she was as good to her grandchildren as Grandmother Alice had been to me, someone would surely name a child after her. This didn't satisfy mother at all! One of my brothers, Sammy, finally did name a daughter after Mother.

<u>*5*</u>

The Old Family Home Place Is Sold

Richard T. Tidwell died at home on October 4, 1917, an auction was held to dispose of his property and personal possessions in the spring of 1918. Family stories relate that the need for the auction was mostly caused by the agitation of Florence A. (Bama) Tidwell's husband William A. Hale under the pretext that he was trying to protect Bama's share of everything and he forced everything to be auctioned off. This is pretty much the same story that Grandmother Alice always told, but Virgiline Tidwell Hale was able to add some particular details. She said that there were some hogs in the pig pen that Richard T. had given to his sons before he died. Bill even went to the pig pen to get the hogs for the auction but John Dee Tidwell stepped in according to Virgiline. John Dee apparently told Bill Hale that there was no way that he was taking those hogs. This story had to have been handed down to Virgiline because this happened before she was born.

Anyway, this is pretty much what happened though the black bog of time has obscured all of the details. Grandmother Alice always said that she and Grandpa had to borrow the money from Bill and Bama Hale to buy the property. What I do know is that the original mortgage was not signed by Grandpa Nathan but by William A. Hale. Could he have been the cosigner for the mortgage? Perhaps he was the administrator. It cannot be determined at this late date.

A copy of the original mortgage follows:

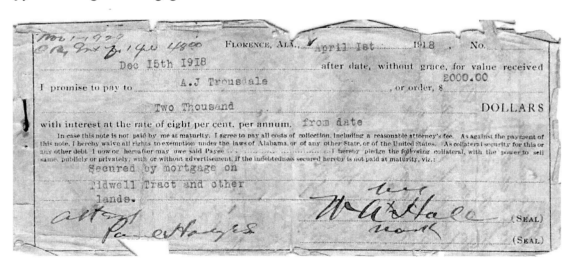

I also have receipts for two note payments that Grandpa Nathan (or Jesse F. Tidwell? Could this have been an attempt to use the gold coins and not attract attention to Grandmother Alice and Grandfather Nathan?) made on the mortgage the first year. They are as follows:

=

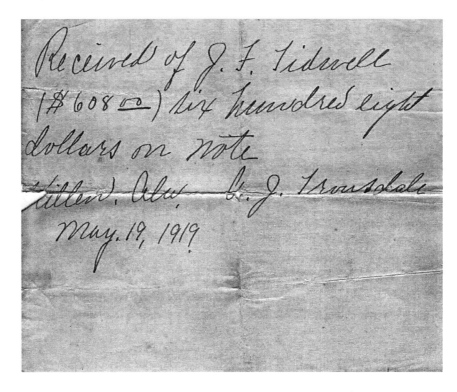

Six Hundred Eight Dollars was a hefty payment back in 1919 on a $2,000 mortgage. Could the gold coins have been a part?

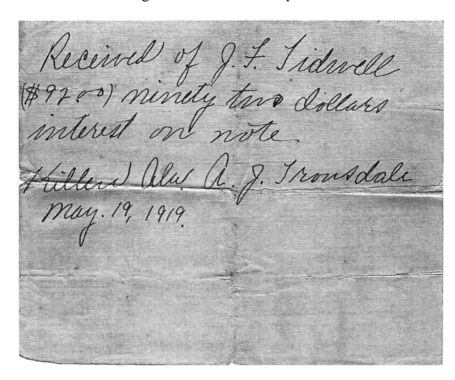

Other interesting documents are two original property tax records that Richard T. Tidwell paid in the years prior to his death.

1904 TAXES.

No. 3098 State of Alabama, Lauderdale County, 11 — 1 — 1904

Received of _R. T. Tidwell_

the sum of _Five 00/100 Dollars_
being in full of amount of Taxes due the State of Alabama and County of Lauderdale for year 1904, divided as follows:

State Tax on Real Estate	8 0
Special State Tax on Real Estate (Maimed Soldiers)	3 2
Special State School Tax on Real Estate	4 6
County Tax on Real Estate	1 2 8
Special County Tax on Real Estate. For Courthouse 10 cts., Bridges 5 cts.	3 2
Road Tax on Real Estate	3 2
State Tax on Personal Property	2 0
Special State Tax on Personal Property (Maimed Soldiers)	8
Special State School Tax on Personal Property	2 4
County Tax on Personal Property	3 2
Special County Tax on Personal Property. For Courthouse 10 cts., Bridges, 5 cts.	6
Road Tax on Personal Property	8
Assessor's Fees	5 00
Collector's Fees	

J. E. Jones

MARSHALL & BRUCE CO., NASHVILLE.   Tax Collector.

From 1904

No. 4334

RECEIVED of _Tidwell R. T._   191__

the sum of _Six + 35/100_ DOLLARS

in full payment of Taxes due the State of Alabama and Lauderdale County 1913.

Total Value of Real Estate	2 7 0	
Total Value of Personal Property	2 0 0	
Tax Rate $1.35 per $100.00 Valuation		
Aggregate Amount		6 35
10% Penalty		
Citation Raise		
Assessor's Fees		
Collector's Fees		
Interest		
Total Tax		

PAID
DEC 11 1913
A. Carson
Tax Collector
Lauderdale Co.

ROBERTS & SON, PRINTERS, BIRMINGHAM.

Tax Collector

From 1913

Two additional documents that I have found are property tax records that Grandpa Nathan (or Jesse F.?) paid on the property. They are as follows:

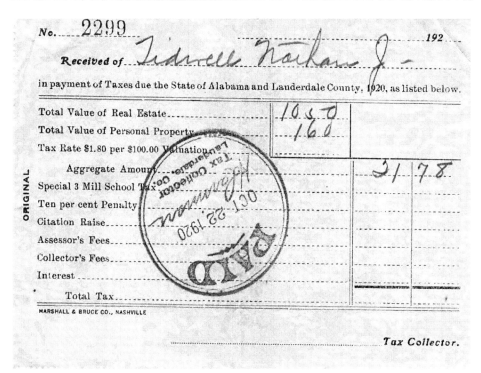

No. 2104
RECEIVED of .... *Tidwell J. F.* .... 191....
the sum of .... DOLLARS,
in full payment of Taxes due the State of Alabama and Lauderdale County, 1917.

Total Value of Real Estate		
Total Value of Personal Property	*143*	
Tax Rate $1.80 per $100.00 Valuation		
Aggregate Amount		*2 61*
Ten per cent Penalty		
Citation Raise		
Assessor's Fees		
Collector's Fees		
Interest		
Total Tax		

PAID OCT 27 1917 Tax Collector Lauderdale Co.

McQUIDDY, NASHVILLE

.... Tax Collector.

No. 2299
Received of .... *Tidwell Nathan J.* .... 192....
in payment of Taxes due the State of Alabama and Lauderdale County, 1920, as listed below.

Total Value of Real Estate	*1050*	
Total Value of Personal Property	*160*	
Tax Rate $1.80 per $100.00 Valuation		
Aggregate Amount		*21 78*
Special 3 Mill School Tax		
Ten per cent Penalty		
Citation Raise		
Assessor's Fees		
Collector's Fees		
Interest		
Total Tax		

PAID OCT 22 1920 Tax Collector Lauderdale Co.

ORIGINAL

MARSHALL & BRUCE CO., NASHVILLE

.... Tax Collector.

I have numerous other old documents that Aunt Jane gave to me that her father had kept in his old canvas ammunition pouch from World War I. It, as well as the documents, are getting old and frail and have the dusty smell of time about them. Grandpa Nathan was a pack rat and kept all sorts of interesting things such as cancelled checks and bank statements. Aunt Jane gave them to me when she found out that she had ALS and was dying. I told her at the time that I didn't know what I would ever do with them. She simply said "You will find something to do with them!"

Aunt Jane and Finney lived with Grandmother Alice in the old family home for years but they had wanted to build a new house for some time. They had purchased 20 acres for this purpose. The holdup was that Grandmother Alice did not want to sell the family home place and move with them to the new house. Grandmother Alice finally decided this move would be best for everybody and decided to sell the family farm around the mid '60s.

She offered it to family members first at a discount. There were no takers. She was only asking $15,000 for it but that was a lot of money back then. There would have been about a $4,000 discount to Grandmother's children as I remember if they had bought it. This was their share and they could have applied it to the purchase price. Few of us could afford it and those who could had no interest. I personally had plans to leave the area as quickly as I could and start a life of my own somewhere else.

Dad wanted it deep down but he and Mother were in one of their perpetual spats that they kept going back then.

Grandpa Nathan wanted Dad to have several acres of the land because Dad had joined the CCC group at 16 and sent his money home to keep the loan on the place from being foreclosed as family stories go.

This portion was split off of the family farm and grandmother sold the rest to Ferrell Allen for the $15,000. I was with Grandma and Ferrell down in the bottom south of the old log house when the deal was reached.

Ferrell cut down and sold the pine thicket that was planted by the CCC boys to control erosion and later built a new house and sold the logs from the old home place to somebody to move and reconstruct. All of the original buildings are gone. Ferrell later built a log cabin down by the creek at the foot of the hill west of the original home place.

I understand that the entire property is now for sale. I doubt that any family members want to or can afford what Ferrell is asking for the place minus all of the memories and family landmarks. All of these are long gone.

<u>*6*</u>

Hog Killing

Our hog killings were traditionally around Thanksgiving. The weather was generally cold enough by then so the meat would not spoil. We later had to move it to just before Christmas because the winters started getting warmer and it was not cold enough to preserve the meat until then. I guess this was the start of global warming and we just did not know it!

Hog butchering is always a bloody, gruesome and dirty mess. I didn't want any meat to eat for at least a week after it was over. I am glad that I don't have to go through that again!

The night of the butchering was always the night for liver hash. This was Aunt Mag's recipe. She would take small chunks of liver, melt, heart, lungs, and a little leaf lard (fat form the intestines) and stew them with a lot of sage and perhaps a little hot pepper. It was quite tasty but was real rich.

Tenderloin and biscuits were also fare for that night and the next morning.

The days following salting the meat down were also very busy. Sausage had to be made and put in sacks, the lard had to be cooked out and the heads worked up into souse meat. Hardly anything was wasted. A lot of good saturated fat and plenty of cholesterol! It's a wonder any of us are still alive after eating all of that!

Hog raising, butchering and preserving the meat with salt was always an important part of family life on Brush Creek. There was no refrigeration in Richard T's day so this was the only way he could preserve meat. We really had only limited refrigeration (the ice man brought a block of ice for the "Ice Box" every week) until I was a good sized boy. I can remember the lines to wire us up for electricity being run out into the country when I was in the 2nd grade or so. It was only after that when refrigeration became common and later than that when we could afford a deep freezer. The original smoke house remained when I was a boy growing up at the log home place. It was a very tight structure with no cracks between the boards. This would have made it very difficult to smoke meat in. It had a concrete floor as well which would have made it almost impossible to build a fire for smoking as well. Things stored in it did not rust so I know it was never used to salt or preserve fresh meat. I do remember cured meat hanging up in it but never it being used for curing purposes. Perhaps the meat was salted and preserved somewhere else and hung without smoke or Uncle Doc cured and smoked it for them. Uncle Doc had a conventional smoke house.

The family affinity for cured meat remains today. I guess it is because of our ancestors having to rely on it for their source of meat during times of no refrigeration that it is so deeply embedded into our roots. We still had to rely on it for our primary source of meat until the 60's or so. We all still crave it I think. Vegetables aren't good unless there is a big hunk of cured pork, preferably smoked, floating in them!

I remember Uncle Ed killing a hog for Dad with me mostly in his way one snowy winter day on the bank of the creek. We had an old wooden barrel sunk into the ground a little way and heated the water to scald the hog over an open fire in Grandpa's old black cast iron wash pot. We then put the hot water in the wooden barrel. We had to dunk the hog into scalding water with a block and tackle. This was supported at the top by a limb from a large hollow beech tree. A single tree, normally used to hook up a plow to a mule or horse, was hooked to the other end of the block and tackle. We cut into the back legs of the hog above the ankle to pull the main leader or ham string free. We then hooked the main leaders to the hooks on the end of the single tree. This allowed us to pick up the hog with the block and tackle, dunk the hog in the hot water until the hair loosened, pull it out and lay it on the ground to scrape it. We then pulled it back up and rinsed it by dumping buckets of water from the creek on it and then removing its intestines and vital organs. We then rinsed the inside of the hog with water from the creek. This was quite a job and took all day.

I later helped dad and Finney Gray do the same thing several times. Finney and I once even butchered a calf the same way, only we skinned the calf instead of scalding and scraping it.

I am sure this was how hogs were butchered in Richard T's day and remained the way we butchered hogs until sometime in the mid 70's at which time dad built a butchering station just northeast of the bridge over the creek by his house. We could only butcher 2 or 3 hogs a day by the old method. Dad dug a small pit and constructed a shallow vat with a metal bottom over it. The vat would be filled with creek water and a fire built in the pit to heat the water. Platforms were built on each side of the vat of rough sawn oak.

After a hog was killed by shooting it between the eyes with a .22 caliber rifle and stuck in the throat to bleed, it was hauled to the vat with a pickup truck. It was then pulled onto one of the wooden platforms. The hog was then rolled into the vat with log chains at each end and worked up and down until the hair loosened on that side. The hog was then rolled onto the other platform with the chains and turned over and the process repeated. We would then pull the hog onto one of the platforms and scrape all of the hair off of it with butcher knives. Once the hair was removed, the hog was then hoisted with the same block and tackle anchored to a piece of metal pipe supported by two small trees. Dad removed all of the intestines and vital organs and thoroughly rinsed the hog with buckets of creek water.

The vital organs were then impaled through the windpipe on a nail driven into a board for this purpose to hold them in place until they dried a little. The liver, heart and lungs were all attached. The melt was removed from the intestines separately. The vitals from several hogs would be hanging there.

Another hog was ready by the time dad had finished with the first one.

This speeded up the process and we killed as many as thirteen hogs and cleaned them in one day by this method. This was really a community affair. All of the neighbors would kill their hogs that day and bring them over to be dressed. I saw people at hog killings that I had not seen since the one the year before.

The hogs were cut down the backbone with a buck saw for pork chops and down both sides of the backbone if they wanted tenderloin and then hung into the smokehouse to cool overnight. We filled up both Uncle Doc's and Dad's smokehouses with hanging meat some years.

Uncle Doc would then take some of the large intestines home to make chitterlings out of them. He would first wash everything out of the intestines and then peel the inner and outer layer off of them. He would then soak them in soda water for several days and change the water frequently. Dad always made fun of him doing this and claimed he could smell Uncle Doc's chitterlings cooking all the way down to his house. Dad's word for chitterlings was chittlins. I vaguely remember him pronouncing it with an "s" in front in early years, especially describing Uncle Doc 's homemade variety. In later years Dad actually bought chitterlings at the supermarket and the family would gather for a chitterling cooking. Thank God I always missed out on the chitterling cooking's!

The meat was then allowed to cool until the next day and then cut up and salted in wooden boxes. The bacon and jowls were sometimes sugar cured on an open bench. Dad's rule of thumb was to leave the meat in the salt box for one week per inch of thickness. This would vary somewhat due to the temperature.

The meat was then washed in the creek to remove the excess salt and hung in the smoke chamber of the smokehouse for smoking with a small fire of green hickory wood and a little sassafras. A conventional smoke house was usually constructed as a small pole barn and sided with rough sawn oak. The siding had to be nailed on while the wood was still green or a nail could not be driven into it. Take my word about this, I have bent many a nail trying to drive them into rough sawn oak after it had dried out. It can't be done. The oak planks would shrink and small cracks would open between them while drying. This allowed for ventilation and allowed the smoke that hit the meat to be cold. The whole area for some distance around smelled very good if Dad or Uncle Doc was smoking meat. It would take several days to get the proper amount of smoke on the meat. They would smoke it again for a half day or so after a damp spell to drive the moisture off of the meat. It was properly smoked when the color of the meat was a deep golden brown and would keep well up into the summer. They could have made a fortune if they could have bottled that smoke and smell and sold it!

Sausage Preserving

Fresh sausage would start to get old and sour tasting after it had been stored in the smokehouse for three or four weeks. It was not hung directly in the smoke room but was close enough to get a little smoke. It would become inedible if not eaten quickly.

This was probably because all that we had to store it in was homemade sacks made from old sheets and pillowcases. Each sack would hold about two pounds of sausage. They were never completely free of bacteria, as was nothing else in the smoke house.

Sausage is best when smoked and aged for about two weeks. We would freeze it at that point after we had freezers.

We never did it but Uncle Doc, Aunt Mag and Grandmother would talk about how their ancestors would preserve sausage well up into the winter.

There were two methods of doing this.

The sausage would first be fried. The methods differ from that point.

Method 1:

The cooked sausage would be stacked into clean fruit jars and the hot sausage grease would be poured over it. The jars were then sealed and kept in a cold place.

Method 2:

The sausage would be stacked in a corn shuck. The shuck would be carefully prepared by removing the ear of corn and then cleaning out the inside. The corn shuck and sausage were tied tightly with some type of cord and kept in a cold place.

A corn shuck: Yuck!!

But remember this was well before we had aluminum foil or plastic wrap!

One method that we particularly liked was to buy some salted and cured sheep small intestines casing from a local German meat market. They would have to order them from Eastern Europe and sold sausage that they had made and smoked in them. These casings costs twenty dollars a pound back in the '70s but we did not have enough sausage every year to use a pound of casing material. We would keep the unused casing material in the freezer from year to year.

This sausage was smaller in diameter than our homemade sausage sacks and this allowed the sausage to dry out quicker. Enzymes in the sheep intestine also gave this sausage a taste of its own. We loved this taste. This sausage would taste better the older that it got. We could keep sausage well up into the spring by this method. The German meat market would keep this type of sausage in their meat cooler and sometimes had it three years old. They charged more for each year that they had kept it refrigerated. It was so dry by that time that it had to be cooked in water to reconstitute it. They would go back into the cooler and cut off what you had ordered. It was always moldy by then. They would simply wipe the mold off with a rag wet with vinegar and sell the sausage to you.

I have not been able to find any sausage made like this in years. I doubt that the FDA will allow it!

Meat curing is basically controlled mummification. The salt and smoke dries it out and the salt preserves it.

Black Cast Iron Wash Pot

The black cast iron wash pot was a much used item both for us and for other country people in our circumstances. It had many uses. Each family had one or more of them.

These pots were cured on the inside by use with animal fats to where they resisted rusting. They, as with all cast iron pots and pans, took on a black sheen with use. This helped protect them from rusting but did not give them complete protection.

The wash pot had to be stored top down with a rock or piece of wood under it for ventilation to keep the inside from rusting. People had to be very careful not to store them upright, especially where water could collect in them. The pot would freeze and crack if water froze in it since it was made of cast iron. You can still see these old pots converted into big flower pots because somebody let them freeze and burst a long time ago. That is about all they are good for once this happened to them.

Our original wash pot passed down from Grandmother Alice to Dad and now Keith has it.

Some of the uses these versatile pots were put to are:

Washing: Of course it was used for washing clothes as this is what it was made for.

Soap Making: It was also used to make soap from hog fat, water, and lye.

Rendering fats: It was used to render animal fat into usable cooking oils or other useful products. We used it to make lard after hog killing. This was the primary source of our cooking oils until vegetable oils became available and affordable. Dad still preferred hog lard to fry fish with all of his life. We would sometimes end up with four or more fifty pound stands (as lard cans were called when I was growing up) of lard after a big hog killing as well as a big pile of cracklings. We used this lard for our cooking oil into the next year. It would start to get rancid by midsummer due to becoming oxidized. This is when the old people would have used it to make soap.

Cooking: These old pots are still used to cook soups and stews for family gatherings and fund-raisers and for a fish fry where large volumes are to be cooked.

Wash Day On The Bank Of The Creek

Wash day before electricity was a special day. I am sure that the women had other words than special for it! Women from all families had to do pretty much the same thing.

I remember Grandmother Alice and Mother doing this on the bank of the creek, the same place where the hog killings took place, by setting up the old black cast iron pot and several wash tubs to wash our clothes every week. Clothes were particularly dirty back then based on how close we lived to the soil or just by living with the chickens and livestock that were always around.

As I remember the process, the first thing that they would do was fill the black iron pot with creek water and build an open fire under it. They would use lye soap that had been made in the same black iron wash pot using bacon grease and any other used hog fat or surplus or rancid lard and lye. This was heated until the lye reacted with the fat and turned into soap. It was then poured into a shallow wooden frame where it was allowed to cool and set up. It was then cut up into small pieces which were shaved into the water boiling in the black iron pot. We would even take baths with the lye soap if we had no other soap. It was not very gentle but would get the job done.

Particularly dirty clothes, such as overalls and other extremely dirty work clothes, were then added to the water and soap in the black iron pot and boiled. They had a wooden paddle to stir the clothes and then used it to transfer them to the first wash tub, which was also filled with creek water.

They would then use a rub board and more lye soap in the first wash tub to scrub the clothes clean after the boiling in the black iron pot. Clothes not boiled were also scrubbed clean here.

The clothes were then rinsed in another wash tub and touched up with the rub board if necessary.

After final rinsing, Grandmother Alice and Mother would wring (literally) the water out of the clothes by hand and hang them up to dry. There was an old wire fence that was close to where they washed clothes that was used for this purpose. Grandma also had a clothesline by the house.

Remember, this was before electricity or permanent press.

The clothes were taken inside after they were dry and they had to be ironed, summer or winter. This was done by heating a flat iron on a hot stove and ironing the wrinkles out of everything. The irons were either heated over the cook stove, wood or coal heater, or even by fireplace if no stove was available.

Times and people, men and women, were tough back then.

Baths

Needless to say, people didn't bathe as often back then. It was a real chore to take a complete bath in the winter. People tried to get by with sponge baths. This meant washing places like face, hands, neck and ears regularly and areas that smelled as needed. A Saturday night bath was as frequent as could be expected. This would have been done by taking the same #3 wash tub used to wash clothes and putting it by the heat source used to heat the house and hope it got pretty warm. Water was also heated in kettles to touch up the water in the tub. Everybody would take a bath in the same water.

The #3 wash tub would have been set out on the back porch during the summer and the sun would have warmed the water.

This was before any deodorant was available and everyone probably smelled worse than most of us do today. This didn't matter much because everyone smelled or stunk the same. We couldn't smell each other.

We were lucky that we had the creek. It was ice cold but everyone bathed in it during warm weather.

Social Interaction and Entertainment

Except for visiting relatives nearby, the Methodist Church was the social focal point for our community. Remember transportation was poor and the roads were dirt and gravel out in the country. The county might run the road grader over the dirt roads once or twice a year to keep them passable. Potholes would get big enough to really cause problems with any traffic. There were cars and trucks but most local travel was still done by walking or horse and wagon in the late '40s. This was a very remote area even then. On a calm spring or summer day when the wind was from the right direction, it was possible to hear the car tires hitting the butt plate on the Shoals Creek bridge on Highway 43 about 4 miles away. The diesel engines from the tugboats on the Tennessee River could also be heard if the wind was from the right direction. We would sometimes walk up the hill to visit Uncle Richard's family at night. The neon sign from Angel's filling station in Killen could be seen from the vantage point on top of the hill on a clear night. No sound or air pollution.

In the late '50s, then Governor Big Jim Folsom paved every cow path in North Alabama. Rumor had it that his wife owned interest in an asphalt company but who cared. The roads were finally passable! Mack Riggs' local general store was the commercial focal point of the community. The guys from the community would gather there at night around the pot bellied stove to visit and talk with anybody that would wander in. This was how we kept up with what was happening in the community.

The opportunity for outside social contact improved with the improved infrastructure. We even had a four party phone line in the house in the mid '50s.

Entertainment when I was a boy growing up was very limited. Aunt Jane, Virgiline and Marguerite, Uncle Doc's daughters, would gather at the old home place and roll their hair at night by kerosene lamp light. They would cut strips from brown paper bags to use for rolling their hair. I don't remember how they did it. They would iron their clothes some nights with flat irons heated on the coal heater. They would chatter, as girls do, about what interested them. I don't remember much about their conversations, but it was entertaining to me.

Grandpa had a battery powered radio. We could pick up Nashville WSM at night and would get to listen to the Grand Ole Opry on Saturday nights if the battery was strong enough.

Gardening and Preserving

Grandma and Grandpa always raised a large garden. There were peach trees around the old barn and a large yellow delicious apple tree out by the road on the east side of the old house.

Grandma would pickle and preserve the peaches and dry the apples for fried apple pies. I remember sitting on the front porch trying to help peel and slice the apples for drying and peeling the peaches. Uncle Doc and Aunt Mag would help when they weren't busy with their own canning and preserving. Wild plums and blackberries were gathered and used to make jelly and jams. We would also try to find wild muscadines for juice.

Wild mint grew in a patch down by the creek. It was perfect to make a drink by crushing the leaves and adding them to sugar water. Watercress grew in the stream from the many springs on the hillside. I was more adventuresome than the rest. I gathered it and made a wilted salad out of it with green onions, tomatoes, bacon and boiled eggs. Nobody else would touch it. Dad thought it would poison me.

Wild bees were in the woods to be found. I remember once that Uncle Doc cut down a bee tree and robbed the honey. Uncle Albert did likewise a few years later.

The entire family would pitch in to pick and preserve the garden bounty for the winter. I remember picking, snapping and/or shelling green beans, lima beans and field peas. There were always a lot of potatoes (Irish and Sweet), onions, peppers, cabbage for kraut, corn, tomatoes, okra and various other vegetables. There was always cucumbers and dill for pickles. They would make a lot of soup mixture. All of the canning was done on the hot wood cookstove before electricity and stored away for winter.

We didn't have it to eat in the winter if we did not grow and preserve it during the summer.

Finney Gray would grow Trucker's Favorite corn to eat as roasting ears while it was green and save the dried corn to have ground into corn meal. I remember helping him shell the corn, put it in a pillow case and taking it to the mill near Saint Florian to be ground into meal. Grandmother would store it in a large wooden bin when we brought it back from the mill. This bin was built into the bottom of one of her cabinets. Grandmother Alice could make the best cornbread ever.

We ate very well.

Cooking

Cooking was done before electricity with a wood burning stove. These stoves had ovens built into them somewhere and a flat surface on top for pots and pans. I have heard of some of them with a tank for hot water but I never saw one. The one I remember Grandmother Alice using had an oven down below and warming ovens across the top.

Special covered round bottom pots were made to fit in what was called the "eye" if it was removed. The flat cooking surface had about four of these "eyes" which were simply circular and were about eight inches across. All pots were made from either cast iron or enameled steel. We used mostly cast iron. The round bottomed pots could also be placed into the ashes and coals in a fireplace, like a dutch oven, as they had short legs on them. I have one of these pots today.

This cook stove was used morning, noon and night. It provided a lot of heat which was nice in the winter. This and a coal heater in the living room were the heat sources for the house. It made things miserable during hot weather though. All of the windows were small in the old house. We had to open all of the windows and doors to try to keep the house cool during the summer. Even with this, it was 10:00 PM or after before the house would cool down after a day's cooking to where anybody could sleep. We would all sit out on the front porch that ran the length of the house at night until the house cooled off.

There was a swing at the east end and a bench beside it. There were chairs scattered about. Grandma would dip her Garrett snuff, Grandpa would chew his plug tobacco, Dad would smoke and the children would play on the porch. Uncle Doc and Aunt Mag would sometimes walk down for a visit as their house was hot also.

Uncle Doc and Aunt Mag were Church of Christ members and the rest of us were Methodist. Both groups interpret the Bible a little differently. This resulted in heated religious debates. Some would claim they were actually arguments. The only agreement reached was that they agreed to disagree the next time they got to talk about this again.

Uncle Doc was also a Republican and the rest of the family claimed to be Democrats. I don't think that any of us knew what either the Republicans or Democrats stood for. Our entire family had been historically Democrats so we were all Democrats, except for Uncle Doc.

Uncle Doc just liked to argue! Anyway, it did pass a hot summer evening until everything cooled off except for people's tempers.

The frogs and katydids would sing us to sleep through the screen doors and windows when we finally did get to go to bed.

Churning Butter

Milking cows and taking care of the milk was always a very important part of farm family life. The cows had to be milked each morning and late in the afternoon. Each farm family had at least one milk cow and sometimes more. Our family members always preferred Jersey cows. They were usually gentle cows and gave lots of rich milk.

The milk would be strained and put into gallon jars and cooled some way if it was to be used fresh or put into a churn to allow to sour and clabber so that it could be processed the next day. This always produced a clear liquid, or whey, that we poured out before churning the soured milk and fed the whey to the hogs.

The first butter churns that I remember Grandmother Alice using were made of wood and covered with a top with a hole in it. The dasher went into this hole. The dasher was a simple four bladed wooden propeller with a slight curvature carved into it. It was mounted on a wooden pole that had been carved from a tree branch by hand. This allowed the milk to be whirled around while the dasher was worked up and down in the churn for an hour or two. Aunt Jane and mother would help with the churning. I even got my turn as I got older. Grandmother always finished the butter after the churning was completed. She would rinse the butter curds with water to get as much of the excess milk out of them as she could and then strain them through a cloth. She would then start to press them down with a paddle carved out of heart of red cedar into her 2 part red cedar butter mold. It had a removable top with some sort of design carved into it. I remember hers having a fern pattern. Each butter mold held about 1 pound of finished butter. The butter would then be taken out of the butter mold and placed on a plate and refrigerated. They later used stoneware churns with a glazed finish. These served double duty as vessels to make Kraut in, dill pickles, or wine as Dad sometimes did.

This homemade butter was especially good with fresh cornbread or biscuits right out of the oven.

Grandma Alice would also use it in special vegetable dishes, such as green beans fresh out of the garden, and to make cakes.

She had steady customers for all of her extra butter.

We would refrigerate and drink the buttermilk. Grandpa Nathan's favorite evening meal, or supper as we called it, was to crumble up fresh cornbread into a glass and pour cold buttermilk over it. He would top it off with a little black pepper and salt.

I still top my buttermilk off with black pepper and salt before I drink it.

Grandma Alice ordered an electric butter churn from Sears after we got electricity. It churned the butter much faster but the butter never tasted as good to me.

We fed the extra fresh milk and buttermilk to the hogs in their slop.

The hogs were our garbage disposal. They ate anything that we did not want out of the garden such as things that were too old to be good or had bad places in them.

Nothing went to waste on the farm.

Virgiline Tidwell Hale with a one gallon churn from **Florence A. Tidwell Hale's** old home place. She is holding the dasher and the stoneware base in on the table. Nobody would ever use such a small churn. It was only meant to be a curiosity at the time I am sure.

7

Grandmother Alice's Major Home Improvements

There were three different home improvement projects that Grandmother Alice was involved in. The first one happened while Grandpa was still alive and had already happened before I could remember.

Living in a log house with mud chinking between the logs posed a housekeeping challenge. The mud chinking would come out and fall either inside or outside. It made a mess the wife had to clean up when it fell inside.

I don't know who came up with this ingenious solution to this problem. The old family home place was the only place that I have ever seen or heard of where this solution to the problem was used. It may have been an original!

Grandmother Alice bought a large amount of unbleached muslin cloth (she called it domestic) and sewed it together with her pedal type Singer sewing machine so that it would stretch from floor to ceiling. A frame of one by four boards was then nailed to the log faces to smooth out the irregularities of the logs and the muslin cloth was then stretched and tacked to this frame. This took a lot of sewing and work as they did all of the three main rooms this way. This included all three downstairs rooms.

The ceiling of these rooms consisted of the exposed rough sawn ceiling joist with rough sawn poplar boards nailed to the top of them. These boards also served as the floor for the upstairs rooms.

Everything was then whitewashed. Muslin clad walls, ceiling joists and rough sawn poplar boards.

This looked much better than rough hewn logs inside but also posed another problem, it left channels for mice and their larger cousins to live in and run about unmolested. I can remember that rat poison was used when we could hear the mice running in the walls. This got rid of the problem for awhile but there was a bad smell for several days.

It was an improvement though and worked.

Grandma's second major home improvement was sometime in the late '50s. A friend of the family, Bill Host, brought out his table saw and he, Dad and I went to work. I don't remember if Uncle Finney was involved in this or not. We ripped out the poplar boards from the ceiling of the west room, which was Grandma's combination bedroom and living room, and the dog trot room. We replaced this with ponderosa pine paneling. Bill then made boxes of the pine paneling to fit over the ceiling joists and we nailed them into place. There was some sort of decorative molding on the bottom of the ceiling joist boxes. Bill then put the finishing trim on. It looked real nice. Sheetrock was then put on the walls in place of the muslin cloth and finished out. The ceiling was then varnished and Grandma painted the walls a sandalwood color. These two rooms looked beautiful. It sort of reminded me of what I always thought the captain's cabin in an old sailing ship must have looked like!

I then stacked the probably over one hundred years old poplar boards on a shelf in the cellar for storage. Big mistake!! I found that these old boards had been turned into sawdust by the moisture in the cellar when I went to retrieve them for some other project.

Grandmother's third major home improvement was to put the muslin cloth on the outside of the front of the house on the front porch. She talked me into helping her. I had just started to college in the early '60s when this project happened. We didn't have to do anything to the east side of the house as it already had the original whitewashed clapboard siding on it.

She bought the cloth in bolts and sewed it together. She had an electric Singer sewing machine by this time so this phase went quickly. We then put up the frames and stretched the cloth. This went smoothly. I don't remember helping her apply the whitewash but I may have.

The results were stunning. It was sort of like a movie set. The house looked impressive and substantial from the road. It didn't even look like a log house! You could see the muslin cloth moving slightly in a brisk breeze though if you were close to the house.

It is amazing what can be accomplished with plenty of imagination, a little money and some work.

8

Alice Genova Reid* and Nathan Jerry Tidwell* Family

Alice Genova Reid Tidwell was born on December 20, 1898 in Lawrence County Alabama. She died the age of 82 on April 27, 1981 at the Eliza Coffee Hospital in Florence, Alabama due to the complications from a stroke. She is buried at the Cox Cemetery near Killen, Alabama next to her husband. She married Nathan Jerry Tidwell on October 28, 1917 in Florence, Alabama. There were four children from this marriage.

Nathan Jerry Tidwell

Born December 20, 1894 in Lauderdale County. Died July 19, 1954 at home from the complications due to strokes. He is buried at the Cox Cemetery near Killen, Alabama as are all of his brothers.

Grandpa Nathan served as a private in the army during World War I in France.

| Alice Genova Reid Tidwell | Nathan Jerry Tidwell |

Nathan and **Alice Tidwell**

Nathan and **Alice Tidwell**

Nathan Jerry Tidwell holding **Terry Glen Tidwell**

About 1952

9

Walter Glen Tidwell Family

Walter Glen Tidwell

Born November 27, 1918, **Died** September 24, 1986 of acute respiratory failure. Walter served in the Army during World War II, Korea, and three tours in Vietnam. Buried Serenity Memorial Gardens, Mobile, Alabama, with full military honors.

Mattie Marie Faires Tidwell

Walter **married** Mattie Marie Faires on April 16, 1938 at the Harrison Chapel Methodist church at Brush Creek, Alabama. Marie was **Born** on December 18, 1918 and is the daughter of John Henry Faires, **Born** September 18, 1853, **Died** July 27, 1927 and buried at the Wesley Chapel Cemetery. She is the daughter of Margaret Francis Spain Faires **Born** February 17, 1885, **Died** May 14, 1967 and buried at Killen, Alabama.

There were three children from this marriage.

Edith Jane Tidwell, born January 4, 1941 at the Eliza Coffee Memorial Hospital in Florence, Alabama. She **Died** on November 20, 1942 at the age of 22 months. She is buried at the Cox Cemetery near Killen, Alabama.

Martha(Marti) Laverne Tidwell, Born October 31, 1943 at the Eliza Coffee Memorial Hospital in Florence, Alabama.

Terry Glen Tidwell, Born June 30, 1952 at the Eliza Coffee Memorial Hospital in Florence, Alabama.

Clockwise from top: **Marie, Walter, Marti** and **Terry;** front **Walter** and **Marie**, back **Marti** and **Terry;** bottom **Walter,** probably **Edith** and **Marie.**

Clockwise from Top: **Marie** and probably **Terry; Walter** and probably **Marti; Walter** and **Marie,** and **Walter** with horse.

Walter in his Army uniform at various times.

10

Richard Almon Tidwell* Family

Richard Almon (Mutt) Tidwell was born May 2, 1922 in Lauderdale County Alabama. He died on November 2, 2002 of pancreatic cancer. He is buried in the Cox Cemetery near Killen, Alabama.

Dad acquired his nickname of "Mutt" early in life. Walter was about four years older than Dad and was taller. Family members nicknamed Walter "Jeff" for the comic strip Mutt and Jeff. Jeff did not stick to Walter, but Dad became "Mutt" for the rest of his life.

He married Evelyn Elois (Luna) Holloway* born January 5, 1923 in Tifton, Georgia. Mother died on December 25, 2008, Christmas day. She is buried in the Cox cemetery, near Killen, next to dad. Elois was the daughter of Ludie Wise and Myrtice Ilene Spurlock Holloway. There were six children from this marriage.

Mother was living at the Lauderdale County Nursing Home near her and Dad's old home place when she died.

Mom and Dad's Old Home Place in the mid '70s after a heavy snow

Evelyn Elois (Luna) Holloway Tidwell and **Richard Almon Tidwell**

Mother was born Evelyn Elois Holloway and legally changed her name sometime in the late '70s to Luna Elois after her grandmother Spurlock. Mother was told in childhood that her mother wanted to name her after her grandmother but her father didn't. We later found out that her grandmother's name was not Luna but this was only a nickname. This did not faze mother. She still kept the name Luna.

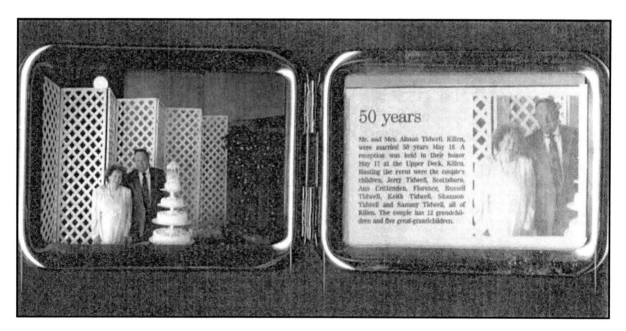

Dad and Mom at their 50th wedding anniversary

Dad at his retirement party with brothers **Shannon** on the left and **Russell*** on the right.

The Ammunition Truck

This happened at a time during the start of the cold war. The Korean War had ended and the country was trying to adjust.

We all just knew that the communist were out trying to get us.

We never had any drills in schools where we had to crawl under our desks. We just had a student civil air patrol outside by the flagpole looking for Russian airplanes. I don't know how these students were chosen. They never asked me to stand outside and watch for the enemy. Could it have been because of the way my mind would wander due to my very active imagination? Whatever the reason, we never saw the Russians!

I must now tell you about the model 12, 16 gauge Winchester pump shotgun! This design was patented in 1912 and was simply called the Model 12.

Well, Dad had a fondness for this gun. He bought the first one while I was in grade school. I still remember him haggling about the price with a guy I think was named Anderson. Anyway, he ran a hardware store in Florence. Dad ended up giving him nearly one hundred dollars for the gun. This store was in the old Studebaker showroom.

Dad also had a habit of buying something that he wanted and saying it was for me. I remember a rod and reel and such. I never did get to use them but dad said they were mine!

Dad traded off the first Model 12 when I was of an early age but he got another one. I don't know the logic behind this trade but I suspect that he needed the money!

He finally did get one and gave me the gun when I was in the 7th grade and I still have it.

What does all of this have to do with the ammunition truck?

Well, after the Korean War was over, there were a lot of 18 wheelers hauling loads with a tag on the back that said explosives. We never questioned this. We just assumed that it was all normal. The trucks were all army drab and we just thought it was a message to confuse the Russians.

Wrong!

What they were actually doing was to move explosives around to permanent storage after the Korean War!

One morning, one of the trucks developed a tire problem about two miles from home on Highway 43. A rear tire on the 18 wheeler caught on fire. It caught the other rear tires on fire but the driver saw what had happened and cut the tractor loose from the trailer and left it on the side of the road and escaped. He knew what he was hauling and what was about to happen! He just flat headed for high ground and hunkered down!

This was by no means the end of it. The fire started cooking off the live ammunition in the trailer with a series of loud reports.

All of this awakened Dad and he grabbed what was then my model 12 Winchester pump and headed off to fight the Russians. He was in WW II and recognized the sound as live armaments going off. Dad only had bird or small game loads to shoot back at them.

Well, so far, so good. The racket did not wake me up!

When I got up at the regular time, mom told me about everything. I was concerned that Dad was no match for the Russian's with high powered rifles! What I was really concerned about was my Model 12 Winchester getting home safely. There were no sounds of explosions by then!

Well, I got up and got ready for the school bus. We lived in a particularly hilly area of north west Alabama with lots of valleys.

All of the valleys had what looked like dense fog in them on the way to school. It was not fog but smoke from the ammunition truck!

This demolished trailer sat on the side of the road for about a week. People came from miles around to see it!

It was completely ruined and had all kinds of holes in the sides. I don't think that a modern recycler could have recovered much from it. It was a mess!

Well, needless to say, my Model 12 Winchester pump got home safely. There were a few more 18 wheelers with the explosive signs on them, but not very many, at least in our area. We all gave them a wide berth whenever we saw one.

The Russians never did attack. I am glad because I would have probably lost my beloved Model 12 Winchester shotgun.

The Pear Tree

The pear tree has a storied history.

Dad planted fruit trees along the driveway as soon as he thought he could afford it after the house was built. This was in the early '50s.

He had a pear tree near the road on the right side of the driveway followed by a peach tree.

On the left side he had some plum trees.

This was about 1952 or a little later.

At that time I had a job cutting Aunt Jane's grass with Dad's lawnmower. She paid me $1.25 each time I cut it.

Dad borrowed my money as soon as I earned it.

One time after he planted the fruit trees, about one and a half years as I remember it, dad was going to town. He owed me about twelve dollars.

There was a bow and arrow advertised in the paper for $7.95. Boy, did I want a bow and arrow!

Dad asked mother what she needed as he left. She gave him a short list.

I reminded him that he owed me money and what I wanted him to buy while he was in town. I even showed him the picture of it from the newspaper.

Boy, did he blow up! He did not even tell me why he could not do it! He just marched out to his prized pear tree and cut it down!

He cut the limbs off on the way back and gave me what he called a "Mule Beating." It was a very good frailing! I pity the poor mules if dad ever gave them one of his "Mule Beatings." I now suspect this was something Dad had been told when he was growing up and he used the terminology himself later.

I learned to be a good southern democrat after that. I spent my money as fast as Aunt Jane gave it to me! Keep the economy moving!

Well, the pear tree grew back. It had two spikes instead of one. It took several extra years before it bore fruit. I don't remember it doing much until after I was gone. Dad in later years would gather a 5 gallon bucket of pears, peel them, and give them to mother. She would make pear preserves out of them! The family still brags about them!

The peach tree produced copious amounts of peaches with worms in them. Nobody cared because all of the peaches raised back then had worms in them. Nobody sprayed their trees back then. We just ate around the worms. A small owl made his home in the peach tree. He hooted at anything that went by after dark! We accepted the owl as part of the family until he died of old age.

We made plum jelly out of the Damson plums that dad had planted.

This should be the end of the story, but it is not.

I left home about 1966 and forgot all about this.

Everything went back to normal. Dad never did repay me what he had borrowed. It did not matter because I was living in Indiana and had made a life of my own up there. I did not need the twelve dollars.

The twin spikes of the pear tree kept growing and finally made a good-sized tree. I did not care as I had my own worries!

Cousin Michael Gray gave me the following of a later development with the pear tree. I never knew about this as I was cut off daily happenings with the family after I left home.

Michael's message:

I was thinking of the time Aunt Eloise chased Russell around the front yard with a broken limb off the pear tree for something he had done. She wore that thing out on him. (When I say limb I don't mean a switch either.)

Seeing that in my mind's eye still has me rolling on the floor.

Aunt Eloise, as small (about 5 feet) as she is, chasing Russell with that limb that was bigger than her, while swinging it at him and making good contact, splinters and chunks flying everywhere.

What a sight that was, Russell hollering every time she made contact.

Michael

Russell was not as big a problem to them as I was, or at least he came along eight years later after I had worn them down considerably!

11

Mother's Poems

Mother always had a strong religious inclination from my earliest memories. She wanted to go to church almost every time the church doors were open. Religion filled a psychological need for her that she was never able to fully achieve in real life.

Mother was raised in the Pentecostal Assembly Of God church and always leaned toward their way of thinking. She went to our local Harrison's Chapel Methodist Church with the rest of the family but always wanted to attend the Assembly of God church in Florence, Alabama, every chance she had. She went by herself and took what family members that would go with her after Dad lost interest in going to church.

She always believed in having a personal relationship with the good Lord and was always talking to Him and claimed that He would answer back to her and reassure her that everything would turn out alright. She talked about her relationship with the Lord every chance she had and to anyone who would listen. I and some others knew how she was and would just tune her out while secretly rolling our eyes. I could never understand her love for the Lord and her personal relationship with him. I never had such a personal relationship with him and was unable to fully understand.

Mother was a strong fundamentalist in her beliefs and really lived for her religious experiences.

It is fitting that mother passed away and went to be with the Lord she loved and worshiped so fervently on Christmas day in 2008, the day we celebrate as being His birthday.

Mother was always writing religious poems praising the Lord and celebrating her personal experiences with him when I was growing up and she continued to do so for much of her life.

I asked her to write down her best ones and I typed them and had them published for her in 1979 as a booklet. She was very proud of the way the booklet turned out and gave copies to family members and church friends. This was one of her proudest achievements in life up until that time.

My maternal grandmother, Myrtice Holloway, was so proud of her copy of the booklet that she wanted to be buried with a copy of it in her hands, and so she was.

I am going to include a copy of mother's booklet of poems as a memorial to her memory in this work. I have scanned one of the last two known surviving copies of mother's booklet and it is as follows:

These will not seem to be poems to anybody who has been trained in poetry and who knows all of the rules and requirements of the various types. They are the most lovely poems ever written in the world to me as they came from mother's heart. This is what she thought and reflect what she truly believed and her love for the Lord that she truly worshiped all of her life.

Inspirations From God

— *Poems by* —

EVELYN ELOIS TIDWELL

1

INSPIRATIONS FROM GOD

— by —

Evelyn Elois Tidwell

MAY these poems be as much
of a blessing to those
who read them as they have
been to me in writing them.

Thom Henricks Associates
Birmingham, AL   U.S.A.

*This book is lovingly dedicated
to my mother
          Myrtice Holloway*

Copyright 1979 by

EVELYN ELOIS TIDWELL

A CALL TO WORSHIP GOD

The Master bids me come,
From a world of care and stress.
He bids me come
To a place of perfect rest.

O'er fields so rich and green,
O'er mountains so high and steep.
He bids me rise
O'er every obstacle in my path.

He bids me His voice to obey,
To carry out His perfect plan.
And to help others along the way,
He bids me follow Him today.

He asks me to show His love,
And to lighten every load.
He asks me to lay down my life,
So that others might know His life.

THE NEW BIRTH

When I see a soul
Born into the kingdom of God,
I begin to see
A beauty directly from God.

I see a life
Reborn from the old life,
I hear a voice say
"Behold, all things become as new."

I see a love,
That can only come from above.
For it is in God's love
That men can be set free.

I see a changed life
That comes into the heart.
For it is God's Spirit
That has come to dwell within us.

I see the mercy
Extended from God above,
Who seeks men out
Because He first loved us.

HAPPINESS IN GOD

Happiness courses through my veins,
Joy is flooding my soul!
My spirit is soaring
To higher heights!

For my soul has found rest,
And my spirit has found peace!
My heart is joyful in God
For His Perfect Grace!

I sought long and hard
To calm this troubled soul.
Finally my will crumbled
To find this Wonderful Lord!

He is such a Wonderful Lord!
To give us such happiness
And to give us joy in our soul
And to give us His Perfect Grace.

WHEN JESUS COMES TO ME

Jesus comes to me
After a long weary night.
He comes to me
In the wee morning light.

He comes to show
His love for me.
He comes to show
That He cares for me.

Oh! The tender love
And the tender care
That He bestows on me.
As His child He sought me out.

MY FRIEND

Friend of mine
Your friendship
Has been as the freshness of dew.
You have been as true
As the skies are blue.

We have fought many battles together
Because we have been bought
With the Blood of the Lamb.

Nothing can ever separate us
From God's love,
Because God has given us
"Victory in Jesus,
Through Jesus, our Lord,
Who loved us,
And saved us,
And gave His Life
A ransom for many.

GOLD

Plenty of gold I have found,
As I searched along the ground.
And as I searched,
I found
A Pearl of great price.

I clutched it to my heart,
For indeed it was a priceless
Treasure.

Gently, a voice spoke to my heart.
"You can have happiness
Beyond measure,
If you will sell all thou hast."

As I unclutched my hands
To give to the poor and needy
In Spirit,
I found that my own spirit
Began to soar o'er the lands.

It was then that I found,
That by giving of my gold,
That I was rich in God,
And I had found treasure in Heaven.

"A TRIBUTE TO ELVIS PRESLEY"

There was once a little boy,
Whose clothes were rags
And his feet were bare,
But this little boy
Was destined to rise
And become a star.

One day he began to sing,
And to put feeling into his song,
And to put his whole soul
Into his singing.
Then the people began
To catch his spirit in song.

Now this well known star
Is dressed in shimmering garments,
With boots on his feet,
Because God made him a Star.

Now God has taken him home
To be re-united with his mother,
Where he is still singing,
With feeling in his song
Throughout all eternity.

10

HOLY SPIRIT OF GOD

What is this lingering presence?
This sweet presence I feel?
It is the presence of Jesus
Sent to comfort and assure me.

He comes to give me joy!
When I am sad.
He comes to bring me hope
When I am in despair!

But most of all, He came,
To give me Life!
Eternal Life!
And to save me from my sins,
And to make my heart right.

And now my heart is singing,
And my life is ringing
With praises unto God!
Who Loved me
And gave me
A home in Heaven with God!

"LIFE"

As I sat musing
In utter despair,
Over circumstances
Beyond my control,

A voice so tenderly said to me,
"I am your life."
Suddenly my spirit soared
With an unspeakable joy.

For indeed He is my life.
And this is His life.

What joy!

To know Him
In the fellowship
Of His sufferings,
And in the power
Of His resurrection.

12

HIS PRESENCE

I felt His Presence today,
As I went on my way,
He came in my heart so gently
That it felt like freshness of day.

I rejoiced in Him
Because I knew
He had seen my need,
And would give me the desires
Of my heart

I had been to see a friend,
And together we had shared
God's Love;
And it was while I was on my way
That I felt God's Love.

It is wonderful to have friends,
But more wonderful still
Is to have God as our friend
And to know He cares for us.

13

ETERNITY

There is no need to fear
The great unknown,
For you will never lose sight
That everything will be all right.

Even though you may feel
That you are all alone
In the vastness of space,
You will need to know
That Jesus is there.

He will come
And take you by the hand,
And lead you
To that Promised Land.

You will dwell with Him
Throughout all eternity
And you will never lose sight
That Jesus is there.

14

HE GAVE HIS NAME

He gave His name

To you and me

Oh! Bless be His name

That saved me from my sins.

His name is Jesus,

The Solid Rock,

Who loved me,

And died for me,

Oh! Blessed be His Holy name.

15

CALVARY

He gave His life for you and me,
He paid it all
On Calvary's Tree.
Oh! Praise His name!
He loved me so,
He gave His all
For you and me.

He loved me so,
He died for me,
He loved me so,
He bled for me.
He gave His Life
For you and me
On Calvary's Tree.

But now He lives forever more,
Triumphant o'er every foe,
And now He reigns within my heart,
To dwell with me forever more.

80

17

FIVE LOAVES AND TWO FISHES

There was a little boy
With five loaves and two fishes
And this little boy wanted to share.

Then Jesus said:
"Shall we buy bread
That these may be fed?"
Then the little boy
With much joy
Gave his lunch to Jesus to share.

Jesus gave thanks
Over the five loaves and two fish,
And gave to the hungry to eat.
The little boy gave thanks
That through Jesus
He had been able
To help fill the hungry.

"FOOTSTEPS—LIFE JOURNEY"

Lord,
We have walked many miles together.
Most of the miles
Have been happy ones.
Some of the miles
Have been weary ones.
But through it all,
You have been
Our Faithful Guide!

You have kept my feet
In the straight and narrow path.
Thank you Lord for all of this
You have kept my feet
From falling into dangerous paths.
Thank you Lord for all this.

Sometimes we have grown weary,
And the nights have been dreary,
But You have been with us,
And gently led us
To that Great and Perfect Will
Of Thine.

JESUS LOVES THE LIL' CHILDREN

She is just a little girl,
Waiting to hear the Word of God,
With eyes so bright
And a heart so right,
Waiting to hear the Word of God.

He is just a little boy,
Waiting to hear the Word of God.
With a smile so light
And a mind so bright,
Waiting to hear the Word of God.

Then Jesus came by one day
And gathered the children
Around His Knee, and said
"Suffer the little children
To come unto me
And forbid them not,
For of such
Is the Kingdom of Heaven."

JESUS LOVES THE LIL' CHILDREN
(Continued)

Then to others He turned and said,
"Except ye become
As little children
Ye cannot enter
The Kingdom of Heaven."

Then the children began to open
Their hearts and minds to Jesus
Who is the giver of Life.

Oh! Such joy and gladness
As the Word of God went forth.

A FLOWER

When I see the wonder
And beauty of a flower,
Then I wonder
With delight of the radiant beauty
Of a flower.

For it is God
That sends such beauty
To enrich my soul
And gladden my heart
With the fragrance of a flower.

ALL I WANT IS JESUS

Some people want fame,
And some want world aclaim,
But all I want is Jesus,
And to know my name
Is written in Heaven.

All I want to do
Is to praise Him,
And to adore Him,
And to say He is mine,
And I am His!

I want to lay
My all at His feet,
And to meet
Him in the air,
And to reign with Him for evermore.

22

JESUS

He was only wanting
To save people from their sins.
But He got hate
Instead of love.

He was only reaching out
To try and soothe
Some of Earth's problems.
Instead He was slapped down
To suppress the truth.

But truth!
Though crushed to the earth
Will rise again,
With a victorious shout,
O'er all her enemies.

For truth strengthens the soul
And makes glad the heart!

MY SAVIOUR'S HANDS AND FEET

They pierced His Hands and Feet,
But it was these hands
That blessed the multitudes.

It was these hands
That set men free
And healed the sick
And raised the dead.

It was these hands
That blessed the children
And soothed the hearts
Of the sorrowing.

It was at these feet
That Mary sat
And learned of His love.

It was at these feet
That Mary broke
The alabaster box
And wiped His feet
With her hair.

It was these feet
That walked the dusty roads
To bring comfort and love
To a lost and dying world.

24

WHEN I SEE JESUS

If I owned all of earth's riches,
It would profit me nothing,
But to see and know Jesus
Is worth every loss I might sustain.

When I see Jesus
Everything I had hoped for
Grows strangely dim.

Everything I had hoped to do
Seems to fade away
When I fully see Jesus.

2008 Ms. Alabama Nursing Home Pageant

Mother was in the Lauderdale County Christian Nursing Home and had been for about a year when this episode unfolded. They took excellent care of her and she seemed to enjoy her stay there.

This nursing home is a member of the Alabama Nursing Home Association, Inc. This association has 232 member facilities.

The association has held a Ms. Alabama Nursing Home Pageant every year for the past twenty-six years.

Mother's nursing home held a pageant of their own to select a representative to represent them at this year's pageant. Mother was chosen to be their representative for this year.

Each statewide contestant must undergo preliminary judging based on their written entries and 3-5 minute videotape interviews. They are then judged by a panel of judges who are knowledgeable in long term health care on a specified list of criteria such as activities, attitudes and opinions. This judging took place in Montgomery on July 30. The scores for each contestant were then tabulated and the top 10 finalists were chosen.

Mother was getting nervous before the top ten finalists were chosen but settled down and decided to enjoy the festivities once she did not make this list.

And festivities there were!

All the contestants were made to feel like queens all during the pageant.

The pageant was held at the Wynfrey Hotel in Birmingham this year.

Three people, Grace Crotts, Activities Director; Carol Hargett, Activities Assistant and Lela Holderfield, volunteer, accompanied mother to Birmingham this year. The nursing home staff always looks forward to this pageant every year.

The Wynfrey is a very nice hotel! It has a five star rating!

My sister Ann and brother Shannon also went down with her.

Mother and entourage were down there two days. They were given nice rooms, were wined and dined in style and the contestants were given facials and their hair was done nicely. Mother looked better than I have seen her in years!

Left to right: **Shannon Tidwell, Josh Hancock, Jerry Tidwell, Ann Crittenden, Sonya and Katherine Mitchell, Shelby Hancock.**

I joined the group on August 5, the day of the pageant. My daughter, Sonya, and her daughter Katherine joined us in Birmingham. Two of my other grandchildren, Shelby and Josh Hancock also wanted to ride with Grandpa in his truck to Birmingham. We had a large group present for the pageant.

Left to right: **Josh** and **Shelby Hancock, Mother** and **Jerry Tidwell**

The ballroom at the Wynfrey was crowded the day of the pageant. Seating was at a premium.

The very beautiful and talented Miss Alabama 2008, Amanda Tapley was Mistress of Ceremony for the pageant. She is an accomplished pianist and has a very beautiful singing voice. Getting to see her was worth the trip to Birmingham by itself for a tired old man.

Amanda Tapley answering questions from the floor.

Mr. Robert (Bob) J. Coker, Jr. was Master of Ceremony as he has been for a number of years. He is the Greene County Nursing Home Administrator.

The 2007 Ms. Alabama Nursing Home Pageant winner, Ms. Elizabeth Gamble of Florence, also rose to the occasion by singing a rendition of "Saint Louis Blues" with a clear, lusty voice. It was reassuring to realize that an 88 year young woman could still sing like that!

There were seventy contestants in all from all across the state. Their ages were from 33 to 99. Everyone had a hoot, especially the contestants!

A different panel of judges chose a winner from the ten finalists. Their choice was based on such criteria as attitude toward life, alertness, personality, ability to show happiness with life in a nursing home and demonstrated interest and continuing contributions to others.

Ms. Trina Ward from the Roanoke HealthCare Center was crowned 2008 Ms. Alabama Nursing Home.

According to what I picked up on the internet, Ms. Ward was born in Washington state where she was the first physically challenged student to be fully integrated into a regular classroom. She often spoke to elementary students about her condition, Arthrogryposis, and her physical challenges. Arthrogryposis is characterized by reduced mobility in many joints of the body due to the overgrowth of fibrous tissue in the joints. At Roanoke HealthCare Center, Ms. Ward is active in church services, Bible study, reads to her fellow residents and makes necklaces for her friends.

She was 33 at the time of the pageant.

The Birmingham TV Station WBRC Fox 6 videotaped the pageant and was supposed to air it on the local channel 6 news. I am not sure that it was ever aired in its entirety.

Mother being interviewed after the pageant.

WBRC wanted mother to wait until they could interview her after the pageant. They thought she had had an interesting first job just out of high school and could have a story about that. Her job was as a chicken sexer at a hatchery. They wanted to know more about that!

I remember mother telling us stories when we were little about that job. She was proud that she had a very high percentage of accuracy and was recognized for it and received a commendation. Apparently egg farmers don't want a bunch of roosters around when they are trying to get their hens to lay eggs! They just want hens and they want them to lay eggs.

We took several photographs of mother after the pageant while we were waiting for her interview.

Left to right: **Katherine** and **Sonya Mitchell, Mother.**

Katherine Mitchell giving **Great Grandma Tidwell** a big hug.
Lela and **Grace** can be seen in the background.

The day was not over yet. Grace, Carol and Lela wanted to stop in Cullman for dinner. They always look forward to dinner at this restaurant every year. The name of the restaurant is All Steak and it is indeed a very fine restaurant. It is in the 4th floor in a bank building downtown. It is way off of Interstate 65 but is worth looking up!

Shelby and Josh were in for more than they thought when they left for Birmingham with Grandpa in his red truck. Neither of them had ever seen an escalator and had only been on an elevator once before when I took them to visit the Vulcan. The Vulcan elevator went up pretty high and had a glass front for viewing, or getting frightened in Josh's case. They both walked back down the spiral staircase inside the Vulcan.

We had to take both the elevator and the escalator at the Wynfrey. Josh never did quite get comfortable with the elevator but they both thought the escalator was fun.

We had to take an elevator up to the restaurant in Cullman. Josh looked at it uneasily and asked me if there was another way. He did get on though.

They both thanked me for a fun day when we got home.

We took several photographs during dinner.

Mother with my brother **Shannon Tidwell**

Shelby and **Josh Hancock** waiting for their dinner

Lela and **Grace**

Mother getting ready to blow out the candle on her cake at the end of the meal.

Josh Hancock, who is normally very shy, just had to give **Carol** a big hug as we were leaving. Carol is such an outgoing person that Josh just couldn't resist her charm.

Left **Jerry Tidwell** with sister **Ann Crittenden**

This was a most enjoyable day for all.

Gardening On Brush Creek

Dad always tried to raise a large garden. He always had at least two or three patches for different things. There would sometimes be one in the bottom between our house and Grandmother Alice's. We always had one on the other side of the house and across the creek in the bottom over there.

We would always catch Dad's old mule early in the spring and put it up in a barn stall until we had our garden planted and only needed to plow it occasionally. The mule had been allowed to roam free anywhere in the pasture it wanted all fall and winter.

The mule was especially frisky early in the spring. It knew what was in store for it and would lower its long ears flat back on its head and start running around the pasture fence as soon as it saw us coming in the spring with his bridle in our hand. Don't be mistaken, mules can move fast when they want to!

The mule would make at least three trips around the fence with us in hot pursuit. It would finally tire of the game and would usually just go and get into the barn stall. We would then just have to walk up and close the stall door.

This was a game we had to play with the mule every spring!

Dad would always take the old mule and break up the garden with his breaking plow and smooth it all down with his harrow. He would then plant everything.

He would usually get busy at work after the garden was planted. He would never turn down an overtime shift. He never seemed to have time to cultivate the garden once it was planted. The grass and weeds seemed to grow faster than the plants we were trying to raise.

We had to take our push lawn mower and cut the grass out of the middles so that we could see what we were trying to grow. We had to do this several years. Uncle Doc always got a big kick out of this and made all sorts of jokes about it.

Dad always planted more than we needed and we always had everything we wanted. We also raised some prime grass and weeds.

Dad's first mule was Toby. He was a small male mule and was especially tolerant and gentle. He was the mule that I learned to plow with. He was even tolerant of my mistakes while I was learning the fine art of plowing with a mule.

Toby would respond to my voice commands. I very seldom had to touch the plow lines while plowing with Toby. Toby was old when we got him and Dad traded him off for a younger mule after several years.

There was a succession of other mules after Toby. Most of them were large female mules. None were as gentle and tolerant as Toby. They would work and follow commands but I had to rely on the plow lines a lot to get them to behave. They also liked to take a nip or two regularly out of a corn stalk while plowing. It was always more than a gentle nip. They would entirely take out the top of a stalk of corn.

Dad turned over a lot of the job of cultivating the garden to me while I was in my early to mid-teens.

Perhaps it was because I was big enough by that time or perhaps Dad finally got tired of Uncle Doc's jokes about his gardening efforts. I don't know.

We had the proper mule drawn implements to break up the garden and smooth it off. We didn't have all of the specialized plows, such as a double shovel, scratcher, and a middle buster, needed for cultivating.

I would have to borrow them from Uncle Doc. I would check with him in advance to be sure that he didn't need them the day that I planned to plow out the garden.

I would harness up the old mule and lead it up to Uncle Doc's place. We would load up what I needed for that day's work in his homemade sled. This was a wooden platform nailed on to the sled runners which were nothing more than rough sawn red oak or other hardwood two by eight timbers with a forty-five degree angle cut into the front of them. Uncle Doc had made sideboards for the sled so nothing would fall off. I would then take everything home and go to work.

This was my job until my late teens. Dad would sometimes have time to cultivate but I did a lot of it.

Dad did not have a mule by the time I was in my late teens. We would have to borrow Uncle Doc's mule, Lize, as well as his implements.

We grew some fine gardens but there was still a lot of grass and weeds!

13

Hunting With Dad

Dad always hunted any wild game that moved in the outdoors. He was also one of the most avid fishermen that I ever met.

If it ran around wild outdoors or swam in the water, he was out there trying to put it on the table.

While Dad would sometimes fish for the sport of it, he never fished *just* for the sport of it. He would always try to catch as many fish as he could. He didn't rely just on a cane fishing pole or rod and reel entirely but would meat fish as he called it. He would put out multi-hook *trot lines* baited with live minnows. I helped him put out a two hundred hook trot line in Scottsboro once. He would catch anything that swam by using this method.

Dad and Uncle Ed even tried their hand at shocking fish to the surface once. They used the magneto from an old crank type telephone and would turn the handle with electrodes lowered into the water. I don't think they ever did much good with it. This was highly illegal but that didn't stop them. He never used dynamite to my knowledge but this was about the only thing he didn't try.

Dad always caught more fish than anyone else in the boat. It could have been that he fished from the front of the boat while everyone else had to settle for what he had missed. It could have been because of his natural native cunning. I could never understand this. He would tell me, "Son, you have to be smarter than a fish to catch one!"

One of my memories of Dad at his peak of fishing prowess was when I was in my mid-teens. He had taken up fly fishing by then. He had an old split bamboo fly rod. I was big enough to be his *trolling motor* by then. Electric trolling motors hadn't been invented yet! He would sit in the front of the boat and point to the weed bed or overhanging bush that he wanted to fish around. I would paddle the boat in that direction while he was busy casting the fly.

This method was most productive when the willow flies were hatching out. They would hatch out in huge swarms several times a year. Bass, bluegill and other top feeders were very actively feeding at this time. We didn't pay any attention to the limit. We just fished until it got too dark to see what we were doing. Dad would then fire up the old small outboard motor and we would go back to where he had rented the boat. We sometimes did not want to clean the fish when we got home. In cases like this, we would wake up Uncle Doc. He went to bed very early. Uncle Doc was always more than happy to get up and clean what we had brought home.

I think that the whole family must have been like this while Dad was growing up. This was just instilled in the older generations. Some of my younger brothers and their sons were and are like this as well.

The countryside was bare of game around our house while I was growing up. There were a few brave rabbits, or maybe they were crazy, and an occasional wandering squirrel but the larger game had long since vanished into someone's stomach.

Dad always kept hunting dogs around while I was growing up. There was always a possum hound at first. Some bird dogs and packs of rabbit hounds followed.

About the only thing that I never knew of Dad hunting were wild ducks and geese. This never mattered because Dad had friends that hunted them. They would just throw the dead birds in the freezer when they got home and give them to dad. Dad would bring them home and it was my job to thaw them out and clean them. It took me a little time to figure out the best method to do this but I soon caught on.

My first hunt with dad, and the one that I remember most vividly, was my first possum hunt with him. I was not in school yet but I got to tag along.

The dogs soon picked up the trail and we listened to them baying as they were trailing the possum all through Uncle Doc's woods. They soon treed it. We followed to where they were jumping up the tree trunk, to no avail, trying to pull the possum down. It was a fairly small tree but the possum was able to climb high enough to stay out of the dog's reach. Although this tree was not large, it was too big for Dad to push it over and shake the possum out. There was only one thing to do at this point. The tree had to be cut down. All that we had brought with us was a tow sack, or burlap bag, to bring the possums home in. We didn't have an axe.

There was only one thing to do. Dad had to walk back to Uncle Doc's place and borrow an axe. I would have only slowed him down so he left me sitting on a tree stump near where the dogs had the possum treed. Dad would walk back to get the axe.

Dad took the carbide lantern with him, the only light that we had. There I was, left alone in the pitch black woods with the scary sounds all around me. I had not even started to school yet, let alone been out in the woods at night by myself. The night seemed to suddenly get colder and the strange sounds in the woods were getting louder and louder.

I didn't know what was making them. I would have tried to run back home but I didn't know which way home was and couldn't run back in the dark.

So there I was, sitting alone on my tree stump and getting more scared by the minute. This was the most scared I had ever been in my life up until that time.

I could finally hear Dad coming back and could soon see the warm glow from his carbide lantern. I was really relieved to see him.

Dad and I went possum hunting together many times after that. Dad would never even try to eat possum. We always gave them to Uncle Albert.

Uncle Albert would come up to the house to get them. He would usually take them home and feed them for a while to fatten them up and take as much of the wild taste out of them as was

94

possible. Sometimes he would kill them in our front yard by placing a pick handle across their neck and breaking it. It depended on how hungry he was I suppose.

I did see them cooking possum several times. They would simmer it in a pot of water with whatever seasonings one uses to cook a possum. There would always be a small bundle of sassafras twigs in the pot as well.

I never ate any but it sure smelled good cooking.

Dad bought me my first shotgun when we were living in Kentucky. It was a single shot .410 shotgun. He taught me how to use it safely.

We saw a squirrel run up a tree on our first hunt. I was given the chance to shoot it out. I walked up to the tree and looked high and low for the squirrel. It was then that Dad taught me my first hunting lesson. The squirrel was moving around the tree while I was looking for it. Dad made a loud noise to confuse the squirrel. I could then walk around the tree and find it. This was the first time that I had ever killed anything.

I guess that one has to be smarter than a squirrel to be able to kill it as well!

The second thing that I killed was a rabbit. Dad had the ability to spot any wild game immediately. He told me to go get my shotgun and then tried to show me the rabbit sitting in some grass by the side of the driveway. He had seen it while driving up to the house in the car. I like to have never been able to see it. It was only after he told me to look for its eyes that I was finally able to spot it. This was my second hunting lesson. We had fried rabbit that night for supper.

We had an Irish Setter while we lived in Kentucky and we went quail hunting many times. I would even shoot down a quail occasionally.

Dad hunted until old age slowed him down. He always enjoyed himself while in the woods and fields hunting or on the water fishing. He always said, "Son, the good Lord doesn't take any time away from you while you are on the creek fishing."

It was after I grew up that hunting organizations began restocking things like deer and raccoons back into our countryside. Deer are now more plentiful there than rabbits were back then.

Sausage Making in the Late '60s

I would always try to come home for visits on Thanksgiving and Christmas after I moved to Indiana. I did not get to do this every year but I tried.

I remember a visit one Thanksgiving and Dad was on the front porch when I got home with his hands and arms sunk up to just below his elbows in a #3 wash tub of sausage. Dad had had the sausage ground somewhere and he was trying to work the seasoning into it. He started by adding prepared seasoning that was added by adding so many packets per pounds of sausage. He would then thoroughly mix that in and prepare a few sausage patties for mother to fry. He did this with the sausage still clinging to his hands and arms. After mother fried the patties everyone would sample them and decide if the seasoning blend was correct. Normally dad would have to add more sage or red pepper until everything tasted just right. The sausage would then be stuffed into cloth sausage sacks or sheep small intestines that had been soaked in water overnight. The sausage would then be hung in the smokehouse.

Dad was sampling sausage patties with the raw sausage clinging all over his hands and arms that particular day when I drove up. I had been away from the farm long enough by then that this entire scene looked extremely base to me. A more appropriate word would be gross!

They tried to talk me into sampling some of the sausage but the entire scene on the front porch revolted me. I wanted no part of the sausage sampling that day.

I have seen documentaries on TV recently about how meats are processed today in slaughterhouses. These documentaries are full of gruesome scenes. I guess there is no pretty way to make sausage even today.

14

Reba Jane Tidwell Gray* and Finney Gray* Family

Reba Jane Tidwell was born November 13, 1927 in Lauderdale County Alabama and married Oscar Finney Gray (born January 30, 1923 In Lauderdale County Alabama). Finney is the son of Gus and Mamie Gray.

Finney in his trademark overalls. **Jane** in a Christmas sweater.

The only child from this marriage, Michael Finney Gray born January 22, 1962 in Lauderdale County Alabama. Their only grandchild is Constance Michael Gray born September 18, 1989.

Reba Jane died on July 16, 2000 from complications of ALS. Finney died on October 8, 2005 from an extended battle with pneumonia.

Both are buried in the Cox Cemetery in Killen, Alabama and are buried next to each other.

Front left to right: **Constance, Jane.** Back row: **Finney** and **Michael**

The Rabbit Hunt

Dad had a friend, Bill Host, who worked with him at the TVA Service Shop in Muscle Shoals, Alabama. Bill and his wife, Wanda, and their two sons Johnny and Billy and our family visited back and forth from my earliest childhood memories. They had a small Airstream travel trailer that they would park in Grandmother's yard sometimes for an extended visit during the summer.

Bill wanted to buy a new Studebaker truck about 1950 but did not want to borrow the money from a bank. Aunt Jane, Dad's sister, loaned him the money to buy the truck and made a little more interest than she was getting at the Savings and Loan where she had her money. I remember Bill and Wanda coming out every month to make their truck payment to Aunt Jane. Bill drove this truck until it completely died of exhaustion and he then parked it at his farm near Iuka, Mississippi. It may still be there.

Aunt Jane was dating the man she eventually married at that time, Finney Gray. Finney had several brothers who could sell ice to Eskimos. They all had a gift of gab except for Finney.

Two of them were actually salesmen and one established a furniture store that was quite successful. His family still operates it near Florence, Alabama.

Finney was exceptionally quiet. He would occasionally get excited and say something that was as near to a cuss word for him as he ever would utter. His most common expressions during times of extreme excitement were "John Brown" and "Son of a Buck." Finney was so quiet that I don't know how he ever proposed to Aunt Jane.

Bill had somewhere between 250 and 300 acres way out in the country near Iuka, Mississippi. A creek ran through it and the land near the creek was mostly marsh land. One thing that I do remember was that the original Natchez Trace ran along the creek in places. It was just an old overgrown sunken road but it gave me a strange feeling walking along it and realizing the history that had been played out there. Bill's son, Billy, went to Auburn and got a degree in Agriculture and farmed the areas that were not swampy for several years. This was well over one hundred acres. I remember that he grew mostly corn and some of the tallest cockleburs that I have ever seen. They must have been over seven feet tall. This was well before the time of herbicides.

They built a fairly large concrete block one room building with a loft above on the farm. They had a large wood burning heater downstairs that served for both cooking and heating the cabin. There were a number of beds up in the loft. Bill was originally from Michigan and knew how to get the most heat from this heater. Instead of the stovepipe going straight up to the flue like all stoves and heaters that I had seen in the South before, he used a series of short straight pieces of stovepipe with elbows to give it four or five turns back and forth. There was very little heat that went up the flue from all of this twisting and turning. The cabin had electricity for lights and to operate a pump they had installed in a spring nearby. It had running water. Billy lived there during the summer while he was farming the place.

The other thing that I remember about this farm was there was a large population of rabbits along the creek and brambles bordering the trees that grew in and along the swampy area. These were not ordinary rabbits, which the locals called "hillbillies," but what they called "cane cutters" or swamp rabbits. They were much larger than normal rabbits. Their habits were different from regular rabbits which will be gone into later.

During the fall and winter, during rabbit season, Dad and some of my brothers, some of Dad's cousins and Finney Gray would go to the farm for an all weekend hunting event. Dad had always had a pack of beagles trained especially to hunt rabbits. We would load up the pack of dogs in the trunk of Dad's old two-door 1951 Pontiac and there was room inside for four or five people to make the sixty miles or so journey to the farm.

The normal rabbits we hunted around home were just regular rabbits. The dogs would jump them up and they would run around in a circle and come back to near where they jumped up from. The dogs never ran out of hearing. All that a hunter had to do was just stand near where they were jumped and wait on them to come back.

Not swamp rabbits. They would always bed down near the creek and seek an area where there was water all around. They would seek out a small mound sticking up a few inches to one foot above the water. They would just sit there while you walked up and not move. If you got close enough, or the dogs got close, they would jump up and head straight for the creek. They would swim it in an effort to lose the dogs. They would then head for the next county if this failed. They would run so far that you could not even hear the dogs chasing them. They would finally start to make their circle and you could just hear the dogs as they started to get closer and closer. They would finally get back to where you could hear the dogs well enough to judge how far off they were and get ready for the rabbit to return.

One effective method of hunting swamp rabbits was for everybody, except one person, to move through the swamp together spread out about a hundred feet apart. One person would lag behind about a hundred yards.

The rabbits would sit tight while the first party moved through unless they came very close to them. This unnerved them though and they were ready to leave when the second person came stumbling through. The rabbits would jump up and head for the creek when the second person came through. The person lagging behind would usually get a shot at the rabbit as it ran off. If they missed, the dogs would then take over.

We always hunted with shotguns, mostly 16 gauges. Some of the locals would sometime join us and they always carried .22 rifles. They always shot the rabbits in the head and scoffed at us for using anything else.

Swamp rabbits were extremely large rabbits as I described earlier. They were always nice and fat since Billy left plenty of corn in the fields for them to feed on at harvest time. He didn't do this on purpose but this was the result of the crude harvesting equipment at the time.

Everyone would loosen their belt and slip the rabbit head under their belt when they killed one. The rule was "If you kill it, you carry it." A rabbit has a notch in the lower jawbone that would hold the rabbit under your belt once in place. The rabbits were so large that their hind legs would sometime drag the ground once you had tucked them in under your belt. The weight got so heavy after you had four or five under your belt that you begged to go back to the cabin. That was the bag limit for rabbit hunting down there, no more than you wanted to carry out!

We would then carry the rabbits back to the cabin. There was an old dilapidated barn there where we would hang the rabbits up after we had field dressed them. Folks think that Mississippi is a southern state and never gets cold! Wrong! This is northern Mississippi and the rabbits would always freeze during the night.

We would then finish dressing the rabbits when we got back home and mother would freeze them. Dad always made good money for the area and time but our family was large. We depended on the game we brought home for a good part of the meat we ate during the winter. I remember having to eat so much rabbit one winter that I still can't stand the thought of eating it. I like tame rabbit in good recipes at a restaurant but not wild rabbit. This experience completely turned me off of eating game of any kind. I have a gun collection and used to target practice up until ten years ago but had to quit because there is no area around where I live that I can shoot. I have not shot a gun in earnest at another living animal in well over forty years.

We would sometimes stay longer than just a weekend and I would miss school on Monday. This was not a problem for most of my teachers, but Miss Wilson in Biology was different! There were all kinds of weird looking mosses and lichens and evergreen shrubs that grew down there in the swamp that nobody back home had ever seen. I would always take something new back to school for her. She would then give me a book and make me identify it and give a report to the class. This worked out pretty well!

One particular rabbit hunt stands out well in my mind. Not only in my mind but all of the participants remembered it until the day they died. We would often talk about it when we met, except for Finney Gray. Finney would talk about it but he did not do it with much enthusiasm. I am the only member of this hunt that is still alive, so I guess that I can give the details to others and not embarrass anyone.

There was Dad, Finney, William Tidwell and me on this particular hunt. William was Dad's first cousin and had a particularly dry sense of humor.

One of Finney's particularly windy brothers had a long-legged beagle that was by no means full blooded. He convinced Finney that this dog was the best rabbit hound that had ever hit the woods. Finney brought this dog along. I don't remember the dog's name, but we ended up calling him "Old Long Head" for reasons explained below.

This was an extremely cold day, even for northern Mississippi. We had on all of the clothes that we had brought and were still miserably cold tromping around in the swamp.

Bill and Wanda Host had joined us but had sense enough to stay in the cabin and keep the fire going in the stove.

"Old Long Head" would wait until one of the other dogs hit a trail and started baying and following it. He would then head in the opposite direction baying his head off. The other dogs would then quit their trail and go to him. We couldn't get anything going with this dog causing such a ruckus.

Finney normally wore bib overalls, or "overhauls" as we called them. On this particular day he was either wearing blue jeans with a belt or had brought a belt along to carry the rabbits with. I don't remember just what he had on but he had a belt with him. He finally got enough of "Old Long Head" and caught him and used the belt as a leash. He had a number of derogatory comments to make about the dog but I don't remember exactly what they were. Needless to say, he was highly agitated with the dog.

There Finney was, leading "Old Long Head" through the swamp with his belt. We came to a log across the creek and most of us had already crossed over to the other side. It was Finney and "Old Long Head's" turn to cross. Finney let the dog go first and he was following with his shotgun held safely so nothing would happen. "Old Long Head" led the way until they reached the middle of the creek. He then decided to go in the opposite direction and headed back at full steam through Finney's legs. The belt got tangled up and Finney tripped. Finney, "Old Long Head," shotgun and all ended up in the waist deep water. Finney still had both shotgun and "Old Long Head" in tow but he was wet clear up to his armpits. It took a while for everything to register with everyone but Finney gave the belt a good yank and said "You Son of a Buck, if you were mine I would drown you"

Wait, this is not the end of this story. It gets better!

101

Remember, this was a bitterly cold day. Bill and Wanda Host were back at the cabin. Wanda had the habit of wearing a dress on top and blue jeans on the bottom to stay warm in cold weather.

Finney's clothes were completely frozen before we got far. He was extremely cold and his clothes were frozen completely stiff by the time we got back, shoes, underwear and all. I don't remember if "Old Long Head" was still in tow or if Finney had turned him loose hoping he would get lost.

Dad gets back to the cabin first and I am right behind. We start to relate to the Hosts what had happened. Finney came stumbling in about that time. Wanda had a heart as big as all outdoors.

Finney just wanted to get close to the heater and thaw out. Wanda would have none of that. She insisted that Finney put on the warm, dry blue jeans she had on the bottom. Finney got red in the face and politely refused. He wanted no part of getting in that woman's pants! He moved closer to the heater.

Wanda would not take no for an answer. She backed up to the door and started removing her ample sized blue jeans. Her pants were down and her dress was up and her backside was facing the door. Cousin William came in the door at that time. There he stood for a second surveying everything, looked at Wanda's backside, and just said "Good Morning."

William never said anything else about this incident.

Anyway, this tale got funnier and funnier every time it was told and retold. Finney's face got redder and redder with each retelling.

I don't remember if Wanda ever did get him into her pants!

"Old Long Head" never did go hunting with us again. Finney quit bragging on him. He was just repeating his brother's words before the hunt when he did brag on him. In retrospect, I suspect that Finney's brother was just trying to sell the dog to him.

We did have many more enjoyable hunting trips down there, none that we remembered as well as this one though. Perhaps I will recall the details of some of them someday.

I don't think Finney ever went back with us again.

My friend, Fred Thebus, sent me an email documenting his experience in hunting swamp rabbits around Newport, Arkansas. He worked at the Revere Foil Division in Newport at the time. Fred most graciously gave me his permission to cut and paste it to my story. It is as follows:

Jerry,

Great story. It brought back memories of hunting swamp rabbits in Arkansas.

Jim Partney, the rolling General Foreman (I bought his house when he left in 1963) had four Walker Beagles.

I recall one hunt where three of us and the dogs crossed the Black river in a fourteen foot flat bottom boat. We hunted in about a thousand acres of woods (the next year the woods were gone and the land planted in soy beans).

The legal limit was eight rabbits apiece, but nobody wanted to tote that many. We carried out thirteen rabbits and that was a load. We always gutted and cut the heads off (with a little practice, we could do this without getting our hands bloody), this cut the weight in half. We hunted with 12 gauge shot guns and would not shoot if we did not get a head shot (usually the rabbit would circle and come around again).

On another hunt, the biggest rabbit I ever saw, circled us three times, always just out of range (he did not get that big letting people shoot at him).

If the dogs pushed the rabbit too hard, he would hole up. Usually in a hollow log or tree. The dogs would let you know where he was. Standard procedure was to cut a six foot sapling with a fork on the end. Each branch of the fork was cut about an inch long and given a sharp point. We would jam the stick into the hollow tree until we hit the rabbit and then twist the points in his fur, then pull Mr. Rabbit out.

Katie usually made Hasenpfeffer (sour rabbit) out of swamp rabbits. The rabbit was marinated in vinegar, browned, stewed until the meat came off the bones, sour cream added, and served on noodles. Yum yum (but I didn't have to eat this every day).

Fred Thebus.

Thanks Fred!

Owen Reid Tidwell*

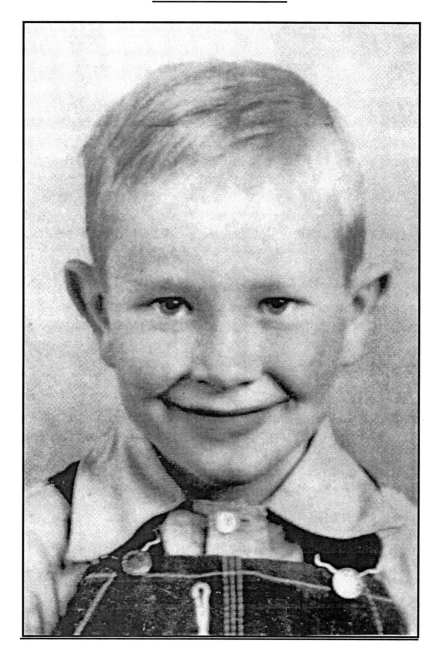

Owen died of a ruptured appendix as an 11 year old youngster. He is buried in the Cox Cemetery near Killen, Alabama.

Part Two

I yearn to go back
To the simple way of life and pleasures of my childhood
I think this must be human nature and must exist in all of us
I know that I can never go back
To this place that only survives in my memory
Our modern way of life is very hurried and full of dangers
That could not even be imagined in years past
We must strive to remember
That less is more
Always chose simplicity over complexity
Enjoy life to the fullest with what you have
Try to remember and enjoy the simple pleasures
We once had but did not treasure

The author

15

John Dee Tidwell* Family

The author quotes excerpts from a work by Joanne Tidwell Forsythe in this section. Her work was published in the Heritage of Lauderdale County, Alabama Vol. 39 and is titled "History of The Tidwell Family in Lauderdale County." Joanne is Richard McBride Tidwell and Louise Agnes Gist Tidwell's only daughter and youngest child. She offers details about the Tidwell Family that were unknown to the author during much of the writing of this book. He discovered this only while doing his final editing.

Joanne Tidwell Forsythe has many old photographs in this work that were unavailable to the author. Her work is well worth reading in its entirety and should be by anyone interested in the Tidwell Family history. I have used this work to flesh out the sparse information that I have about John Dee Tidwell's family.

John Dee Tidwell was born May 1, 1856 in Lauderdale County Alabama. He died on May 20, 1918 from kidney disease.

He married September 28, 1884 **Derendia Ann Billingsley**, who was born March 11, 1866, daughter of **John Powers Billingsley** and **Mary (McBride) Billingsley**. They are buried in the Cox Cemetery near Killen, Alabama, and were the parents of seven children listed below:

1. **Emma E. Tidwell*** was born September 12, 1885; she married **E. Guy Cox*** born January 1, 1887, died November 10, 1964, and they had two children. She died May 29, 1970. Emma and her husband are buried in the Cox Cemetery near Killen, Alabama.

2. **Beulah M. Tidwell*** was born August 16, 1888; she married **H. Irskine Grigsby*** born June 3, 1885, died December 21, 1962, and they had eight children. She died August 5, 1973. Beulah and her husband are buried in the Cox Cemetery near Killen, Alabama.

3. **Ella V. Tidwell*** was born July 29,1899; she married **Ray M. Cox*** born March 5, 1891, died March 24. 1949 (brother to Guy) and they had two children. She died July 16, 1949. Ella and her husband are buried in the Harrison Cemetery near Killen, Alabama.

4. **Mattie S. Tidwell*** was born August 27, 1897; she married **John B. Myrick***, born July 27, 1892, died August 9, 1963 and they had five children. She died May 18, 1980. Mattie and her husband are buried in the old Killen Cemetery in Killen, Alabama.

5. **Doxie Oliver Tidwell*** was born January 15, 1892; he married **Maggie Reid*** born July 10, 1902, died January 28. 1978 and they had four children. He died July 6, 1978. Uncle Doc and his wife are buried in the Cox Cemetery near Killen, Alabama. The stories of this couple are covered in the body of the book.

6. **Richard McBride Tidwell*** was born February 25, 1901; he married **Louise Agnes Gist*** born January 13, 1907, died December 18, 1995 from heart failure. Louise was fifteen years old

at the time of her marriage according to Joanne Tidwell Forsythe's work. She was the daughter of Christopher and Ida (Russell) Gist and they had four children. Richard died October 6, 1987 from kidney failure. Richard M. and Louise are buried in the Tri-Cities Memorial Garden in Florence, Alabama. According to Joanne Tidwell Forsythe's work, Richard received his middle name from the maiden name of his grandmother, Mary Elizabeth (McBride) Billingsley.

Richard M. and Louise Tidwell's four children are listed as follows:

A. **Richard Kenneth Tidwell*** born July 6, 1923, died November 6, 1995. Kenneth and his wife **Marjorie Thompson Tidwell*** are buried at the Tri-Cities Memorial Garden in Florence, Alabama.

B. **James Carl Tidwell** born May 4, 1925, married **Mildred Lanier** and they have two sons, **Glenn Ray Tidwell** and **Jerry Don Tidwell**. Carl and Mildred Tidwell are still living and reside near John Dee Tidwell's old home place.

C. **Charles Allen Tidwell*** was born on November 19, 1928, died March 28, 2003. Charles married **Betty Greenhaw** and they have three daughters **Patricia Ann Tidwell, Charlotte Jean Tidwell** and **Deborah Joyce Tidwell**. Charles is buried at the Tri-Cities Memorial Garden in Florence, Alabama as Betty will be.

D. **Joanne Tidwell Forsythe** Born May 31, 1937. Joanne married **Marvin Forsythe** and they have two children, **Phillip Allen Forsythe** and **Donna Sherea Forsythe Burns**.

    All of the information about Joanne and her brother's families was copied directly from her work.

7. **Anna Laura Tidwell*** was born on October 27, 1910; she married **Alan William Stutts*** born January 5, 1905, died September 12, 1974, and they had no children. She died May 14, 1992. Anna Laura and her husband are buried in the old Killen Cemetery in Killen, Alabama.

The author knows of only one photograph of John Dee Tidwell that survives and it is too faded to copy.

Uncle Doc* and Richard McBride Tidwell's* mother, **Derendia Ann Billingsley Tidwell*, John Dee Tidwell's*** wife. **Derendia** was born March 11, 1866, died July 20, 1912 in Lauderdale County Alabama of pneumonia.

The following two photographs are from Virgiline Tidwell Hale's collection that she graciously let me borrow and copy.

Virgiline related the story to me that all of John Dee and Derendia Tidwell's children planned a visit to the old home place of John Dee Tidwell. This was the only time that they had all been back with their spouses at one time since they had been married. For some reason Richard McBride's wife Louise didn't want them to all congregate there at the same time. Richard sent word down the hill to Uncle Doc and Aunt Mag to stop them there, which they did. They all had their family get together at Uncle Doc and Aunt Mag's. Virgiline related that the following was the only group photograph of the extended family together at one time that she knows of.

108

Left to right: Beulah and Erskine Grigsby, Ella and Ray Cox, John and Mattie Myrick, Anna Laura and Alan Stutts, Emma and Guy Cox, Doxie O. and Maggie Tidwell*. The only child and spouse missing from this photograph is Richard M. and Louise Tidwell. *

Left to right: Emma Tidwell Cox and Beulah Tidwell Grigsby. This photograph shows part of Uncle Doc and Aunt Mag's house in the background and was also taken during the family get together.

Uncle Doc* and Aunt Mag*

This photograph was taken just after the couple learned that their only surviving son, Bud, had to go into service during WWII. Virgiline said she could tell they were both worried to death.

Over time, I grew to think of Uncle Doc as my surrogate grandfather after Grandpa Nathan died in 1954.

Uncle Doc and Aunt Mag were very self sufficient people. I don't know if he ever did anything except farm and there was not much money in that. They grew most everything they ate and did not need to buy much. I remember Aunt Mag peddling her Singer sewing machine and smoking a corncob pipe. They both smoked corncob pipes that Uncle Doc had made. She made a lot of their clothes and they didn't need to go to town often.

Uncle Doc had an old Ford truck that he drove to town when he needed to go. He would take calves and pigs to the sale barn occasionally and hauled things for us when we needed him to. He used the truck around the farm and did what running around he had to until he decided that he was too old to drive anymore and sold the truck. Their children would occasionally take them to town and they would walk across the hills to buy what daily needs they might have from Mack Riggs, who ran the community general store. This was probably limited to basic needs such as some coffee, tea, sugar, pipe tobacco and perhaps a few other things.

They raised their own cow for milk, had chickens for meat and eggs, mules for farming and gardening, pigs for sale and their own meat requirements, and were the only people that I ever knew that would raise veal calves each spring for sale. They would clean out the barn and hen house each spring to fertilize their gardens and they grew enough corn and hay to feed their animals.

Their son, Bud, bought a big old Allis Chalmers tractor and they used it for various things from time to time. I remember there was a bush hog and a hammer mill for grinding feed for the livestock. They set this hammer mill up in the barn. It was an awesome thing to see. They were the first that I ever knew to grow soy beans for hay.

Uncle Doc had his own blacksmith shop and made a lot of his own plow points and other metal necessities for himself and his neighbors. He would use old odds and ends such as automobile leaf springs to make things from.

Uncle Doc always wore old worn cardigan sweaters in cool weather and always had on a cotton striped cap, the type that railroad engineers wore. It was basically a light color and had narrow black stripes in it. It was not made of thick cloth and didn't offer much protection during cold weather. His daughters told me later that they teased him because he would stuff it with newspapers during cold weather. He had the same good looking haircut that I do, and was bald on top.

Uncle Doc was not appreciative of most modern conveniences of the time. He would not allow a radio in the house. His daughters could never understand this and were embarrassed by it. I don't ever remember them having a TV.

Uncle Doc always shaved with a straight razor. I doubt that he ever owned a safety razor. I thought this must be the coolest way to shave that I had ever seen.

I bought a straight razor when I got old enough to shave. I had the local barber, Jess Fritz, order it for me. I bought the razor strop as well.

I took it up to show it to Uncle Doc. He stropped it up good and told me how to use it.

He said "You don't pull straight down, you just slide them off this way" and made the appropriate gestures to illustrate the technique to me.

I went home, lathered up and started to shave. I forgot the sliding motion at first but remembered it when I got down to my neck. One gentle sliding motion was all that it took. I like to have whacked my head off!

I retired the straight razor at that point and went back to using a safety razor. It was a long time before I asked Uncle Doc for any more advice!

They originally heated their house with a fireplace but got a wood burning heater much later. I would visit them on cold winter nights. We would sit around the fire and talk. They always kept their living areas warmer than we did. I would leave later and walk back home, with the cozy warmth from their fireplace or heater radiating from my bones, or it seemed that way to me.

Uncle Doc always cut his own wood from his ample woodlot and would spend much of the late summer and early spring getting enough stocked away for winter. He would rack it up and let it dry. He had the only woodshed in the family.

Uncle Doc was Doxie Oliver, John Dee's oldest son. Aunt Mag was Maggie Earline, Grandmother Alice's youngest sister.

Uncle Doc was in World War I and was born on January 15, 1892 In Lauderdale County.

Uncle Doc in his WW I uniform.

Aunt Mag was born January 10, 1902 in Lawrence County. She and her four sisters and two brothers were the children of John Wesley Reid and Emma Jane Owen Reid who were farming near Town Creek, Alabama and listed in the 1900 census. Aunt Mag was born Melinda Magnolia but changed her name to Maggie Earline before she married. The family had moved to Brush Creek in Lauderdale County by the time that Grandmother Alice and Aunt Mag married. The old house that they lived in on Brush creek is still standing. It has been remodeled several times and still looks pretty good.

This couple married September 17, 1919, seated on a buggy on Royal Avenue in Florence, Alabama, by Justice of the Peace Joe Brewer.

Maggie Earline Reid Tidwell*
Just before she had to take her bed rest.

Aunt Mag died January 28, 1978 and Uncle Doc died on July 6, 1978, surviving Aunt Mag by four months and eight days. They are buried next to each other in the Cox Cemetery near Killen, Alabama.

Uncle Doc and **Aunt Mag.** Date unknown.

Uncle Doc and **Aunt Mag** taken on December 25, 1977.

 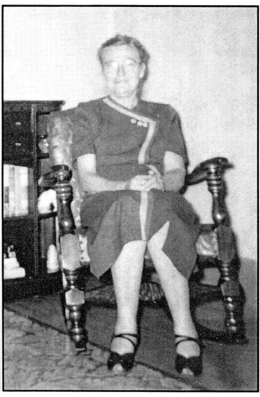

Uncle Doc   **Aunt Mag**

Uncle Doc, Aunt Mag, and Dog Sitting in the Flowers

There were four children from this marriage.

Earl Eugene Tidwell* who died as a young child and is buried in the Cox Cemetery near Killen, Alabama.

Emma Virgiline Tidwell b. February 6, 1922 married **J. T. Hale*** b. May 11, 1924, d. July 24, 1993 on March 11, 1950. No children. Virgiline is the only surviving child.

Virgiline as a young woman.

Floyd Arvel (Bud) Tidwell* born January 3, 1925. Married Katie Lucille Cross, born September 11, 1925 on December 26, 1945. Bud died November 18, 2008. Buried Cox Cemetery near Killen, Alabama.

Bud with his oldest son **Donnie Tidwell.**

Note the old cast iron wash pots set up behind and to the left of the bush for some purpose.

Helen Marguerite Tidwell* born January 23, 1928, died April 14, 1999. Married **Gilbert Trousdale*** born November 23, 1917 on July 5, 1960. Marguerite died December 2, 1988. No Children. They are buried at the Antioch Cemetery, Killen, Alabama.

Marguerite, Uncle Doc, Virgiline. Both daughters were extremely attractive young women.

16

Uncle Doc and Aunt Mag's Home Place

John Dee Tidwell died on May 20, 1918. He had two surviving sons, Doxie Oliver and Richard McBride.

John Dee's farm was split, with Richard McBride getting the upper portion with John Dee's home on it, and Doxie Oliver getting the lower portion along the creek. Uncle Doc's parcel was split into two parts by a sliver of land belonging to Richard so that he had access to the creek as well.

Uncle Doc and Aunt Mag had to build a house on this property as well as a barn.

The house they built was impressive for the time. It had six rooms and was constructed of frame and siding of rough sawn timber. The siding on the outside was one by twelves that ran up and down and had strips nailed where they joined together to seal the crack. It was finished on the inside nicely but I don't remember with what. It was covered up with wallpaper and some rooms were painted.

The front two rooms were a living room and bedroom that shared a common chimney with a fireplace on each side. There were French doors between the living room and dining room.

The middle two rooms were a dining room and a bedroom.

The back two rooms were a kitchen and another bedroom that shared a common flue so there could be a wood burning cook stove in the kitchen and a heater in the bedroom.

There was a nicely finished cellar that covered about one third of the area under the house. Access to the cellar was through a trap door in the floor in the middle bedroom. The walls were plastered and it had a concrete floor. Uncle Doc built shelves to store Aunt Mag's canned goods as well as bins to store potatoes, onions and other root crops. It functioned as a true root cellar. There was one window in the cellar facing south. It had a well constructed stairway down into it.

There was a full width porch with a concrete floor across the front and a porch of identical size with a wooden floor running across the back.

The roof for the front porch was supported by wooden columns that Uncle Doc had built. They had a masonry base that was about three feet tall and the columns were on top of this.

Uncle Doc had several souvenirs from World War I sitting on top of the masonry bases. There was a steel helmet and several pieces of ammunition dating from this time. There was also an old Civil War artillery shell that he had found on his property. There was a large metal screw on the very point of it that was the detonator and had failed to detonate when it was originally fired. The fuse must have been defective. Anyway, one could still hear the black powder rattling around in it when shaken.

Uncle Doc said that he had tied it to a chain and tied the chain around the neck of his milk cow to keep her from running off or straying too far when he first found it. I can just imagine instant hamburger if the cow had somehow hit it against the wrong thing.

I tried to steer clear of it. I think that Bud, their son, has it now. It belongs in a museum, after it has been decommissioned.

There was a swing, bench and several chairs on the front porch. There were numerous shade trees out front and this was always a cool place to spend an afternoon once the daily chores were done. We would sit out front and talk. We would look at the occasional car that went by and wave to the people in it.

The back porch had a wooden floor and this is where Uncle Doc and Aunt Mag prepared the bounty from their large garden to be preserved. Uncle Doc had mounted an old sink to the wall to wash things as they brought them in. It had a drain pipe that went underground to a ditch out back.

There was a large cast iron diner bell mounted at one end of the back porch. Aunt Mag would ring it every day at noon when she had lunch prepared. Uncle Doc would come in from the fields when he heard the dinner bell for lunch and to take a noonday nap and to give his mules a break.

That dinner bell could be heard all over the creek bottom when Aunt Mag would ring it. It let everyone know it was lunch time. All of the children who came to visit always wanted to ring the dinner bell. Aunt Mag always tried to keep us away from it. She said that Uncle Doc would think there was something wrong and come home if he heard it.

There were plenty of windows and each porch had two doors leading out onto them with screen doors on them.

It was a well thought out and constructed farmhouse.

The first barn they built burned and killed most of their livestock. Uncle Doc blamed it on his putting some baled hay that was too wet into the hay loft. The hay went through a heat and caught the hay and barn on fire. Uncle Doc said this liked to have wiped him out. It was a tremendous loss for the young couple just starting out.

The barn was rebuilt and a corn crib, blacksmith shop with an attached wagon shed, chicken house, wood shed, smoke house and well house were built. A garage for Uncle Doc's old Ford truck with a workshop behind it was built later. There were numerous other small buildings.

One thing that I remember about Uncle Doc's garage was that the bumblebees really loved it. They had tunneled into it and built nests everywhere. As children, Ann and I would go up to Uncle Doc's for bumblebee hunting. Uncle Doc had carved paddles for us to use to knock the bees down while they were flying and then stomp on them. We killed bees many afternoons until we got tired of doing it.

Uncle Doc's Homemade Paint

Uncle Doc painted the house with some homemade paint. He painted it only once but it never needed painting after that. It never did completely dry and you didn't want to lean up against the house even into the '50s or '60s. The paint was a deep barn wood red and it would rub off on anyone's clothes that were unlucky enough to brush up against it.

I was inquisitive about how he had made it in later years and asked him. He said that he got the formula from the county agent and it was a mixture of used motor oil, or burnt motor oil as we called it, and iron oxide. Iron oxide is nothing but iron rust!

Uncle Doc had brushed it on and let the wood soak it up as much as it could. That was why it lasted so long and why it never did completely dry.

I imagined at the time that this must have made the wood very flammable but thought nothing more about it. In retrospect, this may have contributed to a later happening.

Soda

Uncle Doc was the only person in the immediate family that was still actively farming by the time I could remember. Everyone else had taken jobs in the industries that flourished in the area with the construction on Wilson Dam and during and after World War II. All that anyone else was doing was gardening.

Uncle Doc always discussed things and paid close attention to the county agent.

At one point, Uncle Doc became a firm proponent of using sodium nitrate fertilizer with his corn. He would apply the fertilizer to the middles the last time that he plowed it. The fertilizer application was called "side dressing" and the last plowing was called "laying by."

Up until that time, the most common fertilizer was 4/10/7. Everybody used it for everything and it came in cloth bags. It was a common joke at the time that you could tell a country girl by the fact that her dress had 4/10/7 across the chest. Fertilizer bags and cow feed bags were all cloth back then. Fertilizer bags were white and cow feed bags always had some kind of printed pattern on them. The cloth bags were made into clothing. I have worn several "cow feed" shirts while growing up!

At some point, Uncle Doc started using sodium nitrate fertilizer on his corn. He claimed that it dramatically increased his yields. Nobody could see just how adding soda, as sodium nitrate was called back then, could do anything to a corn crop.

I don't know if this was Uncle Doc's idea or the county agent had recommended it.

Uncle Doc planted a test patch using sodium nitrate when he laid his corn by and another one without using it under the county agent's supervision. The yield with the sodium nitrate was thirty percent greater as I remember it. Anyway, it was significantly larger.

The county agent couldn't believe it according to Uncle Doc's story. He couldn't understand how using it could do anything to the crop's yield.

Every corn farmer uses extra nitrogen when growing corn now. They have increased the nitrogen content by switching from sodium to ammonium nitrate.

This makes a good story and I know for a fact that Uncle Doc was the first in our immediate area to use this practice.

17

Farming and Gardening

Uncle Doc always used mules to farm and garden. He also used them to pull his farm wagon. He always used two mules to pull his farm plows and wagon but he only used one when gardening. He finally got too old to farm but he always gardened as much as he could.

He had one mule that he kept as long as I can remember. It was a large female mule by the name of Lize.

According to Uncle Doc, Lize was so well trained that he didn't even have to put plow lines on her. He could just talk to her and she would do exactly what he needed her to do.

There were only four basic commands that you needed to control a mule anyway. They were "get up, whoa, yea to turn right, and haw to turn left." I later found out that Uncle Doc was right about Lize all along when I borrowed her to plow out Dad's garden. You just needed to talk to her.

I never visited Uncle Doc much when he was working in his fields but I was always around while he was gardening. He had a large garden directly behind his house and a smaller one by the side of the house. He would sometimes plant one across the creek near an apple tree but not often.

The large garden had a six foot high net wire fence around it to try to keep the chickens out. The chicken house was only a short distance from the garden. The chickens were allowed to roam all over the yard and the surrounding woods to look for food.

Uncle Doc and Aunt Mag grew things in their garden that we didn't want to or didn't know how. They always had beets and carrots. They are very small and slow growers at first and require a lot of cultivating. They also grew the staples such as corn, okra, tomatoes, potatoes, squash, melons and always a big pea patch. They would grow all kinds of peas such as crowder, black eyed, purple hull and just regular field peas.

Peas are delicious when picked fresh while they are green and either cooked or canned. They are also good dried.

They would pick and thrash dried peas for the winter. We always did this, but nothing on the scale they did.

They had two or three small resealable metal drums that they used for this purpose. Each drum held at least seven or eight gallons.

They would allow the peas to mature and dry in the field. They would pull cotton sacks behind them and harvest the dried peas before the birds got too many of them. A cotton sack is about six feet long that has a neck and shoulder strap. People pulled them along the ground behind them while picking cotton.

The dried peas, cotton sack and all, would be hung up in the barn until the peas got dry enough to just pop out of their shells with just a little pressure.

They would wait for a windy day before they finished them by thrashing. This included beating the daylights out of the cotton sacks to shell the peas. I sometimes got to help by jumping up and down on the sacks.

The peas, once they had been thoroughly thrashed, were dumped onto a tarpaulin--peas, hulls and all. The peas would then be winnowed by picking them up and throwing them up into the wind. The wind would blow the hulls away and the peas would fall back onto the tarp.

This continued until the hulls were all gone and nothing was left but mostly peas. The bits and pieces of the hulls were then picked out by hand.

The peas were then put into the metal drums filling them about two-thirds full. Uncle Doc would place a saucer on top of them and pour about one or two capfuls of what he called "high life" or sodium bisulfate into the saucers.

The drums were then tightly sealed by forcing the metal tops back on them.

The "high life" would then evaporate and thoroughly fumigate the peas killing all of the weevil eggs and larvae. Weevils will eat holes by tunneling through the peas and ruining them.

We did other beans this way too, notably dried lima beans. They are not as good to eat in the winter as canned beans picked and preserved while green but are a lot easier to preserve.

Fodder Making

Uncle Doc and Aunt Mag did not allow much to go to waste. They had a use for most everything.

One thing that Uncle Doc did that I have never seen anyone else do was to make fodder for his livestock.

He would build wooden shocks and cut his garden corn while still green after he had harvested the roasting ears. The corn stalks were then placed while still green on the shocks and allowed to dry.

Uncle Doc would then cut about the top one-third of the corn stalks off and bundle them together. He would tie it all together with a corn leaf and put it in the hay loft to feed his animals during the winter. Everything still had a green color.

There is nothing like corn fodder to bring an ailing animal around. The first thing that an ailing animal will do is quit eating. They will eat fodder when they won't eat anything else.

We would trade Uncle Doc out of a bundle or two of fodder especially when we had an ailing mule. We would soak the fodder in creek water to reconstitute it before feeding it. The mule would eat that and then usually start eating properly again.

Guaranteed.

Growing Tobacco

Uncle Doc would occasionally grow some tobacco for his own use. He and Aunt Mag both smoked corncob pipes. I didn't know until then that tobacco would grow this far south.

I remember Uncle Ed participating in this too.

They would first prepare a seed bed by burning wood and leaving the ashes. The bed would then be worked up and the seeds planted. This was done close to the house so it could be kept watered.

When the plants grew to the proper size, they would set them out.

I was too little to remember much that happened after that.

Uncle Doc had quit growing tobacco by the time we moved to Kentucky.

Our neighbor in Kentucky had grown tobacco for a number of years and still had a tobacco barn. They would split the tobacco stalks after they had been harvested and hang them up in the barn to dry and would smoke the tobacco with wood smoke to further speed up the drying process.

Our neighbor had kept a big stack of cured tobacco in the barn for his own use. He smoked a pipe as well. It was a dark, ugly looking stack with a foul odor I thought!

Dad took a good quantity of it for Uncle Doc and Aunt Mag to smoke in their pipes during one of our visits home.

It produced an odor while being smoked in a pipe much like a strong smelling cigar. It was enough to make a young boy gasp for breath while tears were running from his eyes!

Aunt Mag's Homemade Hominy

Aunt Mag was the only person in the family that made hominy. I never saw her do it but she told me how to do it. She would add shelled corn, water and hardwood ashes from the fireplace in the black iron pot and build a fire underneath. She would let everything simmer for a while until it was done.

She must have tied the wood ashes in a cloth bag since there was never any traces of them in her finished product.

She would then thoroughly wash and rinse everything with water.

The lye in the wood ashes dissolved the corn husk and fluffed up the corn kernels. She would then share a quart or two with family members.

This was the best hominy that I have ever eaten! It was nothing like the canned stuff that you buy in the supermarket.

She only did this once a year but we always waited for it in anticipation!

Sassafras Tea

Uncle Doc would always scour the countryside late in the fall to dig sassafras roots. Just any sassafras root would not do. It had to be red sassafras roots. He would call some white sassafras and some he would call red. Only the red sassafras roots made the proper tea and they had red colored bark on the roots.

Uncle Doc would then place the roots in a dry place and let them dry out over the winter. He would cut them up into short pieces in the early spring and use a hatchet to splinter them.

Aunt Mag would then take the splintered roots and boil them with water until the water took on a light pinkish brown color. She would then mix the proper amount of sugar with the tea minus the roots and they would serve it hot.

They called it a spring tonic to purify the system.

I don't know anything about purifying my system but it sure did taste good! I got some roots from them every spring so that we could make our own tea.

Lana and I used to buy chopped sassafras roots in a plastic bag from the supermarket in the '70s and '80s, but I haven't seen any in a long time.

There were several sassafras thickets growing on Grandmother Alice's old farm. These were uprooted by Dad's friend with the bulldozers when the old place was cleaned up.

Uncle Doc had called them white sassafras up until that time. They had a red color after the bulldozer pushed them up. Uncle Doc said that he had been searching the country side for red sassafras all of this time and it was close by all along.

Apparently the sassafras roots do not turn red until after they get old enough!

Uncle Doc's Economic Policy

Uncle Doc claimed to be a Republican in a family full of Democrats. That made us wonder about him at times. His major economic policy was that the government would have to issue new money and void all of the current currency in circulation. He said that they had to. There

125

was no way that they could repay all that they owed for World War II and all of the government programs unless they did.

They would have to just wipe them out and issue new money.

There is no way that anyone can continue on borrowing money and never paying any of it back, he thought!

With the current debt and economic problems and all of the promised bailouts currently dominating the news and the election, I am beginning to wonder if he might not have been right all along.

18

Auction

After Aunt Mag's death, but before Uncle Doc's, an auction was held in their home to dispose of what their children did not want. I understand this was mostly household goods and personal items. The land had been divided in their will and I suppose the children had already taken what they wanted. Uncle Doc and Aunt Mag had moved in with their son, Bud, when Aunt Mag could no longer function. Aunt Mag died three days later.

I was living in Scottsboro and did not attend. I don't remember if I even knew about it before hand.

Some items had been removed the day of the auction, but I understand that there was a lot left. A fire broke out the night of the auction and burned everything to the ground. Everything was a total loss.

The cause of the fire was never known. I wonder if Uncle Doc's homemade paint contributed to the inferno.

This was a sad end to a grand old couple that I learned so much from and that had shown me so much love and understanding while I was growing up. I am saddened especially by their passing and the loss of the house that I had grown so fond of.

Uncle Doc and **Aunt Mag's** house the day after the fire. Photo taken on March 5, 1978. **Lucille Tidwell,** Bud's wife, is in the foreground.

127

Lucille and **Bud Tidwell**

Bud in his Navy uniform.

19

Virgiline's Stories

Emma Virgiline Tidwell is a very special lady who was 87 years young on February 6, 2009. She still lives by herself and keeps an immaculately orderly, clean and well decorated house. She does all of her own yard work, gardening with a tiller, canning and freezing and has the reputation as a most wondrous cook.

She farmed with her own tractor and did her own home repairs, such as climbing up a ladder to keep the tin roof nailed down on her barns, well past 80. She still has more energy than a teen-age youth and can run circles around anybody her age that I know of or have ever heard of. Mischief just sparkles in her blue eyes.

She has plants scattered tastefully all through her entire house and hauls plants that are currently filling her large sun porch at the back of her house to and from her yard each fall and spring.

Virgiline is the last surviving child of Uncle Doc and Aunt Mag. Virgiline looks remarkably like her mother and has a personality much like Uncle Doc did. It is hard sometimes for me to realize that I am talking to her instead of Aunt Mag. She has some wondrous stories to tell about growing up on Brush Creek and I will try to relay some of them. She is remarkably alert and tells these stories with a strong voice and is very much interested in telling them. She has a treasure trove of old photographs and has generously shared them with me.

She had to start treatment for lymphoma about five years ago and this sapped all of her energy for a long time. She has since recovered and has most of her strength back. There were signs that the lymphoma could be coming back the last time she had an examination. They plan to do her blood work again after the first of the year and will take a sample of bone marrow for a conclusive test if her blood work does not look any better. This possibility has her concerned but she is not letting it get her down. She is living one day at a time and is ready to face whatever she has to again. She is one very remarkable woman.

Virgiline sold her tractor and retired her ladder shortly after being diagnosed with her illness. She still laments on not being able to climb on top of the barn to nail down the tin that is getting loose in places.

Virgiline was born on February 6, 1922 and is from February to May older than my father. She is twenty years older than I am and she was three years older than her younger brother Floyd (Bud) and is six years older than her younger sister Marguerite. There was one older brother, Earl, who died as a young child and is buried at the Cox Cemetery.

One of the first stories that I ever remember Virgiline telling me was taking me to the mailbox. This was a big chore back then as the mail was delivered about half of a mile from their house and about a quarter of a mile from ours. Someone had to walk down to the mailbox to get the mail or post mail every day.

The mail was delivered by the place where they tried Richard T. Tidwell and supposedly condemned him to hang. Virgiline apparently made the mistake of taking me to the mailbox with her once.

She said that I would wait until I saw her coming down the road going to the mailbox. She said that I would run as fast as my wobbly little legs would carry me when I saw her. She said that I would say "Me want to go with you. Me get a letter from my Daddy." Dad was in the Navy during WWII at the time. Nothing would do but she had to pick me up and carry me to the mailbox and then back.

I told her "Virgiline, I must have been a pest back then." She replied "You were like a little piss ant, no, you were worse than a piss ant back then!" She said for me not to tell Lana what she had said because Lana might get mad. I couldn't resist telling Lana though and she said "You are still like a piss ant!"

Another story that Virgiline told me was that Grandmother Alice and Mother were worried about my not wanting to feed myself when they started trying to wean me to solid food. She said that she was visiting one afternoon when they were trying to feed me. She said that she picked up the spoon and I ate everything that she would feed me. She said that she told Grandmother Alice and Mother that there was nothing wrong with me. She told them just to not feed me. I would start feeding myself when I got hungry enough.

Virgiline also told me two other stories that show how she and Bud bonded at a very young age. They remained very close until Bud's death in 2008.

Shaving Bud's Neck

Virgiline said that this happened while she and Bud were very little children. She said that they were neither any size at all.

One day Aunt Mag went outside for something and Bud said "Virgiline, shave my neck."

Virgiline said that Bud was so small that his feet didn't even touch the floor when he straddled the chair for the shaving. She said that she put a towel around his neck like a barber would do. She tried to do the shaving properly.

She then got a pan of water and Uncle Doc's shaving mug. She lathered up Bud's neck real well in preparation for the shaving. She had never used a straight razor before but this did not faze her! She went to work!

Aunt Mag came back inside somewhere in the middle of the neck shaving and did not say a word. She remained quiet until Virgiline put the razor down and then unloaded. In Virgiline's words "Laid Down The Law!" Virgiline said that she was told never to touch that razor again among many other things!

Bud then chimed in and said "Mama, she is not going to hurt me. She is doing a good job!"

I know that Aunt Mag was afraid that Bud could have been severely cut but he was not.

Virgiline said that neither of them received a spanking and it was probably because Aunt Mag was so relieved that Bud had not been hurt!

Bud later inherited the razor and Virgiline has the shaving mug.

Virgiline's First Driving Experience

Virgiline said that this story took place sometime later but she and Bud were both still very small.

Uncle Doc had an old green Chevrolet at the time with a canvas top. He called the trunk the "Turtle Tail" back then because it reminded him of how a turtle opened its shell.

It was a ritual for him every Saturday to load up the trunk with extra produce from the garden-- eggs, milk and butter to try to sell to his neighbors.

Everything was loaded up this particular Saturday except the milk and butter, which were still in the refrigerator, and Uncle Doc went inside to shave.

Virgiline explained that the road took a different route back then that it does now. It went down hill from their house across the current road, across a deep ditch and wound around down the creek to where it crossed the creek near the old beech tree where we washed clothes and killed hogs. It then ran in front of the old barn and the old log home place of Richard T. There was a wooden bridge across the deep ditch directly in front of their house.

Virgiline said that her legs were too short to touch the pedals but she climbed up in the driver's seat of the old Chevrolet anyway. Bud was pushing from behind, although he wasn't big enough to do much, and got the car rolling. She must have somehow knocked it out of gear. Anyway, it started rolling down the hill.

Uncle Doc heard the commotion and ran outside to see what was going on with soap lathered all over his face. He tried to sling the soap off and started chasing the car.

Virgiline said she was able to cross the wooden bridge but, somewhere along the way, she lost control and was headed for the ditch. The car rolled to a stop before she got to the ditch.

Virgiline said that Bud told Uncle Doc, "Dad there is no need to run. Virgiline is driving!"

I asked Virgiline if she got a spanking. She said "No, but I don't know how I avoided it. I guess Dad was just so happy that I did not run into the ditch!"

Virgiline's Courtship and Marriage

Virgiline married J. T. Hale on March 11, 1950. J. T. had a number of illnesses over the years as I remember.

Virgiline was working at the old Flagg Knitting Mill in East Florence when she met J. T. This is also where Marguerite and Aunt Jane went to work later.

J. T. was working at Simmons Wholesale House also in East Florence and near the Flagg Knitting Mill when they met.

Virgiline said that J. T had sent her a message that he would like to have a date with her. She said that she sent a message back that if he was man enough to deserve a date he would have to ask her himself.

Virgiline said that she had been to lunch one day and was returning to work across the railroad track. J. T. was out on the back porch where they loaded trucks at Simmons Wholesale when he saw her on the railroad track. He jumped off of the back porch and hollered at her. Virgiline said that she stopped and he ran up to her and asked for a date on the railroad track.

Virgiline said that she told J.T. many times during later married life that she bet that he wished that a train had come along and hit her that day.

Virgiline said that their first date was a double date with one of her friends.

J. T. had to walk the whole 4 ½ miles to her house on the second date. J. T. lived on the property where they built a home after they were married.

She said that she and J. T. dated for two years and three months before they married.

We discussed that theirs must have been love at first sight.

Coat

Another story that Virgiline related to me was that once Aunt Mag had bought enough heavy tweed cloth to have a coat made out of. She had intended to see if Doris Rogers could make it for her but Doris could not do it.

Virgiline said that she was visiting one day shortly after her marriage and Uncle Doc told her to go into the bedroom and get the sack of cloth. Uncle Doc said that perhaps she had time to make the coat since she was alone at home all day while J.T. was working.

Virgiline said that she looked the material over and was afraid that she would ruin it. Aunt Mag told her, "You are family and nothing will be said if you do ruin it."

Virgiline said she took the cloth home and made the coat. It turned out beautifully and Aunt Mag wore it for years and thoroughly enjoyed it.

According to Virgiline, Aunt Mag thought this was the grandest coat there ever was simply because she had made it for her. It burned up in the house the night of the fire.

Virgiline and **J. T** taken during their dating years.

Virgiline and **J. T. Hale** taken shortly after marriage.

20

Tour Through Virgiline's Home

Getting to take a tour through Virgiline's home is really a treat. She has antiques from various family members with stories to go with all of them. They are her cherished treasures.

A tour starts off down the hall where the first piece of furniture that Uncle Doc and Aunt Mag bought after their marriage is on display. It was an old oak dresser with an oval mirror that still looks new. She said that they went to Florence in a two horse wagon and paid twenty-five dollars for it at Rogers Department Store and hauled it home.

Uncle Doc's brother Richard McBride Tidwell was not married at the time and they lived with him in his house. They later bought the house at the foot of the hill and moved into it. Virgiline said that the back four rooms was all there was at the time. She says she remembers when they added the front two rooms to their old home place.

Uncle Doc and Aunt Mag moved the dresser along with what other furniture they had into this house in 1919. Virgiline said that it was never removed until she brought it to her house and it has not been moved since.

First piece of furniture after **Uncle Doc** and **Aunt Mag's** marriage.

The next room contains an old Gentleman's chest that Uncle Walter tied on the top of a station wagon and hauled home for Aunt Marie from Missouri when he was stationed there. Aunt Marie would not have it in her house for some reason and he sat it out on the front porch at the old log house. Uncle Doc saw it and knew that Uncle Walter didn't know what he would do with it. He hurried home to tell Virgiline who was dating J. T. Hale at the time and they knew they would soon be married. Virgiline and J. T. went down to look at it and Uncle Walter offered it to them for what he had paid for it in Missouri--twenty-five dollars. They promptly bought it and Virgiline still has it and tells of the offers she has had for it. There were very few of them made and very few of them are still in existence. Probably none of them are in the excellent condition that hers is.

Virgiline's Gentleman's chest. There is a shelf under the dome for things like a gentleman's hat and compartments for things like gloves and other accessories.

The next room holds other treasures. One of them is a cedar chest that Uncle Doc made by hand in his '80s. He made three of them from scrap cedar that Ferrell Allen had left over from lining a closet with cedar. Uncle Doc offered one to Marguerite but she would not have it in her house.

Cedar chest that **Uncle Doc** made from scrap cedar left over from someone else lining a closet with cedar.

Virgiline said that she took one. It is not the fanciest cedar chest ever but it is very precious to her because her dad made it. Lucille Cross Tidwell, Bud's widow, has one and Aunt Mag had the other one.

The next room is the dining room. There are numerous cherished treasures there and among them are her Grandfather's, John Dee Tidwell, trunk and her Mother's vinegar jar. This jar was carried to the general store and filled from a barrel, probably wooden, when empty.

Virgiline's grandfather's trunk.

136

Virgiline with her mother's vinegar jar.

Another treasure is an old ceramic picture from Richard T. Tidwell's home place. It was there when Grandmother Alice moved in and Aunt Mag always admired it. Grandmother Alice promised it to Aunt Mag after she married. Aunt Mag was down visiting one day after her marriage and told everyone that she needed a drink of water before she started home. She came out with the picture and told everyone she was taking her wedding present home.

Virgiline said that Aunt Mag always kept buttermilk in the pitcher in the refrigerator. It has a small chip on one side of the spout where Aunt Mag hit the side of the refrigerator door once when taking it out.

Virgiline with ceramic picture from **Richard T. Tidwell's** old home place.

Table from Richard T. Tidwell's Old Home Place.

This table sits in Virgiline's living room and was originally from Richard T. Tidwell's old home place. Richard gave it Florence Alabama (Bama) when she married Bill Hale. Bama had two tables that were almost identical but the other one is narrow. Virgiline knows that this table came from Richard T's old home but is not sure about the narrow one. She is almost positive that it did as well. The tablecloth has been pulled back to show the details of the table.

According to Virgiline, Bill Hale raised such a stink after Richard T. died about protecting Bama's share of everything that he forced everything to be auctioned off. There were some hogs in the pig pen that Richard T. had given to his sons before he died. Bill even went to the pig pen to get the hogs for the auction but John Dee Tidwell stepped in according to Virgiline. John Dee apparently told Bill Hale that there was no way that he was taking those hogs. This story had to have been handed down to Virgiline because this happened before she was born.

This is when Grandpa Nathan and Grandma Alice bought the farm. A copy of their original note on the farm was made out to Bill Hale and is elsewhere in the book. There are also copies of some early property tax records made out to Richard T. also.

Bama Hale had to be hospitalized for two weeks with pneumonia late in life. Bill had apparently talked her into going home but there was no one at home to take care of her. The doctor agreed to let her leave but only if she went to Virgiline's house to stay until she had fully recovered.

138

Bill didn't want to come at first but finally decided to come also. Virgiline fixed up a room for them and they moved in. Virgiline said that Bill was really hungry that first night.

He was also extremely dirty. So dirty that Virgiline didn't want him sleeping in one of her beds. She told him that he needed to take a bath and clean up and that she would run his bath water. Bill refused and Virgiline lost her temper. She told him that she could take his clothes off and force him to take a bath but she would wait until J.T. got home from work and let him take care of it. Bill reconsidered his options after a while and decided to take a bath on his own and told her "Girlie, run my bathwater!"

Bill took the longest time to take his bath and told Virgiline that he didn't know he was that dirty and that the water looked pretty bad when he had finished.

Virgiline said that she had to take Bama back to the doctor in two weeks and Bill had apparently talked her into going home. She lived about six more months. Malcolm Hale, Bama's only child, went through all of her things and threw most of them way after she died. He at first brought Virgiline the narrow table but his wife did not like the wide one so he brought it to Virgiline and took the narrow one to his wife. This is how Virgiline ended up with this table.

Bama is buried in the old Killen cemetery in Killen, Alabama.

This is a lot of information not associated directly with this table but the story ties in with information elsewhere in the book. It needs to be told.

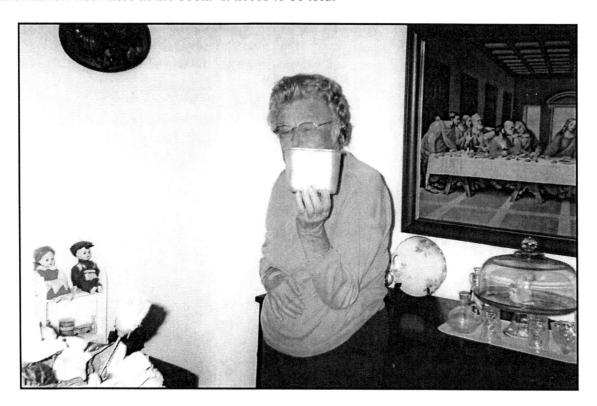

Virgiline with a part of **Uncle Doc's** mess kit from WW I.

21

Virgiline's Early Life

Virgiline had the normal upbringing of any young lady growing up on a hardscrabble farm for the time and area.

She told me about going to the cotton gin with Uncle Doc after they had picked a bale of cotton in the fall. A bale of cotton took about 1500 pounds of picked cotton to yield about a 500 pound bale of cotton and about 1000 pounds of cotton seeds, which were used as animal feed after ginning. The cotton sacks, also used to harvest dried peas, were weighed with an old beam and balance scale when they were full and dumped into the wagon which had side boards attached.

They would then hook up a two mule team to the wagon and set off for the gin. There was a considerable wait at the gin until their wagon could be worked in. Virgiline said that it would sometimes be after dark and getting cold when they finished at the gin and started for home. Uncle Doc would scoop out a hole in the cotton seeds which were still warm from the gin for her. She would sit there in her warm nest in the cotton seeds and look at the stars overhead. She thoroughly enjoyed their trips to the gin!

Virgiline's life as a normal childhood on the family farm came to an end when she was in the 6th grade. Her mother became ill and the doctor put her to bed for a rest which lasted for 6 months. The first doctor thought she had tuberculosis but a later doctor thought it was pneumonia and scars on her lungs from scarlet fever. Anyway Aunt Mag was very run down and ill and had to have bed rest. She had to take things easy for some time after she was allowed to get out of bed.

Uncle Doc had three children to care for and a farm to tend. He had to have help. He hired a colored woman to do the housework and cooking that winter but he still needed help with the farm. He could not afford to pay for a woman to help in the house and someone to help him farm so a decision had to be reached and they discussed the options.

They could continue with keeping the woman and let Bud drop out of school to help Uncle Doc with the farm or Virgiline could drop out of school and do the housework and Uncle Doc could hire someone to help him farm. They couldn't possibly afford to keep the woman and hire a helper for Uncle Doc both.

Virgiline volunteered to drop out of school. She thought it was more important for Bud and Marguerite to finish school than it was for her. Virgiline said she had already failed two grades.

So, this is what happened. Virgiline had to transform from being a school girl into becoming a woman with enormous responsibilities overnight at the ripe old age of about 15 years. She immediately had to start doing the chores of housekeeping, cooking and clothes washing on an old rub board.

Virgiline said that her mother could not help her but could tell her how to do something. She had helped her mother enough that she knew the basics of cooking but didn't know the fine details of seasoning and things like that. Her mother told her she would just have to use her judgment until she found out. She said they will have to eat it anyway whether they like it or not. It didn't take Virgiline long to catch on.

Virgiline recounted how two women came to visit Aunt Mag one wash day. She had planned to open a jar of canned hog head and make hog head hash for dinner. The women stayed and stayed. Virgiline had about worn her fingers down to a nub on the old rub board and still had to cook dinner. None of the women offered to help.

Virgiline said that she went down into the cellar and got some potatoes to put in the hash, which she normally did not do. It didn't matter how it tasted, that was all she had to cook. She said she added the potatoes and some extra water to make it be enough for everybody. The women claimed it was the best hash they had ever tasted.

Another story she recounted that after one hog killing she was making chitterlings. Grandmother Alice came by and saw her doing it. Nobody had told Virgiline to make the chitterlings, she just knew they would go to waste if she did not and they all liked them.

Grandmother Alice promptly marched into Aunt Mag's bedroom and started complaining about them making Virgiline make chitterlings. Aunt Mag listened to all of this she could stand and told Grandmother to shut up and get out. Nobody had told Virgiline to make the chitterlings, she had done it on her own. In fact, Uncle Doc had told her not to do it. Grandmother Alice didn't help Virgiline make them, she just went home.

Virgiline then went into how to make chitterlings. She said they had to be soaked in water for three days and the water had to be changed every day. She said they also had to be tied in a special manner. She said that she did not know how to do it but Aunt Mag showed her how to do it with a strip of cloth and then she had no trouble.

She said that years later she made chitterlings for Clint Freeman and her husband J. T. Clint Freeman bragged about them and J. T. had never eaten them but had heard bad things about them. Clint told J. T. that you had to know how to prepare chitterlings for them to be any good.

I told Virgiline about Dad always making fun of them for making chitterlings. She thought that was funny because Dad always came up and ate chitterlings with them and thought they were good! She got a good laugh out of that.

Feeding the Animals

Virgiline said that she and Bud were a lot alike, but Marguerite always took things seriously.

Virgiline said that the children all had chores to do on the farm. One of their chores was to feed the animals.

Bud's chore was to climb up in the hayloft and throw down hay for the animals. Marguerite's chore was to take the hay to the mangers in the stalls for each animal. Virgiline said that her chore was to go the corn crib and get corn for all of the animals.

Marguerite always took pride in her hair. She was constantly washing it and pinning it up in pin curlers. She had just finished with her hair before it was time to feed the animals on this particular afternoon.

Bud decided that he had to take a leak after he had thrown down the hay. There was a big crack in the hayloft floor over one of the stalls. He started to relieve himself through the crack.

Little did he know that Marguerite was directly underneath. He completely wet her head and her hair before she could move.

Marguerite began to let up a howl and hollered so much that she could be heard all the way to the house. Marguerite was as mad as a hornet and made such a ruckus that Aunt Mag came running from the house to see what was wrong.

Virgiline said that this was truly an accident, but that Marguerite was convinced that she and Bud had planned it. She would not consider anything else. Virgiline said that Marguerite went to her grave still believing that she and Bud had made up for this to happen.

Ornery Mule

Virgiline told me some stories about an ornery mule that she and Bud were trying to harness one day in the barn. It didn't want to be harnessed and reared up to get away but hit its head in the process. It tore a triangular piece of skin and flesh off that was hanging down. They got a piece of black sewing thread and a needle from the house to sew everything back in place. The mule didn't want any part of this either so they had to tie a rope around its nose and twist the mule's head down and hold it in place while this sewing operation took place. I can just see this frightened mule trying to get away in my mind's eye!

Anyway, the operation was a success and the mule healed up. The only problem was there was a ridge where they sewed everything up. Uncle Doc showed the ridge to the man who eventually bought the mule from him and told the story of the black sewing thread. This didn't hurt the value of the mule and the man bought it anyway.

Virgiline and Bud had this mule hitched up to a plow near home one day and were trying to get it to behave and plow. This mule was prone to kicking spells and took one that day while hitched to the plow. Bud kept trying to control the mule but couldn't and got mad. He told Virgiline to get something to beat the mule with which she did. Bud held the plow lines tightly, trying to get the mule to go and Virgiline beat it. The mule finally settled down but Bud was mad. He said "I am going to kill this mule; I am going to work it to death."

He had Virgiline sit on the beam of the plow to make it sink into the ground deeper and make the mule work harder. Aunt Mag saw what was happening and was afraid the mule would start kicking again and kill Virgiline, but the kids continued as they were. Aunt Mag told Uncle Doc the story when he came home and he went to check on everybody. He came back and report to Aunt Mag that everything was OK. Everybody was still standing.

Virgiline said that both she and Bud had decided to try to work that ornery mule to death and sweat was running off of the mule when Uncle Doc went to check on everything.

Helping Around the Farm.

Virgiline also told some stories about helping Uncle Doc around the farm. One story was that she would harness up her team while Uncle Doc harnessed his. He would do the plowing and she would run the two gang wooden section drag harrow to smooth the land once he had plowed it. This was a wooden frame with metal spikes set into it. There was a handle to set the angle of the teeth as the spikes were called.

Another story was that she was once running the harrow over a newly planted field of potatoes to smooth off the top. The potatoes were planted in a furrow and then covered by running a breaking plow down each side of the row. The top of the resulting ridge had to be knocked off with a wooden top harrow when the potatoes started to come up. Marguerite was with her and kept pestering to let her do it. She said that Marguerite was not strong enough to control the harrow but she let her try it anyway. Marguerite started letting the harrow wander and started digging up potatoes. Virgiline said that she made Marguerite stop and replanted the potatoes and finished the job herself. Uncle Doc saw what had happened and asked Virgiline about it. She told Uncle Doc but he did not get mad.

Another story she told was that John Mance came by one cold winter Sunday evening and wanted to buy a load of firewood. Uncle Doc had the wood cut but did not have any back sticks cut. He told the man he would deliver the wood the next day if he could get someone to help him cut down a tree for back sticks. Back sticks were what people commonly refer to today as back logs. They are larger than firewood and are put at the back of the fireplace where they burn slowly all day. They are not dried and seasoned but are always green logs and are covered up with wood ashes at night and the fire can be revived by scraping the ashes off of them each morning. This makes it easier to get a fire going every morning.

Virgiline said that she told Uncle Doc that she would help him cut down the tree as they needed the money. The ground was frozen and she and Uncle Doc got the cross cut saw and headed for the woods. Uncle Doc picked out the tree and they started sawing.

Virgiline had on a dress and had to rest her bare knees on the ground. When they had finished cutting down the tree and Virgiline got up there were two depressions where her knees had been. There was water puddled in both of them.

Uncle Doc recounted this story to Aunt Mag and said that the two depressions looked like little duck nests. He said that Virgiline never complained, she just kept pulling on the saw.

One other story that Virgiline recounted was about an old colored man named Tom Houston who had broken his pelvis as a youngster. He had perfect use on one leg but the other just dragged behind. She showed me how he walked. Virgiline said that she noticed that his woodpile was about gone on her way to school and told Uncle Doc about it. Uncle Doc loaded up some wood and took it to him. Tom said that he sure needed the wood but couldn't pay for it. Uncle Doc asked him if he had ordered it and he said that he hadn't. Uncle Doc told him that since he didn't

143

order the wood he didn't owe for it. It was a gift from his daughter. The wood was not split but Tom said that he could do that and was very happy to get it.

22

Review of Stories.

We next reviewed stories from earlier parts of the book and Virgiline verified that they were correct in the way that I had said that things were done.

She got a kick out of the tobacco growing story and had something to add.

She said that Uncle Doc had a tobacco patch across the creek where he sometimes grew things by the two apple trees there. There were a lot of tobacco worms in it and Uncle Doc told Virgiline to pick them off the first thing the next morning.

Virgiline said that she had forgotten all about picking the worms off until midday and it was very hot by then. It was a muggy day and there was hardly a breeze stirring.

Virgiline was afraid Uncle Doc would whip her if she did not get the worms off so she went over there in the heat of the day to do the job.

She said the tobacco was wet and sticky and smelled awful . She got deathly ill but kept on until she had finished the job.

She was still sick when Uncle Doc got home and she told him the whole story. Uncle Doc told her that he would not have whipped her if she had not completed the job.

Activities on the Bank of the Creek

The next stories we reviewed was hog killing and washing on the bank of the creek. She said this was true but Grandpa Nathan had a sorghum mill there and made molasses as well at one time. I had heard stories about this before but had no firsthand knowledge. The cane press and cooking pan were long gone before I came along.

The molasses making operation is accurately depicted in the movie "Sergeant York." The cane press is powered by a mule that goes around hooked to a pole to drive the rollers in the press and the juice is collected there and then cooked in a flat bottomed pan until the water evaporates. Virgiline said that she would carry the cane juice from the mill to the cooking pan and would slosh so much of it on her dress that it would get stiff.

The cooking pan is divided up into compartments, Virgiline didn't remember just how many. A green scum or skim would form on the first sections as the fire underneath the pan boiled the water away. The pan had to be skimmed frequently to remove the scum. Virgiline said that the molasses was not any good to eat unless the skim was thoroughly removed. The molasses would finally reach the final section where it was dipped into containers.

Uses For Lye Soap

We next discussed the making of lye soap. Virgiline said that lye soap was the best soap ever for washing hair. I could not understand this at first but remembered from my chemistry classes that glycerin is also produced by the process of making soap. The glycerin must have acted as a kind of moisturizer or conditioned when washing hair.

Virgiline lamented that she could not buy lye any more at the grocery store.

Virgiline also recounted that Anna Laura Stutts, who was Uncle Doc's youngest sister, had relayed to her that the people in Missouri always used lye soap to wash their hair. Anna Laura's husband, Allen Stutts, and Anna Laura had lived for a time in Missouri.

Ann Laura Tidwell Stutts*, Uncle Doc's Youngest Sister

Hog Head Souse and Liver Loaf

Virgiline also told me how they made hog head souse and liver loaf. It was very similar to the way we made souse but we never made liver loaf.

The basic way to make souse is to split the hog head with an axe to get it into smaller pieces to where it can be pressure cooked. The brain is removed after splitting. Some people always scrambled the brain with eggs but I only sampled it once or twice. Not my favorite fare.

The eyes were cut from the head and the inner ear was also removed. All remaining hair was singed off over a fire. It is important to always cook the ears and feet with the hog head or the finished product will not jell.

After everything is pressure cooked, all meat is removed from the bones and run through a hand cranked sausage grinder. It is then weighed and we then added prepared sausage seasoning by weight and tasted everything after mixing. More seasoning can be added to taste.

Virgiline said their seasonings were sage, salt and red pepper.

The mixture is then placed in a large mixing bowl that is large enough for a dinner plate to be placed on top and a weight, such as a flat iron, is put on top of the plate to press out the grease that will rise to the top. It gets cold overnight in an unheated room and the greased is pressed out into the plate and the souse sets up into a gelatinous mass. It is then refrigerated. It is sliced and eaten with crackers as a snack.

Liver loaf is made in the same way except half of a hog head, two feet and half of a liver are used. It is eaten the same way as souse.

23

Early Christmases on Brush Creek

Early Christmases were much the same for Uncle Doc's family as they were for ours at the old log house. We didn't have much, but we always did something special for Christmas.

Christmas would always start with the cutting of the Christmas tree. We would look the entire countryside over for the perfect tree every fall. It would then be cut about a week before Christmas and was always either a cedar or pine. There was a particular kind of short leafed pine tree that grew on the old home place that never got any taller than fifteen to twenty feet. We called them scrub pines because they were not suitable for anything but a Christmas tree. They just spread out at the base and would make the perfect Christmas tree when a young fellow would climb up in it and cut the top out. The old timers preferred cedar trees and this is what was predominately harvested.

The tree would then be carried home and mounted on a cross made of two by fours that had been made just to mount a Christmas tree and was kept over each year for the next Christmas tree.

The tree would be carried into the house and the women would take over from there. They would move it around to find the perfect spot for it to stand in its magnificent glory once it had been decorated.

Out would come the decorations for the tree that were stored from year to year. There were shiny fragile glass ornaments of all colors that especially looked beautiful at night under the light from kerosene lamps. This was before we had electricity.

Some decorations were made fresh each year. I remembered this after Virgiline jogged my memory. Corn was popped and strung by needle on long pieces of thread. Chains of colored paper were glued together using strips of colored paper and homemade flour paste. This was simply flour mixed with water and used as glue.

The first decorations to go on the tree were always the chains of popcorn and colored paper. We also had a few chains of some sort that were stored over from year to year that were used. Some were silver, red, gold and sometimes an iridescent blue. They were mostly made of some kind of metal foil. We didn't have many of these store bought chains as they must have been expensive back then.

The glass ornaments were hung with care. They were carefully moved around the tree to find just the right spot. A few of these were always broken each year as they were so fragile and the wooden floors, sometimes covered with a linoleum rug, were very hard. We felt a pang of sorrow each time one was broken as they were each remembered from Christmases past.

The last thing to be added were the icicles and the angel hair. Some early icicles were made of lead foil but later ones were made from aluminum foil. The angel hair, or white spun fiber glass that would cling together and look something like snow, was added later. The finished results were always stunning and everyone would stand back and ooh and ahh at the finished results.

Later Christmas trees had colored electric lights on them but I never thought they had the regal splendor of the earlier trees that we had to create from so very little and always turned out so beautifully.

The most meaningful part of the Christmas tree for a young person was when the presents would magically start to show up. Most would not show up until the night before we were to open the presents. They were never elegant but were always meaningful. There might be a new shirt that someone had handmade or perhaps one bought from the Sears Roebuck catalog. Sometimes it would turn out to be a new pair of pants or one year it was a Red Rider BB gun. Santa Claus somehow always seemed to know exactly what we needed.

After the Christmas tree was up, the women would go to work in the kitchen and bake all sorts of pies and cakes. The baking smells permeated the entire house and always made it seem so magical and wonderful. There might be apple, coconut, lemon, chocolate and mince pies, as well as a variety of cakes.

One of our favorites was Grandmother Alice's coconut cake. She would use fresh coconut and would save the coconut milk to pour over the cake. My job was to drain the milk from the coconut and split it open so we could grate it. I got to help grate the coconut later, but I grated more knuckles than coconut in my earlier attempts. I always got to drink any leftover coconut milk and eat the small pieces of coconut that were too small to grate further. Ann and I would fight over who got to lick the bowl after the icing had been added to the cake.

We ate well all year long but special treats were always prepared for Christmas both at Aunt Mag's and Uncle Doc's house and also ours. I discussed the typical Christmas with Virgiline recently and she gave her memories of early Christmases.

She also told me that one Christmas Uncle Doc had to borrow five dollars for Christmas but had a big Christmas for three children.

Virgiline said that their favorite cake for Christmas was a jam cake. Aunt Mag would always make one. She relayed to me how Donnie, Bud's oldest son, recently wanted a jam cake. She said that she did not have everything that she needed to make the cake but Donnie went to the supermarket to buy what she did not have. She made the cake and he thoroughly enjoyed it.

She relayed how they would always boil a cured ham for Christmas in a lard can and told me how to do it. I remember Grandmother Alice doing this but I was too young to remember exactly how she did it. This must be something that Grandmother Alice and Aunt Mag had both learned how to do from their mother.

They would take a lard can and put dinner plates in the bottom to keep the ham from sticking to the bottom of the can. They would then cover the ham with water and punch a small nail hole in the cover of the can to allow steam to escape while the ham was cooking. Then they would simmer the ham for a long time until it was tender. Virgiline said that she still has the platter that they would then serve the ham on. I asked her what they would do with the lard can. She said that nothing was ever thrown away that could be used again. They would store it and use it over and over again until it had rusted out.

Virgiline said that they would then catch a hen from the yard and use her to make chicken and dressing.

She said that this was their yearly Christmas tradition and it didn't take much money to prepare for Christmas as they had everything already on hand from the farm.

We talked about other things they would have for Christmas. She said they always had Christmas candy such as coconut balls, chocolate cream drops, peppermint sticks, a hard candy mixture with peppermint in it, apples and oranges, pecans and English walnuts. This is pretty much what we always had as well.

Uncle Walter was a cook in the army. He prepared a special ham for us one Christmas during one of his visits. I think this was in 1953 when he drove his new red and white Ford station wagon home.

He bought a ham from the supermarket and scored it diagonally to make diamond shaped areas where he inserted whole cloves. He then glazed it with some special glaze just before it was done, honey I think mixed with pineapple juice. He also added pineapple slices that were held on with toothpicks during glazing.

I thought this was the best ham that I had ever tasted. I don't think that I have ever tasted another ham that I enjoyed so much.

Virgiline is shown in the following photographs with some of her Christmas presents from early Christmases.

Virgiline with a ceramic figure that her mother bought from Ona Rogers' local country store for her Christmas present one year. Virgiline said that her mother paid twenty-five cents for it.

This photograph shows left to right a carnival glass vase that I brought **Aunt Mag** one Christmas from Indiana. Middle another twenty-five cent Christmas present that **Virgiline** still has. Right a pitcher that I also brought **Aunt Mag** from Indiana for Christmas in the late 1960's. Similar to the flow-blue pattern popular at that time but without the flow.

151

Virgiline said that her family paid ninety-eight cents for this doll trunk at Rogers Department Store in Florence, Alabama, for her Christmas present one year.

Virgiline said that her parents paid ninety-eight cents for the old cast iron toy wood cook stove at Marion Lyles's store in Killen, Alabama for her Christmas present one year.

The toy stove is sitting on the Bama Hale table from Richard T. Tidwell's old log house in this photograph

24

Bud's Stories

Virgiline relayed to me that Donnie had brought Bud a book at one time to record some of his childhood stories. Bud wrote three stories and Virgiline does not have the book but she recounted the stories to me. Lucille Cross Tidwell, Bud's widow, has the book.

Bud's Christmas

Virgiline thought that Bud must have been 6 to 8 years old when this story took place.

Anyway one late December day, Uncle Doc and Bud were at Marion Lyles' General Store in Killen, Alabama.

There was a pocket watch on display there and it cost a dollar. Bud wanted the watch but Uncle Doc did not have the money. This must have been in between 1931 to 1933 and money was scarce then.

Uncle Doc, ever resourceful, sold a load of firewood to get the dollar to buy the watch for Bud's Christmas.

Bud was delighted with the watch but was puzzled by the ticking sound it made. He asked Aunt Mag what was making the watch tick. Aunt Mag told him there was a little man in there working and making that noise.

Bud decided that he wanted to get the little man out so that he could see him. He took the watch out on the back porch and tried to free the little man with a hammer. Aunt Mag went out on the back porch to see what all the racket was about. There she found Bud hammering away at the watch.

I don't think that Bud ever did get the little man out to where he could see him but he did manage to get him to stop working!

Bicycle

Virgiline said that Bud was about 12 years old when this story took place.

Another story that Bud wrote was about a bicycle that was in pieces that Dee Cox, a cousin, gave him. There were spokes missing from the wheels and the retainer that holds the handlebars in place was missing. Bud replaced the spokes and made a retainer to hold the handlebars in place and put everything together. They painted it a bright red and Virgiline said that it really looked good.

Bud was apparently so thrilled with the way that the bicycle turned out that he rode it to Saint Joseph, Tennessee, then to Saint Florian, Alabama, and then to Florence. This was quite a ride for a young lad on a bicycle.

There was not much traffic on the roads back then but the roads were not maintained very well back then either! I remember having a bicycle at about that age and I would never have undertaken such a ride!

Guinea Fowl

Virgiline said that Bud must have been 15 or 16 years old when this story took place.

Bud had gotten some Guinea eggs from somewhere and put them under a setting hen to hatch them. He raised six to eight guineas from them.

There was a Farm Bulletin that was published monthly back then and it was a listing of all of the items that people across the State of Alabama wanted to sell. I remember reading the Farm Bulletin when I was growing up and I remember the listings were by county. Bud listed his Guineas in the Farm Bulletin.

A woman from Mobile wrote Bud and wanted to buy his Guineas. She sent a money order for them.

Bud built a crate from wooden strips for the Guineas and nailed them in. He then shipped them to her in Mobile.

Virgiline said that Bud could just imagine the woman opening up the crate and not knowing how wild Guineas are. He could just imagine them flying away over the gulf.

Anyway, Bud made enough money off of the Guineas to buy a pig. He then raised the pig and killed it that fall and peddled out the meat. She did not remember how much money that Bud made from the pig.

25

Recipes

Grandmother Alice cooked differently in her early years than she did later on. I think all cooks do. We first start with the basics we have to know in order to prepare what food we have and make it into something edible. We can then start to experiment and improve on the basics as we gain experience.

These recipes are from Grandmother Alice's later period.

Please see Aunt Mag' and Virgiline's recipes for how cooking was done in the '20s to the '50s and perhaps beyond.

Grandmother Alice's Recipes

Grandmother Alice's Yeast Biscuits

5 cups sifted all-purpose flour	3 tsp baking powder
1 tsp soda	3/4 cup Crisco
1 tsp salt	1 package yeast
3 tsp sugar	2 cups buttermilk

Dissolve yeast in 1/2 cup warm water with sugar for ten minutes or until it bubbles. In a very large deep bowl sift flour four different times with soda-salt-baking powder. Cut in Crisco until looks like fine cornmeal. Add yeast and buttermilk in center of flour mixture. Stir till all flour is moist. In large lightly oiled bowl put in yeast mixture and form a ball shape. Cover with clean kitchen towel. Let rise till double. Maybe two hours or so. Punch down and knead. Make amount of biscuits needed. Let rise again in baking pan then bake until golden brown on top rack. Refrigerate left over dough well covered. Let remainder rise again before baking.. Dough will keep almost two weeks in refrigerator. BAKE 400 for 12-14 minutes.

Grandmother Alice's No Crust Egg Pie

1 cup sugar
3 tablespoons butter or margarine
3 tablespoons flour
3 eggs
1 large can evaporated milk
1/4 tsp nutmeg
Pinch of salt

Place all in blender and mix. Pour in lightly oiled and floured pie pan. Bake at 325-350 until set.

Grandmother Alice's Pecan Pie

4 large eggs
1 cup dark brown sugar
1 cup white syrup
1 cup chopped pecans
1 teaspoon vanilla
½ cup unsalted butter
½ teaspoon salt (optional)

Mix ingredients. Put in unbaked pie shell. Bake on bottom rack at 375 degrees for 15 minutes --
Then 300 degrees for 35 minutes or until set. Cool.

Grandmother Alice's Tea Cakes

1 cup sugar
1 cup melted Crisco (cooled)
2 eggs
3 cups flour
2 teaspoons vanilla

Mix cooled Crisco, sugar and eggs and beat lightly. Add flour and make into dough.
Squeeze out small amounts of dough and make into balls. Place onto cookie sheet one inch
apart. Wet the bottom of a smooth bottomed glass and press dough real thin. Bake at 350
degrees.

If you use self rising flour don't add any salt.

Grandmother Alice's Soft Molasses Drops

¾ cup butter or margarine
1 ½ cup brown sugar
3 eggs
1 teaspoon vanilla flavoring
2 tablespoons molasses
3 cups plain flour sifted
1 teaspoon soda
1 cup raisins if desired

Cream butter and sugar until light and fluffy. Add eggs and vanilla beating well. Combine
molasses, soda and flour. Beat well. Drop by spoonfuls on cookie sheet. Bake 10 to 12 minutes
at 325 degrees or until brown.

Grandmother Alice's Green Bean Recipe

To my knowledge this recipe was not written down. It is simple one that Grandmother Alice gave Lana when I brought her down from Indiana to Alabama to meet my family before we were married.

Grandmother Alice would fry a few pieces of bacon until it was crispy but not hard in the pan she intended to cook her green beans in. She would then add the green beans and water to just cover the beans, one teaspoon of sugar and one teaspoon of salt. Cook medium - high heat until the water is evaporated. Add more water if needed until done. Grandmother Alice cooked a quart of home canned green beans to show Lana how to do it. This recipe can also be used for fresh green beans but they must cook longer.

The fat from the bacon will wilt the green beans quickly and make them look and taste like they had simmered for a long time. The family particularly liked these green beans.

Grandmother Alice's Dried Bean Recipe

I remember that Grandmother Alice cooked dried beans this way.

After the beans are soaked, add them to water in the pan you intend to cook them in. Be careful to not add too much water. Check them frequently while they simmer and add just enough water to keep them covered.

Salt and pepper to taste.

Grandmother Alice though the beans had a more intense flavor if the amount of water used was limited.

Grandmother Alice's Beef Recipe

Grandmother Alice never wrote this recipe down but I remember seeing her cook beef this way. She started doing this after she got her first electric range. The early ranges had what was called a deep well in them. This was simply a burner that was recessed ten inches or so into the top of the range and the well was lined with some sort of metal and was probably insulated to conserve heat. The range came with a pot and cover that fit down into the well and sat on top of the burner. This whole configuration was called a "deep well" and was used primarily to simmer things under low heat for a long time. Beef was tougher back then but was tenderized by simmering for a long time with the temperature set very low, perhaps like a crock pot cooks today. The fat had not been trimmed off of the beef as closely as it is today either.

Grandmother Alice would start with whatever beef was handy. It could be chunks of beef that we would call beef stew today or could be a whole roast. Grandmother Alice cooked whatever she could get or afford.

She would first add a small amount of water and the beef. She would season the beef as it simmered with salt and black pepper to taste. This beef would simmer until it literally fell apart. She would then give it a final taste and add the final seasoning. The water would almost be cooked out at the end.

This was always very tender and delicious though always fatty. She would serve it over freshly made biscuits.

This was so good that we always sopped up what little juice there was left with another biscuit.

Grandmother lamented that her next electric range did not have a deep well. She kept the old pot but it did not cook the same without the well.

Hoover Gravy

This recipe was a staple for both Grandmother Alice and also my mother. It was a staple of most families in our area and circumstances.

Take whatever grease is left over from frying either bacon or sausage. Bacon grease was used most often.

Pour off whatever grease you will not need. It was commonly stored in an empty coffee can.

Brown flour in the grease until it gets to the color you want. Some like it more brown than others.

Slowly add milk and stir. Add salt and black pepper to taste.

Continue adding milk until the proper consistency is achieved.

Water can be used if milk is not available.

This was especially good over freshly baked biscuits split open. It would be served with ripe tomatoes in the summer or whatever else you were blessed with to eat!

<u>26</u>

Mother's Recipes

These are some recipes that Mother asked me to type for her in 1997. She was concerned about some of her granddaughters who did not know how to cook the "Southern Basics." Mother learned most of her cooking skills from Grandmother Alice.

Mother was a good cook when she had the time and used it wisely. She would often get distracted and take short cuts such as baking things in too hot of an oven or using the pressure cooker to speed up her infamous white bean recipe.

I don't have her recipe for cooking large dried lima beans but they were always a family favorite. I still cook them and will give my recipe.

Grandma Luna Tidwell's Cornbread Recipe

Cooks one pan of cornbread
2 eggs beaten in mixing bowl
Add 2 cups milk
Put in enough self rising meal to thicken eggs and milk.
Pour into a round, slightly greased skillet and bake at 450 degrees until brown.

You can also half the recipe for a small pan.

Enjoy!!

I always cook my cornbread at 350 degrees on the top shelf of the oven and add a large dash of vegetable oil to the batter. I use a cast iron skillet. Grandmother Alice would always brown a small amount of meal in oil before adding the batter. This acted as a release and kept the cornbread from sticking to the skillet. I still do this. She would always add some bacon drippings, a generous amount, to her batter. Grandmother Alice's cornbread was always the favorite in the family. Perhaps it was because of this extra fat or perhaps it was because she always used freshly ground cornmeal. I use stone ground cornmeal from the Falls Mill in Belvidere, Tennessee. Cornbread is moist and delicious when cooked this way but loaded with extra calories.

Grandma Luna Tidwell's Chicken and Dressing Recipe

Cook (boil) one fryer one hour or one hen two to three hours. You can put one teaspoon salt in this. Bone chicken and set aside.

When cornbread cools, crumble up in a large mixing bowl. Add two eggs, four pieces of toast crumbled up, one teaspoon of salt, one teaspoon of black pepper, one cup chopped onion, two teaspoons of sage, a quarter stick of butter, a half cup chopped celery if desired. You can also add a half pound of uncooked sausage, Grandpa Tidwell likes hot, chopped up apple or a few chopped nuts if desired.

Pour chicken broth from where you cooked the chicken over this until you get the desired thickness you want. Put chicken pieces into this.

Bake in a pan or mixing bowl until done in a 400 to 425 degrees oven.

You can also stuff a turkey or chicken whole with this. You can also half the dressing recipe.

Enjoy!!

Grandma Luna Tidwell's Biscuit Recipe

Sift a medium size mixing bowl half full of self rising flour. In the middle of the bowl, make a small hole with your hand in the flour. Into this add four tablespoons of lard, shortening, or oil. I use lard because Grandpa Tidwell thinks it makes a better biscuit. Then measure a cup of milk and add this gradually into the lard, working it each time with your fingers. Each time you add milk, work a little flour into the lard and milk mixture. Then when all of the milk is poured into the mixture, begin adding more flour until you can work or knead it into dough.

Don't knead a lot, but just enough so you can handle the dough to put it on a lightly floured board where you can cut out your biscuits if you desire. I pat mine out in my hand by adding a little dough at the time and lightly working it with my hands until I can put it in a cake pan, lightly greased. When I get my pan full of biscuits, slightly touching each other, I take my knuckles and lightly pat each biscuit. Bake in a hot oven 450 degrees for 10 to 12 minutes. Take up and enjoy!

Grandma Luna Tidwell's Chicken and Dumpling Recipe

Cook one fryer for one hour. A hen can be used, but cook the hen for at least two to three hours until done. You can put the broth in the refrigerator for awhile and skim off any excess fat you don't want.

Put the chicken back in the broth and bring to a boil with one teaspoon of salt. You can also salt your chicken when it is cooking with one teaspoon of salt.

Prepare your dumplings the same way you prepared your biscuit dough, only use one cup water instead of one cup milk. I use a little less lard, shortening or oil - about three tablespoons. The water and a little less shortening makes a better dumpling.

Put the dough on a lightly floured board and knead slightly. Divide the dough into three or four parts and roll out. Then cut it into squares or strips and put over into the chicken broth a few at the time. Use medium to low heat. Put a top on the pot and let is cook just a little time. Then stir them down slightly, add another layer of dumplings to the pot, let them cook slightly with the top on the pot, and stir them down slightly. Keep doing this until all of the dumplings are in the pot. Cook a short time, then stir down slightly, and take up and enjoy!

Grandma Luna Tidwell's Cream Filling Recipe

1 ¼ cup sugar
2 tablespoons flour or cornstarch
4 cups milk
4 eggs (save whites for meringue for pies or pudding)
1 tablespoon butter
1 teaspoon vanilla flavoring

Stir continually if cooked in a single pot. You can cook this on low heat in a medium sized pot, or you can use a double boiler.

Cook until thickened. For puddings you might not want to cook as long, but for pies such as banana cream pies, coconut pies, you might want to cook it until it thickens.

You can half the recipe for one pie, one small banana pudding, or one pineapple pie or pudding.

Grandma Luna Tidwell's Cheese Sauce Recipe

2 tablespoons flour or cornstarch
2 cups milk
½ stick butter
As much cheese as desired shredded up and add to this mixture

Boil slowly, stirring often until thickened. This is good added to macaroni or anything that calls for a cheese sauce.

Grandma Luna Tidwell's Apple Crisp Recipe

4 cups apple slices
1 teaspoon cinnamon
7 tablespoons butter (works best melted and drizzled while whisking)
1 cup sugar (brown is better)
1/2 cup water (apple cider is better)
¾ cup flour

Butter dish and pour in apples. Pour water and cinnamon over apples. Mix sugar, flour and butter together. Whisk until grainy. Pour over apples and bake for one hour at 350 degrees.

This recipe is good using any fruit.

My Large Dried Lima Bean Recipe

Soak the lima beans overnight in cold water. Thoroughly rinse after soaking. I use a colander and rinse with five pots of cold water from the pan I soaked the beans in.

Cook pork. I prefer ham hocks or country cured smoked ham. Place about a half cup of water in a baking dish, add the pork, cover and cook in the oven at 300 degrees for 2 ½ hours or so. Remove when they start to give off their characteristic aroma. Set aside and cool.

Take the bones, skin and fat off of the ham and discard. Cut the pork into the size that you will use and set aside.

Cover the beans with water, put the beans on the stove and simmer uncovered until all traces of foam disappear. Place the cover on the pot and continue simmering until they are done to your liking. Water will probably have to be added while cooking. Salt and pepper to taste. Add the pork when cooking is finished and remove from heat. The bean flavor as well as the pork flavor can be clearly tasted. Serve with cornbread.

$\underline{27}$

Aunt Mag and Virgiline's Recipes

Virgiline has several small boxes of recipes that she has accumulated over the years. She found the original recipe for Aunt Mag's jam cake during our last interview. My sister, Ann Crittenden, copied these recipes while I interviewed Virgiline about her early recipes.

Virgiline had two extremely old hand written recipes for jam cakes. One was from Aunt Mag and one was from her friend Kathrine Rickard. Both recipes were very old and extremely fragile. There were holes in the creases where the paper had been folded and unfolded to read many times over the years. Both recipes contained very little about the actual mixing and cooking of the various ingredients listed. I guess they thought that anyone wanting to make this cake already knew how to make a cake.

Virgiline gave us some of the cooking details verbally. She said that Aunt Mag used her own recipe for many years but later started using Kathrine's recipe.

Aunt Mag's Jam Layer Cake

4 eggs
2 cups sugar
1 teaspoon cinnamon
1/2 teaspoon cloves
1 cup blackberry jam
1 cup buttermilk
1/2 cup butter
1 teaspoon soda
1 cup raisins
3 cups plain flour
1 cup nuts

Thoroughly mix ingredients. Pour into lightly greased and floured cake pans. Bake at 350 degrees until a toothpick stuck into the center comes out clean.

Icing

2 cups grated coconut
2 grated orange peels
Juice of two oranges
2 cups sugar
1 small can crushed pineapple
Juice of one coconut
2 tablespoons flour

Mix flour, orange juice, orange rind and coconut juice. Add pineapple and one cup of coconut. Cook until thick and spread on cake. Sprinkle one cup of coconut on top of cake.

Aunt Mag's Carmel Icing

2 cups white sugar
1 cup milk
1/2 cup of brown sugar
Lump of butter the size of an egg.

Boil white sugar and milk. Brown a half cup of sugar in a cast iron skillet and add to milk. Virgiline said that store bought brown sugar would not work. It has to be browned in an iron skillet. Cook until it forms a soft ball in water. Add butter and beat until thick.

Kathrine's Jam Cake

1 cup butter
½ cup sugar
3 cups plain flour
1 cup raisins
2 cups nuts
1 cup buttermilk
1 teaspoon of allspice
1 teaspoon soda
1 teaspoon baking powder
3 eggs
Dash salt
1 cup coconut
1 bottle cherries
1 cup blackberry jam

No mixing instructions. Virgiline said to bake at 350 degrees.

My sister Ann said that the two best cakes ever made by family members for Christmas were Grandmother Alice's original coconut cake and Aunt Mag's jam cake.

Grandmother Alice's original coconut cake recipe has been lost to the family. Mother used the same basic recipe but changed it to fit her taste. I think that Grandmother Alice changed the icing in later years to one made from whipped cream and sour cream with some powdered sugar in it. She may have used this icing all along.

I think that a close approximation of this cake recipe can be resurrected by baking a white layer cake with vanilla flavoring and use the hints from the Christmas story and the basics for making a scratch cake found in Aunt Mag's jam cake recipes.

Virgiline's Recipes

Virgiline has boxes of different recipes that she has tried over the years. None of her old recipes are written down.

She does not give specific directions as to the amount of sugar to use. She said it depends on how much you are cooking and how sweet you want it when I asked for specific amounts. She goes by taste in these recipes, like most good cooks do.

I will start with one of her favorite recipes from recent years first. She clipped this one from the newspaper and said it will feed a large group of people when they visit.

Winter Warmer Soup

This is a potato soup.

In 1 quart of water boil:

3 cups of cubed potatoes.
1 cup of diced carrots.
1 diced onion.

Cook until tender. Do not drain remaining water. Add

4 chicken bullion cubes.
1 can cream of chicken soup.
1 can cream of celery soup.

Stir all ingredients until well blended. Add 1 pound of Velveeta cheese torn into small pieces. Stir while cheese melts. Simmer on low for 15 minutes.

Virgiline said this can be kept in a crock pot until served.

Dumpling Recipe

Dumplings are a staple of many southern dishes. I have eaten them cooked with (as mentioned later) a pig tail. They are also cooked with squirrels, chickens and other meats that have been parboiled. They are very tasty.

Mother had her own recipe for making dumplings but Virgiline has a slightly different one.

Make stock from either chicken or a ham bone. Today's ham bones are not like the ones we cured in the smoke house.

Make dumplings with cooled broth and use no grease. Any oil or grease will make them fall apart when they are added to the final recipe.

Roll out the dumpling dough real thin and cut into strips.

Drop into boiling broth a few at a time and push down and add some more. Drop in all of the dumplings and then it only takes about 10 more minutes to cook.

Virgiline mentioned that a hen makes better dumplings than a fryer.

Apple Dumpling Recipe

Do not use Delicious apples for this recipe as they will not work. Only use tart apples such as Winesap or Granny Smith.

Biscuit dough can be made from scratch but Virgiline now uses canned biscuits from the supermarket.

Peel and slice apples. Roll out biscuits real thin in all directions. Add apples and roll up in biscuits and seal by folding the edges. Place in a baking dish.

Put about one cup of water, one cup of sugar and ½ stick of butter in a pot and bring to boiling. Add boiling water and sugar solution to the baking dish. Bake under low heat until brown.

I asked Virgiline about adding cinnamon. She said some people may but she never did.

Dried Apple Roll

Use only home dried apples. Cook apples with water until done. Add sugar until slightly sweet. Cook almost dry. Made biscuit dough and roll out a big sheet real thin. Spread apples all over the top of the dough. Roll up like a jelly roll. Pick up real gently and twirl it around until it is all in a baking dish. Prepare the water, sugar and butter solution like called for in the apple dumpling recipe and add to the baking dish. Bake in a low oven until brown.

Fried Apple Pies

Prepare apples the same as above. Fresh biscuit dough can be prepared and cut into circles using a saucer or small plate or canned biscuits can be used and rolled out real thin in all directions.

Place apples on one side and fold the other side over. Fold the edges and crimp with a fork. Fry instead of bake.

Virgiline said that she had to cook 20 extra fried apple pies for J.T. to take to work whenever she would cook them.

Donnie, Bud's oldest son, always takes some home when he is visiting and she has cooked them. Donnie claims that visiting Virgiline is just like visiting Granny (Aunt Mag). He always gets to take a sack of goodies home.

Fried Corn

Cut corn from cob and scrape the milk out of the corn cob. Put a generous amount of bacon drippings into a skillet and heat. Add water, corn and a pinch of sugar and salt to the bacon grease. Some people also add black pepper. Cook until it thickens and add a lump of butter before you take off of the heat. Virgiline said that this recipe is not good unless you use bacon grease.

Macaroni and Tomatoes

Virgiline said that she learned to cook this from her mother. She said that her grandmother Emma Jane Owen Reid and Great Aunt Jo Billingsley cooked it as well.

Boil macaroni until tender, not mushy. Cut up bacon into small pieces in a skillet and brown. Add enough chopped onions into the bacon drippings to make everything taste like onions and cook until they change color. Add macaroni and a quart of canned tomatoes. Use fresh chopped tomatoes if they are available.

Add a pinch of salt, sugar and black pepper to taste. Eat with vegetables.

Virgilian said that she still cooks this a lot today.

Macaroni and Scrambled Eggs

Virgiline said that her mother and Grandmother Derendia Ann Billingsley Tidwell cooked this recipe as well.

Boil macaroni in water until it is tender but not mushy. Put a fair amount of butter in a skillet and add macaroni and salt and pepper. Cook in butter until it turns color and then scramble eggs into it.

Virgiline says that she now sprays the skillet with Pam so that the macaroni will not stick as easily. She said that the macaroni is bad to stick.

Good!

Golden Oldies

Now we get down to the old time favorites. I don't know but perhaps people had to prepare them and eat them out of necessity. I do know some members of my family considered them to be delicacies. I do like some of these items but some are not things that I would want to eat regularly. One thing that I do know is that certain family members now cook and enjoy them out of preference rather than necessity.

Fried Scallions

Wash, peal and cut up blades and all. Put in skillet with a little water, pinch of salt and a fair amount of grease. Cook until all of the water is cooked out and scramble eggs into it. I asked Virgiline how many eggs and she said, "It just depends on how many scallions you started with."

Virgiline said that she had cooked a fairly large bowl of these just after her marriage. J.T. came in with his brother about the time they were done. He took one look at them and asked her "Are they any good?" Virgiline told him that if they were not she would never cook them for him again. J.T and his brother devoured the entire bowl full.

Virgiline said that you could use this same recipe for polk greens. I know that would be good with spinach as well. I have cooked canned spinach from the supermarket by a similar recipe and I really like it.

Collards and Pig Tail

Boil one fresh pig tail until it starts to get tender. Chop up collards and add. Cook until collards are done. Salt and pepper to taste.

Virgiline said that J.T. took one look at the first collards and pig tail that she ever cooked for him and he didn't know if he would like them or not. He later would tell all of his buddies at work that collards weren't fit to eat unless there was a pig tail floating in them.

I offered to bring Virgiline a cooking of fresh collards once when I was discussing this recipe with her by phone. She said that she probably would not be able to find a good fresh pig tail. She said that she loved collards but they didn't love her anymore since her treatment for her illness. She said that the same thing was true for cabbage but turnip greens did not bother her. She eats them regularly and loves them.

Ann and I discussed our first and only encounter with a cooked pig tail. Mother's mother, Myrtice Holloway, was visiting one hog killing and she saw the pig tail in the scrap pile. She brought it into the house and prepared pig tail and dumplings for us. It was different than anything that Ann or I had even eaten. We only sampled a small amount. Not our favorite fare!

Grandmother Holloway later related a story about her son, Sam, who was living at home while he was attending college on the G.I. bill. Grandmother Myrtice related that Sam told her shortly after graduation "No more pig tails!"

Brains and Scrambled Eggs

I remember Grandmother Alice and Mother cooking brains and scrambled eggs shortly after every hog killing and asked Virgiline if she knew how to cook them. She said that she did and preferred fresh brains over canned ones.

When a hog head is cut up to get it into small enough pieces to pressure cook for souse, the first cut with the axe is always down the middle of the head. The brains are then gathered after this first cut. I have witnessed this many times and they are always a bloody looking goop. The blood is washed away.

Virgiline said that there is a bloody colored skin on the outside of the brains that has to be peeled off. The brains are then boiled with a small amount of water until they are tender. Bacon grease is then added before all of the water is boiled out. She said they are no good unless bacon grease is used. Eggs are then scrambled into the brains using plenty of salt and pepper.

I have eaten a small amount of this several times but it is not my favorite fare! I had no idea how they were cooked.

Dad and mother would occasionally buy brains at the grocery store and cook them this way.

Homemade Hominy

I have outlined how hominy was made briefly earlier in the book. Virgiline gave me the recipe since she knew it and had helped Aunt Mag make it and has made it herself since she was married.

Virgiline said that hickory cane corn makes the best hominy. Wood ashes from hickory wood either burned in a fireplace or stove has to be used. The ashes are tied into a pouch in a piece of clean white cloth. I asked Virgiline how many ashes were required. She said, "It depends on the amount of corn you use."

First the corn is added into water in a black cast iron wash pot and the ashes are added. A fire is built under the pot and the corn and ashes are simmered until the outer husk or skin of the corn will slip off. The corn is then removed from the pot and must be thoroughly washed. The corn is picked up while it is being washed and the husk is removed a small amount at the time with a circular motion between both hands. Not only is the husk removed from the corn but the eye as Virgiline called it. This is the pointed end of the corn that grows next to the cob. Discard the ashes and water solution.

The corn and husk are thoroughly separated and the corn kernels are again thoroughly washed. The corn must be put back on to cook in fresh water for a long time until it is done. Virgiline said that this could take up to three hours.

The hominy is then fried with a small amount of water and meat grease. A lot of black pepper is added.

I asked Virgiline if they ever canned the left over hominy. She said there was not enough left to can. She said that dad would always come up with a bucket to get what they would give him and they ate the rest of it quickly.

Virgiline said that it took all day to make hominy. I can understand from her description of what was involved in making hominy why they only made it once a year. Nobody else in the family ever made hominy.

The freshly made hominy was a favorite of every family member who got to share in the bounty.

Chitterlings from Scratch

The last recipe that I discussed with Virgiline was how to make chitterlings from scratch. Virgiline and her family were the only ones that I ever knew that actually made them. I never saw the whole process of making them.

Virgiline had talked so much that day that she was getting hoarse. I knew that it was time to stop with my questions.

She had this to say when I asked her how to make them. "So you want to go to the hog pen now!"

The first step is to acquire the large intestine from a freshly slaughtered hog.

The next step is to remove all of the "pig poop." This is done by cutting the large intestine into twelve to eighteen inch pieces. Then everything inside has to be thoroughly removed and washed out. She made hand motions of grabbing the pig gut in both hands after water had been added and shaking it up and down and then releasing the bottom end to allow the water and anything in it to empty. I can understand the importance of this step as pig poop is what makes the hog pen smell so bad.

Virgiline said this step is made easier with running water. She made the hand motion of sticking the end of a garden hose into one end of the pig intestine and flushing everything out.

The next step is to cut the intestine down one side to leave a flat piece of flesh. Everything would then be thoroughly washed again and the outer layer or membrane is removed from the intestine. I told Virgiline that I had heard that there was an inner membrane that had to be removed also. She said no, there was only two. The inner part next to the pig poop was all that could be eaten.

After everything was thoroughly cleaned, the inner layer is washed again in cold water and put into either an earthen butter churn or a five gallon glass jar. Virgiline said that the jar has to be kept in a cold place. In cold weather it can be kept in a cold area but in warmer weather it must be kept in the refrigerator.

Virgiline said that the chitterlings had to be removed and thoroughly cleaned every day for three or four days and placed in fresh cold water. I asked her about adding soda to the water as I had been told was necessary. She said that all that she used was just cold water.

The next step is to parboil the chitterlings with salt until they are tender. They are then taken up and allowed to cool enough to be handled.

The next step is what she called linking up. This is the step that she had problems with the first time she tried to make them during her mother's bed rest. Virgiline could not make me understand what this involved so she cut a strip from a rag like her mother had shown her. A hole was cut in one end and then the intestine is pulled through to form a small loop on top. Another loop is pulled through and run through the first loop. The process is repeated until the entire piece of intestine is looped. This adds some substance to the flat piece of flesh. The end product looks something like a braided rope.

The chitterlings are then rolled in corn meal and fried until brown.

I don't know how long ago or who came up with the recipe for cooking the large intestine of a pig. All that I can understand is they must have been awfully hungry to go through all of this mess and work to prepare them.

Virgiline said that she prepared chitterlings for her husband and a family friend, Clint Freeman. She said that the chitterling did not even have an odor during parboiling. J.T. had never eaten chitterlings before and was not expecting much as he had heard nasty tales about them.

Virgiline said that they enjoyed them and Clint told J.T. that you have to know how to prepare chitterlings or they were not good.

The closest thing to chitterlings that I ever ate while growing up was tripe. Someone bought a few cans of it and Grandmother Alice warmed it up. It even came in its own brown gravy.

I thought it was good even though I had never eaten anything like it before. They told me it was the large intestine from a cow after I had finished. I could not believe that anything that tasted so good was the gut of a cow. I had to look it up in the dictionary before I would believe it.

I have never eaten tripe since then.

I don't think it is how anything tastes that makes us like it or not. It is simply that we perceive it to not be good based on what it was prepared from.

Hog Head Hash

Virgiline mentioned making hog head hash in one of her stories. She gave me the recipe by phone.

If there are more hog heads from a hog killing than anyone wants to use for souse they can be canned. In Virgiline's story she intended to open a quart of canned hog head and make hash. The things she would add to the hog head are:

A lot of chopped onions.
Cubed potatoes.
Red pepper, sage and salt to taste.

Red Eye Gravy

Most of the old timers loved red eye gravy. I never liked it and Virgiline says that she doesn't because it is too greasy. This is the way to make it though.

Fry ham or pork chops and take up when done. Remove most of the grease from the skillet and put the pan back on the stove. Get hot.

Add water or black coffee and cook a little while with stirring, remove and put in a bowl. Serve over fresh biscuits.

Egg Gravy

Add grease to pan and brown flour. Don't brown it very much.

Beat an egg thoroughly and add water.
Stir egg - water mixture into the browned flour. Salt and pepper to taste.

Virgiline said that a lot of gravy can be made from one or two eggs and will feed a passel of hungry children.

Old Fashioned Jam and Jelly

Virgiline said that this recipe must be followed closely. It cannot be deviated from. Do not try to double the recipe as it will not work. She guarantees that it will work every time.

For jam, crush up the fruit you plan to usc. Use the amount of crushed fruit called for in the recipe. For jelly, the crushed fruit must be boiled with very little water and then strained.

Add the exact amounts called for in the recipe.

2 cups crushed fruit or juice.
2 cups sugar.
Very little water. Will not jell if too much water is used.

Bring to a rolling boil. Boil for exactly 5 minutes. Do not let it boil over.

Take up and put into containers. Will jell when it cools.

28

Mother's Later Recipes

Cakes and Pies

These are from Mother's later period. These are things that she told Lana the recipes for and Lana wrote them down. Lana did not write down the mixing instructions as she knew the order to mix things. I guess this is why Aunt Mag's jam cake recipe had no mixing instructions. Anybody who knows how to cook knows to do the basics, according to Lana.

Lana proceeded to educate me on the fine art of cooking. She said that the solid ingredients are always added first in the order they appear in the recipe. The liquids are then added in the order they appear in the recipe with plenty of mixing in between each addition. Flavorings are always added last. Simple I guess but it would have never occurred to a chemist like me!

Strawberry Cake

1 box of white cake mix
1 package of strawberry Jell-O
½ cup of fresh strawberries and juice
½ cup water
½ cup of Crisco oil
4 eggs
Red food coloring

Mix ingredients. Bake 350 degrees in an angel food pan about 45 minutes.

Glaze

½ box powdered sugar
½ cup strawberries and juice
½ cup butter or margarine
Red food coloring

Coconut Pie

2/3 cup sugar
¼ cup flour

Stir

Add 2 ½ - 3 cups milk

Separate 2 egg yolks and beat
2 tablespoons butter

Cook and stir until thick. Add 1 tablespoon vanilla and 1 cup coconut.

Put in baked pie shell. Top with whipped cream.

Very rich in taste.

Coconut Cake

1 box yellow cake mix (Mix as directed)

1 tablespoon butternut flavoring or 1 teaspoon of butter flavoring and 1 teaspoon of nut flavoring

1/3 cup sugar

Bake as directed.

Icing

1 cup Crisco
1 or 1 ¼ box of powdered sugar
1 tablespoon vanilla

Mix. Sprinkle cake with coconut and between layers.

Refrigerator Fruit Cake

1 cup white raisins.
1 cup candied cherries.
1 cup candied pineapple.
1 cup coconut
1 cup pecans.
1 large box of vanilla wafers.
1 can Eagle Brand milk.

Crush wafers to powder. Add nuts and fruit, mix well. Add milk and mix. Put in pan of your choice and press well.

Refrigerate several days before eating.

I have to relate a story about the first and only time that Lana made this recipe. It was the first Christmas we were married. She did not have any Eagle Brand milk and decided to substitute 1 cup of bourbon left over from my bachelor party. I remember it being rum, but I don't know.

One thing that I do know is that it burned your mouth and throat all of the way down to your stomach! My stomach even had a nice warm glow. Man, was it good! She had quite a bit of batter left and made it into balls.

It was the tradition at work for everyone to take goodies to the office the last day we worked before the Christmas break. I had not been married before and had nothing to take. This was the first year that I had something to take and brag about Lana's cooking. It was so good in fact that I went from 175 pounds to 205 pounds in the short space from October to Christmas.

Well, I took a good quantity of bourbon balls and some slices of spiked fruitcake that year. Gene Dirker, a friend from the neighborhood and work, had already sampled everything and had warned the women about it. They would not touch it.

Gene had notified the guys though and they were primed for it and were looking forward to it in rapt anticipation.

A line of guys quickly formed as soon as I put it out on the table. They tackled the bourbon balls first and gasped for breath. After a short drink of water they got back into line with a smile on their face.

They completely devoured everything that I had brought that day. There was not much work accomplished after that but all of the men had smiles on their faces!

Lana had never cooked with booze before and didn't know how much of it to add. She didn't drink and still doesn't. She said she planned to add more but the liquid in the batter was about right after she had added 1 cup. After Gene Dirker and I made such a fuss over it the first time we sampled it, Lana said she ate one raisin. It liked to have choked her and burned all the way down. She never tried to eat any more to see how everything blended together. She didn't want any more of that cake!

Poor girl, she never knew just what a treat she missed.

$\underline{\mathit{29}}$

Flash Forward To The Early 21st Century

My early roots in the Shoals area instilled values and preferences from the past that still influence my decisions, thoughts and actions even today! I think everyone must surely be this way. I think that they will always stay with me.

One example is the following recipe for cooking mustard greens. This seems like simple fare but our family looked forward to eating greens of all kinds every year and took growing them and cooking them very seriously, as I still do.

Mustard Greens

We are told there are streets made of gold in Heaven.

We are also told that we will all have mansions to live in.

Will they be the mansions of old made of mud bricks or will they be like our modern McMansions. I don't know. Will they have modern plumbing or outhouses like they did 2,000 years ago and we still did up until about 50 years ago? How will we get around with streets made of gold? Will we be able to use horses with steel shoes or carts with iron wheels? The streets wouldn't last long! Will we be forced to carry everything on our backs like they did back then and they still have to do in third world countries? Will we all have to wear robes like they did back then and people still do in the Middle East?

Again, I don't know!

One thing that I do know, if there is an official smell in heaven, it will be the smell of fresh mustard greens cooking. The good Lord must love mustard greens or he would not have created them!

Mustard greens give off a very delicious smelling pleasant, pungent odor while cooking. The smell alone makes one hungry even if they have just finished eating. I discovered this at Uncle Doc's and Aunt Mag's house while growing up. We never grew mustard greens but they always did. They sure smelled good while cooking!

I have eaten Aunt Mag's mustard greens after they were simmered for at least half a day. They ended up as a green, tasteless, goop like the greens of any kind that Grandmother Alice cooked. They didn't taste anything like they smelled cooking.

I often wondered why this was. How could anything that smelled so good while they were cooking end up tasting like that?

I finally discovered this by accident. I was blanching some fresh greens before freezing them. I had only cooked then about ½ done.

When I thawed the first of the greens, I did not have the time to cook them much more. I only heated them up.

I always strive for at least two tastes in anything that I cook. I want the vegetable taste to come through as well as the meat taste.

I always bake my ham hocks or anything else separately and only combine everything while serving.

The taste of the greens blew me away. I could actually taste the mustard. The natural sweetness of the kale, after it had been hit with some cold weather and frost, was also there.

This grew into further experimentation.

I found that if I cooked ½ curly leafed kale and ½ curly leafed mustard together with vegetable oil until they wilted, all of the taste came through.

I always overdo everything. I froze more than twice as much as I needed that year.

I had much to share with my sister, Ann. She had never eaten greens that tasted like that. I had given her the directions, frozen greens and some fresh ham hocks that I had to travel to near Pulaski, Tennessee to get. She and her entire family raved about them. They finished off all of the frozen greens and ham hocks in no time. I have a standing order from her for ham hocks and frozen greens every year!

Why didn't the old timers do this?

Ann didn't know either. She hated greens while growing up. She couldn't figure out why the family always overcooked them. We came to the conclusion that they learned how to cook from their ancestors and everyone did it that way back then.

I finally realized why. They didn't take care of their teeth and didn't have access to the oral hygiene that we do today. All of their teeth had been pulled by the time they were 40 or 50 years old. They had to cook everything this way to be able to gum it all down.

The only time they wore their false teeth was to church on Sunday.

Another mystery solved! Another culinary delight rediscovered!

If I ever get to go to heaven, I can grow enough fresh mustard greens to keep the place smelling properly. I will need the good Lord to pardon enough sinners, me included, to till the fields and pick the mustard and kale. Everybody else will be playing their harps and singing!

I know that I can garner a lot of converts up there when they realize what lies before them if they don't join in and help me and just how good fresh mustard tastes when properly prepared.

But wait! There may be an unexpected problem as there always is with all of my plans. The good Lord gave the Jewish people their dietary restrictions. No pork! Unclean! Jesus grew up under these dietary restrictions. He won't be able to intervene for me!

I will try to get someone to smuggle in some good smoked pork! Perhaps they can bury some with me in my casket! I can then prepare some proper mustard greens for the good Lord. I'll bet he may change his mind when he gets a good taste of them!

He may still think that pork is unclean but he may make the goats and sheep that I am sure he will want me to use taste like cured smoked pork!

Remember, Jesus turned water into wine!

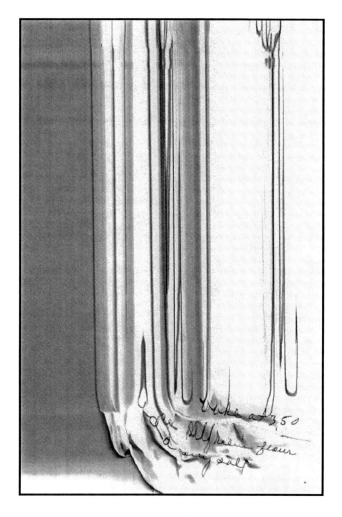

30

Cooking Blues
Original Artwork (if it can be called that) by **Lana Alsman Tidwell.**

Lana calls this *Cooking Blues* because of the blues that having to cook three meals a day for their family imparts on many women. Perhaps nightmares would be better terminology.

I think that it has a surreal almost dreamlike modern art quality. I think that each viewer can see all sorts of symbolism in it for various things in their own lives. As an optimist I see an upward uplifting trend. On the other hand, I can see that a pessimist would see a downward trend with somewhere to bottom out. It is to be interpreted by each viewer in their own way.

Even though Lana took art lessons briefly and dabbled in painting for awhile, I didn't know that she was particular artsy and as it turned out, neither did she. I don't know exactly how she created this but it had something to do with a jam in the scanner/printer that she was using to try to copy some of Grandmother Alice's recipes, written with a blue ballpoint pen, for me to type. Someway the ink was smeared all over the page. She left it for me to look at and I liked it and thought it deserved to be in the book. With its upwardly flowing theme, it symbolized to me the upward struggle our family has had over the years in growing, preserving and cooking the foods that we needed for survival. This is a common theme that resonates through all parts of my book.

There have been many things that have changed since 1845 for different members of our family. They have had to use their ingenuity to adapt to more modern things that came along.

We were always closely dependent on livestock and had to learn how to care for them. We depended on them for our meat, eggs, milk, butter and to pull our farm implements.

There was an old ox yoke used to plow oxen in Uncle Doc's barn. Somebody in the family, I thought, must have had to plow oxen at some point in time. Then horses and mules were used, now tractors. I now simply use a garden tiller that gets its horsepower from an internal combustion engine.

I later found out from Virgiline that Uncle Doc had made this ox yoke from memory having seen people use oxen as a boy growing up. He had never used it. It was sold at the auction.

Cooking has also gone through a similar revolution. It had to start with cooking over an open fire with a cast iron caldron. Dad had a small one that was supported by a metal tripod that he used while I was growing up to fry fish and cook stews outdoors. Dad called it his "Gypsy Pot." I bought three similar pots at first Monday in Jackson County over the years but family members wanted two of them. I now only have one left.

Cooking then progressed to fireplaces with special features cast into cooking pots of the time. I still have some of these. Then we progressed from fireplaces to wood burning cook stoves and kerosene stoves to electric ranges. And now microwaves.

Nobody in the family before mother had a microwave oven. Certainly not Grandmother Alice or Aunt Mag. Not even Aunt Jane. Virgiline does have one now. She has successfully made the transition from making hominy in a black cast iron wash pot over an open fire and making chitterlings from scratch to cooking in a microwave oven all in one generation. **What a remarkable woman!**

I could not possibly have imagined back in 1950 when we had a four party phone line that we would now all have cell phones, most even take photographs. Nobody had anything like that back then except Dick Tracy in the comic strip with his two-way wrist radio!

It boggles my mind when I try to think what changes the next 66 years will bring. I would like to be around to see more of them than I will.

One thing is certain, our family will adapt and embrace them. They may even use their ingenuity to try to improve on them or use them in different ways.

31

The Reid Connection

As discussed earlier in this book, Grandmother Alice and Aunt Mag were sisters and were the daughters of John Wesley and Emma Jane Owen Reid. I heard stories of Christopher Columbus Everett Reid and John Wesley Reid while growing up on Brush Creek.

Two of their nieces, Annie Reid Blacksher and Ada Lorene Reid Spencer undertook a years long journey of tracking down the genealogy of their families. This was a remarkable undertaking as resources from the internet did not exist then. They obtained their information from talking to people who were still alive and searching out old records.

Annie Mae Reid Blacksher

Ada Lorene Reid Spencer

Their dedication paid off as they traced general information of the Reid family migrations back to 1513 in Scotland and 1611 in Ireland where the family stayed for over a hundred years before they immigrated to America. The earliest Reid they found in America was of a John Reid living in Virginia in 1698. The later Reid families apparently first settled in Pennsylvania, then some moved on to Virginia, North Carolina and after the Revolutionary War they were granted land in South Carolina and Georgia for their services in the war. They were both truly remarkable women in their dedication and perseverance in their efforts. I am at a loss to be able to comprehend how they accomplished what they did without computers or the internet. They had to manually type their manuscripts on an old typewriter with cursive type. Remember, these were two little old ladies from Lawrenceburg, Tennessee.

Here is a summary of some of their work pretty much as they had written it. I offer the results of my internet search to try to clarify some of the few things that they were unable to resolve and *I include this information and my comments in italics.*

They start their work with a general description of the Reids in Scotland and Ireland. The Reids originally came from Scotland. Their connectedness is with the totality of forces that operated within the clans of the "Scottish Highlanders" of the tenth century and were of the clan Robertson. There we find the Reids of Scottish nobility with a reputation for moral and physical strength, energy, ingenuity, piety, resourcefulness, and the ability to direct others.

The Reids and their allies were loyal to the Stuarts and followed them with the clang of color and weaponry during all of their misfortunes. They took part in the battle of Flodden, where the English won the victory near Branxton, Northumberland, in 1513. In fact, this battle was the beginning of Scottish genealogical records.

The Reids were driven from Scotland as political refugees, along with their friends and other noble families of Scotland. Their properties were confiscated by the victorious government. For them it was farewell to the "land of brown heath and shaggy wood."

The Reids of Scotland were of the Presbyterian faith.

After the Reids left Scotland, most fled to Northern Ireland. Later, Irish intermarriage is found with immigrant ancestry going back to Thomas Warsop, Lord High Chancellor of Ireland. Some of these Reids went to England to live at one period where they spelled their name Reed. They later returned to Ireland. One of their old estates, "Lincolnholt Manor" is still there in England and still being held in escrow.

In 1611, King James I of Britain, offered land to the Reid family to colonize Northern Ireland. The lands were available for new ownership when the Irish rebellion, instigated by Phillip II, King of Spain, failed. He had seen in the Catholics of Ireland allies to redeem the defeat of the Armada and by strategy to regain the English Throne for the Catholic Church.

Thus the Reids became known as "Scotch-Irish" since they spent a hundred years in Ireland before coming to America. After the 1700s, most came through Pennsylvania. While some stayed in Pennsylvania, others moved on south to Virginia and North Carolina. Many Reids were Revolutionary War soldiers. They were granted land in South Carolina and Georgia for their service.

They then traced the lines of our branch of the Reid family back to Alexander I and wife Margaret McCay Reid, both born in the 1690s in Northern Ireland. Alexander I and Margaret McCay Reid, along with his family and several brothers left Ireland in 1745 to Port Philadelphia and settled in Lancaster County Pennsylvania. Some of them advanced down the Blue Ridge Mountains. Some settled permanently in Virginia while Alexander I Reid and family continued to the Salisbury District, Rowan County, North Carolina along the Yadkin River Valley. This movement of settlers occurred in 1750. Alexander I Reid bought land there in 1756. His sons did likewise with son Samuel in 1753, Andrew in 1762 and George in 1763.

According to court records, Alexander Reid I was "old and very infirm" in Rowan County, North Carolina when he filed his will on January 11, 1775. His will was proved in 1777 and lists his family as follows:

Wife Margaret Reid.
Alexander Reid II received the Plantation.

Seven additional children received one-seventh of his property. Samuel, Andrew, John, George, Hannah Knox, Frances Hall, Mary Wilson (or her children Alexander and Margaret Wilson). Sons: Andrew and Samuel were named executors.

Our branch of the Reid family comes from Alexander Reid II born in Ireland in 1726 and died in Jasper County, Georgia in 1813. Annie Reid Blacksher and Ada Lorene Reid Spencer have traced the movements of some of the additional brothers and list all of the children from Alexander Reid II on. Their work gets a little confusing because there is so much information about various families and some of the same given names keep reappearing from generation to generation. I will take the time to sort it all out sometime.

It would perhaps help if I would construct a family tree.

I have copies of two of Annie Reid Blacksher and Ada Lorene Reid Spencer's fairly large manuscripts and each agree on most things but they differ somewhat on others. I suspect that the one they both signed and dated March 30, 1982 in Lawrenceburg, Tennessee, was the final version but I will try to resolve the differences by doing what research I can on the internet. Unfortunately I do not have copies of all of their supporting documentation, only what they included in their manuscripts.

I will summarize some of their material and supplement some it with family stories and my internet research. I have already found two misspellings on the internet of some known last names and the internet apparently has reported their information as the Reid sisters had typed their manuscripts. Whoever entered everything on the internet also has at least one date of death wrong. I know where the cemetery and grave marker are and have included a photograph of the grave marker in the Family Memorial section.

I will only include information on Christopher Columbus Reid and John Wesley Reid, with a mention to Freeman Reid in this work, as I heard stories about them when growing up and will relate what I remember.

Family stories I heard while growing up mentioned an infant on the Reid side who was half Indian. No one was exactly sure of the details. The pertinent facts had been lost in the fuzzy, deep and endless bog of time--even back then. Some family members denied it, while others readily embraced it. Some claimed the baby was the result of a willing relationship, while others claimed it was the result of rape. No one was sure if the baby was male or female. One thing I do know--Grandmother Alice had the complexion and facial structure of someone with Indian blood. Dad evidenced this trait as well by his easily tanned complexion. I also tanned easily in my youth and so does one of my daughters.

The story was told that the half breed infant was thrown into the hog pen to be devoured. Providentially, a neighbor happened by just in time to rescue the infant from its fate.

Just look at the photograph below of Matilda Caroline Brown, C. C. E. Reid's wife. It is evident to me that this woman had some Indian ancestry.

Perhaps our family wouldn't have graced the face of the earth had this baby not been rescued.

Christopher Columbus Everett Reid*

C. C. E. Reid was born in 1838 in Green County Georgia and died on November 30, 1864 in the Federal Civil War prison at Alton, Illinois. He is buried in a common grave in the cemetery where all of the Confederate soldiers who died at the Alton Prison are buried. His name is listed on a bronze plaque on the Confederate Monument whose inscription reads:

Erected by the United States

To mark the burial place of the 1354 Confederate Soldiers
Who died here and at the Smallpox Hospital on the adjacent island
while prisoners of war, and whose graves cannot be identified.

C. C. E. Reid was the son of Freeman Reid and Nancy Ray Reid, married on December 10, 1835 in Green County Georgia.

He married Matilda Caroline Brown of Troup County, Georgia on February 17, 1856 in Troup County. Matilda was born in Georgia 1834 died about 1908 in Clay County Alabama. She was the daughter of Elizabeth Brown of Troup County, Georgia. The Brown family was listed in the 1850 Troup County, Georgia census as follows:

Elizabeth Brown	f	48	Ga. 1802
Matilda C. Brown	f	16	Ga. 1834
Elizabeth Brown	f	15	Ga. 1835
James Brown	m	13	Ga. 1837
Jane	f	11	Ga. 1839

Matilda's father is not listed with the family. It is unknown to us if he had died or what his name was.

C. C. E. Reid enlisted in the Confederate Army on August 5, 1861 in Troup County Georgia with Jeff Faulkner's Independent Cavalry. A roll call dated October 31, 1861 at Camp Beauregard, Kentucky, shows Private C. C. E. Reid. He served with the 25th Alabama regiment, Company G, which was a mounted company. He served with the 29th Alabama Regiment, Company A when he was taken prisoner on May 17, 1864 in Calhoun, Georgia. He was sent to the Alton Illinois Prison and died there on November 30, 1864 of Phthisis which was an old term meaning Pulmonary Tuberculosis.

Christopher C. E. Reid's Civil war record is listed below. This is from the State of Alabama Archives and History and Matilda C. Reid's pension application May 5, 1887, Clay County, Alabama.

Enlisted as a private August 5, 1861. Troup County, Georgia, Jeff Faulkner independent Cavalry.

Answered present Roll Call Camp Beauregard, Kentucky October 31, 1861.

Company G 25th Alabama Infantry.

Battle of Pittsburgh Landing, Shiloh, Tennessee April 6 - 7 1862.

Operations against the advance and siege of Corinth, Mississippi April 29 – 30, 1862.

Engagement Farmington, Mississippi May 9, 1862.

Skirmish near Farmington, Mississippi May 12, 1862.

Skirmish Bridge Creek before Corinth Mississippi May 28, 1862.

Retreat to Boonville, Mississippi May 30 - June 12 1862.

Retreat from Perryville to London, Kentucky October 10 - 22, 1862.

Operations against the advance on Murfreesboro, Tennessee December 25 - 30 1862.

Battle of Stones River, Murfreesboro, Tennessee December 30 1862 - January 3 1863.

From the National Archives.

Company A 29th Regiment Alabama Infantry, Pollard, Alabama, present at Roll Call.

Company Muster Roll Call April 1863, present.

Company Muster Roll Call July and August 1863, present.

Company A. was nicknamed Walker Reynolds Guards.

Company A 29th Regiment Alabama Infantry.

April 30, 1863, Eastern Division Department of the Gulf.

August 1, 1863, First Brigade Western Division Department of the Gulf.

Mobile Alabama early 1964 garrison duty serving both as Infantry and Heavy Artillery. Ordered to join the Army of Tennessee.

April 30, 1964, Cantey's Brigade unattached, Army of Tennessee.

Atlanta Campaign May 1 - September 8, 1864.

Combat. Sugar Creek near Resaca, Georgia May 9, 1864.

Battle of Resaca Georgia May 14 - 15 1864.

Captured May 17, 1864, Calhoun, Georgia.

Appears on Roll of Prisoners Of War, May 22, 1864 Nashville, Tennessee.

Arrived Military Prison Louisville, KY, May 22, 1864, Alton, Illinois, May 25, 1864.

Received in U. S. A. Post and Prison Hospital Alton, Illinois June 24, 1864. Runs fever. Returned to quarters July 2, 1864.

Received in Post and Prison Hospital Alton, Illinois October 31, 1864. Phthisis.

Died November 30, 1864. Phthisis is an old term meaning Pulmonary Tuberculosis.

The prisoners that died are buried in a common grave. All that died November 30, 1864 would be buried together in the same grave.

As for the children from this union, Annie Reid Blacksher and Ada Lorene Reid Spencer make the following entry:

"We have record of three children for Christopher and Matilda Reid, Fannie Reid born 1854, John Wesley Reid born 1856 and Robert Reid born 1858."

In another entry they note "His widow Matilda Reid with son Grissom Christopher (G. C.) Reid is living with his mother while the other son John Wesley Reid is living with his grandmother." They offer proof of Grissom Christopher's interaction with family members in this entry.

In yet a third entry they give the following information "Grissom Christopher Reid born December 1857 in Troup County Georgia son of Christopher C. E. Reid and Matilda Caroline Brown, sometimes called Bob, died August 18, 1918 in Clay County Alabama after an explosion in the Pinckney Mines. "

Annie Reid Blacksher and Ada Lorene Reid Spencer had listed Grissom Christopher Reid as a son in their earlier manuscript and had traced his family. The Grissom Christopher Reid I found on the internet was born 1863 in Clay County Alabama died 1918 in Clay County Alabama. This is undoubtedly the same man as the same names for the wife and children are given in both cases.

The Reid sisters apparently had difficulties in finding records to verify the exact names and birth dates of C. C. E. and Matilda Caroline Reid's children. I experienced the same difficulty in my internet research. The only one of their children that I could find a record of was a Francis Reid born 1854 in Georgia. I could find no other mention of her. Apparently many records were lost or destroyed in the turmoil in the south caused by the Civil War and the Reconstruction period afterward. The Reid sisters did have the knowledge they could gain from discussions and interactions with living family members which the internet does not offer. I accept their version as fact at this point. This makes their efforts and dedication to their task more remarkable and awesome due to the lack of resources at their disposal versus what is now currently available and the results of what they were able to achieve!

Matilda married Robert J. Reid (no known relationship to C. C. E.) after C. C, E. Reid's death in the Civil War. Robert J. Reid had served in the Confederate Army Company G. 26th Alabama Regiment, Alabama Volunteers. They moved to Clay County, Alabama and were living there when Robert died in 1877. Just when Matilda left Georgia and moved to Alabama is unknown. They are first listed in the 1880 Clay County, Alabama census.

On February 25, 1877 Alabama passed a law to pay a pension to needy Confederate Soldiers, Sailors and their widows.

Matilda C. Reid made application for Christopher C. E. Reid on May 5, 1887 in Clay County, Alabama. This was twelve years after the Civil War was over. There is no record that any money was ever paid. (Alabama State Archives.)

On February 10, 1899 Alabama approved a law, thirty-four years after the war, to pay a pension to needy Confederate Soldiers, Sailors and their widows. Matilda made application for her husband Robert J Reid on March 31, 1900 in Jefferson County, Alabama. She listed her net worth as $35.00:

One cow and calf $10.00.

Household and kitchen furniture $25.00.

In 1904 a pension was paid of $22.65, 1905 $30.00, 1906 $30.00 was paid. In 1907 - 1908 $12.50 when she died. (Alabama State Archives.)

It is remembered that in 1941 her grandson John Irvin Reid, his wife Ada and three of their daughters made a visit to the family of her son Robert Reid. It is believed that she lived with his family. We were taken to a very old cemetery where Matilda and many other Reids are buried. This is believed to be in Georgia since all of the graves were covered with small wooden shelters. This is an old custom in Georgia, not seen in Alabama.

For more clarification the author feels that it is necessary to type in a section from their work in its entirety to tie in Freeman Reid, Christopher C. C. Reid and John Wesley Reid and their associations with the early family.

Freeman Reid and Nancy Ray

Freeman Reid, Born 1810, Oglethorpe County Georgia married Nancy Ray on December 10, 1835 in Green County Georgia. Nancy was born 1821 in Georgia and died 1885 - 1888 in Clay County Alabama.

Freeman Reid died 1837 - 1840 when Nancy was listed with her son aged two. Nancy would marry two more times but this son, Christopher Columbus Everett Reid, born 1838, would be her only child.

2nd marriage January 6, 1843 Nancy Reid married Patrick O'Kelly in Green County Georgia. The 1850 census lists Patrick O'Kelly, age 40, born in Ireland.

This marriage must have been a "bad" one since we find Patrick O'Kelly living alone in the 1860 census and Nancy O'Kelly with her son Christopher Reid, age 12, living in the same area.

In the 1860 (*1870?*) census we find that Nancy O'Kelly age 39, seamstress, is living alone.

3rd marriage On April 15, 1874 Clay County Alabama, Nancy O'Kelly marries James G. McCain.

1880 Clay County Alabama. This is long after the death of Christopher C. E. Reid 1864 in the Civil War, his widow Matilda Reid with son Grissom Christopher (G. C.) Reid is living in Clay County Alabama while the other son, John Wesley Reid is living with his grandmother.

James G. McCain ---- 72, farmer
Nancy McCain ------- 52, keeping house
John W. Reid --------- 22, grandson

1881 John W. Reid marries Emma Jane Owen.

1883 Grissom Christopher Reid marries Susan C. Welch.

After their marriages, a tract of land that was owned with their mother, Matilda C. Reid, was sold to John B. Ray. There were many more deeds for land for G. C. Reid and wife Susan, nothing more for Matilda C. Reid.

John W. Reid continues to live with the McCains. In January 1885, John W. Reid filed in court an agreement he signed with his grandmother, Nancy McCain, that he would take care of her and continue to support her in the manner that she was accustomed to. In return, at her death he would receive 160 acres of land.

James G. McCain died in 1884 and is buried next to his first wife in Clay County Alabama. Nancy McCain died 1886 - 1887. Her grave has not been located.

In 1887 Matilda C. Reid filed for a widows pension for the death of her husband Christopher C. E. Reid. No money was ever paid. It is believed that she died in 1887 although no grave has been found. *A later entry corrects this. She died about 1908.*

G. C. Reid continued to live on in Clay County Alabama with his wife Susan and raised a large family until his death in 1918.

In 1888, John W. Reid and wife Emma sells the 160 acres to the Alabama Graphite Company for $30,000. He then, with wife Emma and son Alfred, moves to Lawrence County Alabama where he buys a tract of land, 320 acres, near Town Creek, Alabama.

This land was sold in 1903, moving across the Tennessee River *with several pit stops along the way* into Lauderdale County. Emma Reid died 1928, John Wesley Reid in 1932. Both are buried at the Cox Cemetery near Killen, Alabama.

The Reid sisters ended one of their manuscripts with this thought "The Reid, Owen, Brown and Cottle families were all very large families. From the old records that we have checked they all came to Georgia from North Carolina. They are all listed in the 1805 Georgia land lottery records. The Reid and Owen families were all in Georgia in the 1790s. The O'Kelleys are first listed in the 1830 Georgia census.

Since all of these families were OUR FAMILY we are happy to have found all of them living in Troup County Georgia 1850."

John Wesley* and Emma Jane Owen Reid* Family

Emma Jane Owen Reid

John Wesley Reid

Annie Reid Blacksher and Ada Lorene Reid Spencer made the following entry about the Reid family in one of their manuscripts "The Reids moved a lot. For many they were looking for a better life for themselves and their families. However, in Georgia when they had both land and money, they still moved on. For these they had to see the other side of the mountain."

John Wesley Reid must have inherited a double dose of this trait from his ancestors.

Born in Troup County Georgia May 1, 1858, died in Lauderdale County Alabama October 17, 1933 and buried in the Cox Cemetery near Killen, Alabama. He was the son of Christopher C. E. and Matilda Caroline Brown Reid.

John Wesley married Emma Jane Owen born March 22, 1858 Randolph County Alabama, daughter of Alfus Daniel Owen and Martha Ann Cottle. Emma was born Emily Jane Owen and was named after her father's sister Emily, as were some of the other family named after family members. As she grew up she changed her name to Emma. Now in the family there are two of her granddaughters named for her (*Emma Virgiline Tidwell Hale and Emma Nola Reid .*) Emma died March 4, 1928 in Lauderdale County Alabama and is buried beside her husband.

It is believed they were married in Randolph County Alabama since Emma was listed on the 1880 census living with her family. The Randolph County court house was destroyed by fire in 1894 and all old records were lost.

It is not known when this family left Georgia but they are listed in the 1880 census as living in Clay County Alabama. An old deed shows John W, his brother Grissom Christopher and their mother Matilda C owned a tract of land. In 1882 John sold his share of this land. In March of 1888 he and Emma bought a farm near Town Creek, Lawrence County Alabama where eight of their nine children were born. The two oldest children died as infants. From the keepsakes of John W. and Emma Jane Reid is a small black card printed in gold

In Loving Remembrance of Our Dear Children

Doner Mable Reid -- Died September 29, 1882 age 9 days.
Ronnie Lee Reid -- Died July 29 1884 age 8 months 14 days.
Clay County Alabama
Purchased by Mr. and Mrs. J. W. Reid

This little card is still kept and treasured by one of their granddaughters.

This is the family as listed on the 1900 census for Lawrence County Alabama.

John W. Reid - M   - May 1858   - 44   - farmer - Ga.

Emmer	- F	- March 1858	- 44	- keeping house - Ala.
Maud	- F	- July 1888	- 12	- Ala.
Alfred C.	- M	- July 1886	- 14	- Ala.
Claud	- F	- Aug.1889	- 11	- Ala.
Buler	- F	- Jan. 1884	- 6	- Ala.

John   - M   - Dec.1895   - 5   - Ala.
Alice   - F   - Dec.1898   - 2   - Ala.
Maggie the youngest child was born 1902.

The 1910 census from Tishomingo Mississippi is as follows:

John W. Reid age 54
Mrs. Emma J Reid age 52
Claudie Reid age 18
Beulah Reid age 15
John E. Reid age 14
Alice Reid age 11
Maggie Reid age 7

Approximately 1904, John W. sold this farm and moved the family from Lawrence County Alabama to Golden Mississippi to educate his children he said. This move did not work out so he moved to Walker County Alabama. Again this move did not work out and by 1910 or 1911 he moved the family to the Brush Creek community near Killen, Alabama. Emma Jane died there March 4, 1928 age 71.

Ten months later he married Susie Lash of the Springhill community near Killen Alabama. This marriage proved to be of short duration ending with John Wesley walking away with his plow lines in a pillow case and his crops in the field. *Virgiline Tidwell Hale relates a story about this that offers many more details. She said that John Wesley was living with them at the time of his marriage. Uncle Doc was digging something in preparation of building his truck shed. John Wesley had spruced himself up and had shined his shoes. He went out to talk to Uncle Doc and looked at what he was doing. He then said "Boy, I would help you but I would get my shoes messed up." Uncle Doc replied "We don't want you to mess up your shoes!" John Wesley then ambled off down the hill toward Grandmother Alice's house. Uncle Doc hollered for Aunt Mag when John W. was out of earshot "Mag, you had better come out and see this. This is the last time you are going to see your dad before he gets married!" Aunt Mag's response was "Who would want to marry that crazy old coot?" Uncle Doc said "I don't know, but he is going to get married!"*

Susie Lash was a widow and was much younger than John Wesley. The family knew she was living just north of the Tennessee state line in the early '60s but nobody from the family ever tried to visit her. I often wondered why. I guess they figured they would not be welcomed after her experience with John Wesley Reid!

Anyway Susie Lash's husband had left her with a farm, a new Florence wagon and a daughter. John Wesley promptly took out a mortgage on the farm and the Florence wagon without telling Susie about it. The bank was about to foreclose on everything and John Wesley put the leather wagon lines in a pillow case and left the country. Stories that I heard while growing up and that Virgiline reiterated was that John Wesley took off his shoes and waded creeks as much as possible so that Susie could not put bloodhounds on his trail! He headed straight for Grandmother Alice and Grandfather Nathan's place. He should have known that Brush Creek was the first place that she would have looked if she really wanted to find him. John Wesley had no other place to go!

Both manuscripts say that he then lived with his daughter and son in law Alice and Nathan Tidwell until his death October 17, 1933 age 77 where he was laid to rest beside Emma Jane Reid in the Cox cemetery.

Virgiline Tidwell Hale says that John Wesley would visit with his children and stay awhile after his wife Emma Jane Owen Reid died. While staying with Aunt Mag and Uncle Doc, after his marriage to Susie Lash, John W. made plans to visit with Alfred in Kentucky. Aunt Mag forbid him to visit and told him "You will hurt yourself if you go up there and I will have to go up there to bring you back home". John Wesley replied "Whoowee daughter, you are trying to boss me around. I will not be bossed around!" So off to Kentucky he went. John W. was in an accident while in Kentucky, he was hit by a car or truck, and broke his hip. There were not many phones in the area then and Alfred called Emma Cox to get the message to Aunt Mag to meet John Wesley at the train depot in East Florence as he was hurt and was coming home on the train.

When the train pulled in and Aunt Mag went aboard to check on John Wesley he pointed to a fruit basket and he said to her "Whoowee daughter, look what a nice fruit basket they gave me." Aunt Mag replied crossly "You Crazy Old Coot, I am not interested in your fruit basket!"

John Wesley Reid then lived with Grandmother Alice and Grandfather Nathan until his death.

The children from the marriage between John Wesley and Emma Jane Owen Reid who grew into adulthood are given below:

Alfred Claborn Reid

Alfred and Eula Reid

Born July 17, 1886 Lawrence County Alabama (*must have been Clay County due to his birth date*) died January 26, 1956 Harlan County Kentucky. Buried Rest Haven Cemetery, Keith, Kentucky. He lived for many years in rural Caywood and like his father always a farmer.

Married 1st Eula Bradley, Lauderdale County Alabama. Two children. Howard Reid died as a young child and Roy Reid adopted by Schermahorn from Eula's second marriage.

Married 2nd Louise Cdword in Caywood, Harlan County Kentucky

Lelia Maud Reid

Born May 27, 1888 Lawrence County Alabama died February 19, 1963 Lawrenceburg, Tennessee. Married December 8, 1907 Lauderdale County Alabama Robert Henry Young born July 26, 1864 died November 12, 1940, Lawrence County, Tennessee. Both are buried in the Mars Hill Methodist Church Cemetery, Lawrence County Tennessee.

Four sons were born to this marriage.

1. Orion Owen Young born March 16, 1909 died June 4, 1972, buried Mars Hill Cemetery.

2. Alsie Carr Young born April 22, 1911, died February 8, 1983. Buried Mars Hill Cemetery, Lawrence County, Tennessee.

3. Thomas Jerome Young born February 12, 1916, at Springer Station Lawrence County Tennessee. Died December 27, 1973. Buried Mars Hill Cemetery, Lawrence County, Tennessee.

4. Loran Richardson Young born February 5, 1921 Lawrence County Tennessee.

Cornelia (Claud, Claudie) Reid

Lloyd Danford and Cornelia Toole

Born August 1889 in Lawrence County Alabama *married Lloyd Danford Toole born 12 August 1886 in South Carolina, died 27 August 1961 in Richmond County Georgia. According to*

Virgiline Tidwell Hale, John Wesley Reid was a very mean man and this had something to do with Cornelia leaving home. Virgiline said that Cornelia had joined a "lonely hearts" club and corresponded with Lloyd by mail for some time. He traveled to Alabama and married her. They moved to Richmond County Georgia.

There were six children from this marriage.

1. *Nora Ellen Toole born 10 May 1914 in Richmond County Georgia.*
2. *James Allen Toole born 20 February 1917 in Richmond County Georgia.*
3. *Loree Toole born 26 June 1919 in Richmond County Georgia.*
4. *Eunice Verdell Toole born 13 February 1923 in Richmond County Georgia.*
5. *Charles Edward Toole born 9 August 1925 in Richmond County Georgia.*
6. *Thomas Lloyd Toole born 5 August 1928 in Richmond County Georgia.*

Virgiline said that Cornelia only came home once to visit with the family after she left home. That was while Uncle Doc was away from home in World War I.

As I was growing up I heard Grandmother Alice mention her name occasionally but she did not elaborate on the details of her leaving home.

Beulah Reid

Left to right: Maud Young, Beulah Moomaw, Alice Tidwell, Maggie Tidwell. This photograph was taken by the author with and old Kodak camera at Grandfather Nathan and Grandmother Alice' s old log home place in front of a purple lilac bush sometime in the 1950s. The author still has this camera but film for it is no longer available.

Born January 8, 1894 Lawrence County Alabama died September 1, 1974 Buried Pisgah Methodist Church Cemetery, Lauderdale County, Alabama. Married Edward D. Moomaw born May 1, 1892, died September 4, 1965, buried Pisgah Methodist Church Cemetery, Lauderdale County Alabama. Ten children from this marriage:

1. James Elias Moomaw born December 4, 1916 died September 16, 1960, buried Green View Cemetery, Lauderdale County, Alabama.
2. Grace Kathleen Moomaw born December 20, 1918 died August 8, 1944, buried Stony Point Church of Christ Cemetery, Lauderdale County Alabama.
3. Floyd Moomaw born July 6, 1920, died August 12, 1920.
4. Oscar Fielder Moomaw born September 6, 1922.
5. Stevenson Wesley Moomaw (Ted) born July 17, 1924, died March 27, 1945 WWII War Battle of the Bulge, Baston, France. Buried in Alabama.
6. Lois Geneva Moomaw born March 8 1926.
7. Lillian Inez Moomaw born October 1, 1928
8. Doris Evelyn Moomaw born April 28, 1931.
9. Ava Pearl Moomaw born October 24, 1933.
10. Dottie Ann Moomaw born October 26, 1937.

John Irvin Reid

John Irvin Reid

Born December 16, 1895 in Lawrence County Alabama died November 4, 1950 Lawrence County, Tennessee, buried Center Point Cemetery, Lawrence County Tennessee. Married Nellie Ada McDow born April 27, 1900, on October 22, 1915 in Lawrence County Tennessee. Eight children from this marriage:

1. Annie Mae Reid born November 12, 1917, died April 2, 1989. Buried at the Center Point Methodist Church Cemetery, Lawrence County Tennessee.
2. Gladys Luella Reid born April 13, 1918.
3. Wilma Irene Reid born December 15, 1919.
4. Emma Nola Reid born November 5, 1921.
5. Floyd Edward Reid born February 15, 1923.
6. Ada Lorene Reid born February 8, 1925 Lauderdale County Alabama.
7. James Irvin Reid born September 10, 1926 died August 12, 1927 buried Paducah, Kentucky.
8. Helen Marie Reid born April 5, 1928 died August 7, 1948 Lawrenceburg Tennessee. Buried Center Point Med. Church Cemetery Lawrence County, Tennessee.

Alice Genova Reid

Alice Genova Reid was born on December 20, 1898 Lawrence County Alabama died April 27, 1981. Married Nathan Jerry Tidwell born August 25, 1894, died July 19. 1954. Both are buried at the Cox Cemetery near Killen Alabama. There are four children from this marriage that are listed elsewhere in this book.

Maggie Earlene Reid

Born July 10, 1902 Lawrence County Alabama died January 28, 1978. Married Doxie Oliver Tidwell born January 15, 1892, died July 6, 1978. Both are buried side by side in the Cox Cemetery near Killen, Alabama.

Four children from this marriage that are listed elsewhere in this book.

John Wesley Reid Stories.

Some of these stories I heard while growing up but the most detailed ones were related to me by Virgiline Tidwell Hale. Virgiline knew John Wesley while she was growing up and others were passed on to her by Aunt Mag.

The first one was relayed to me by Grandmother Alice. At some point John W. decided to move his family to Searcy Arkansas. I have driven through Searcy several times in my travels and unlike a good part of Arkansas that is flat, it has rolling red clay hills much like northwest Alabama. John W. would have had to pass through some of the most valuable farm land now in Arkansas to get to Searcy. It is suitable for rice farming and most anything else.

I don't know how he ever heard of Searcy Arkansas. Again I don't know how he picked any of the places where he moved!

Anyway John W. had loaded up the farm wagon with the family and what belongings he could carry and headed out. John W. always punctuated his sentences with Whoowee when he was excited or wanted to make a point. Aunt Mag, the youngest child, was sitting in the back of the wagon and said "Whooowee, I can ride anywhere you can drive!"

John W. didn't get far and was back home by nightfall as I understand it.

Another story about John Wesley that dad told about while I was growing up was about John W's habit of using the chamber pot, or thunder mug, every night before he retired. The chamber pot was kept in the unlighted far room at Grandma Alice and Grandpa Nathan's old log house. John W. would go into the far room and light a match while he relieved himself standing up. He would then throw the lighted match in the chamber pot when he had finished.

Dad and Uncle Walter got the bright idea to pour a bottle of rubbing alcohol into the chamber pot one night shortly before John W's nightly visit. John W. did his normal routine and the chamber pot flamed up as soon as he threw the lighted match in. John W. let out his constant Whoowee and called the entire household in to watch. They all gathered around and watched as the flames slowly died down and John W. turned to Grandmother Alice and proclaimed "Whoowee daughter, I told you there was something wrong with my kidneys!"

Virgiline Tidwell Hale said that John Wesley was ill tempered, rude, and cross with his family members, including his grandchildren. She tells of a time when John Wesley was visiting with them. Uncle Doc was trying to teach his children table manners and to say please and to politely pass the food to someone else when asked. John Wesley wanted some potatoes and Virgiline says that she started to pass them to him but he just grabbed them out of her hands like a hungry hog. John W. proceeded to tell her to just eat what was in her dish and not to touch anything else. Uncle Doc called John Wesley on this and told him that he was trying to teach his children table manners and that John Wesley should obey them while visiting. John Wesley's reply was "Whoowee, I can't teach them anything!"

Virgiline also said that John Wesley would always start looking for someplace else to farm the next year as soon as he had laid his present crops by. He was never satisfied anywhere. He would disappear for days at a time after the crops had been gathered and nobody would know where he was or when he was coming back. The girls all thought that he was with another woman and Aunt Mag would beg her mother, Emma Jane, to not let him back in the house when he would finally drag in. They never knew where he had been or what he had been doing.

The last story that Virgiline related to me was once, while Aunt Mag was having to take her bed rest and Virgiline was doing the housework and cooking, John Wesley showed up for supper. John Wesley loved green fried tomatoes and Virgiline went out to the garden to pick some tomatoes that were just starting to turn to fry for him.

John Wesley did not have any teeth and was hungrily trying to gum them down. He got choked on the green tomato peelings that had been left on the tomatoes and ran out on the small back porch they had at the time. John Wesley bent over the side and started trying to heave them up. Virgiline said that he was going Whooawk, Whooaukh, Whooackk every time he would try to heave. Virgiline said that the peelings would come out of his mouth like a snake's tongue with every heave. Everyone was doubled up with laughter at the sight except for Uncle Doc.

Aunt Mag's chamber pot had been emptied, washed out and left outside to air out on the back porch. Uncle Doc ran his finger into John Wesley's mouth to rake as many of the peelings out as possible. John Wesley tumbled backward about this time and ended up on his back side and slid up against the side of the house with the chamber pot on his head. The bail just slid under his chin as a solemn flourish.

John Wesley gathered his composure as much as possible, looked around and said "Whoowee, you were just going to laugh yourself silly while I choked to death. I would have too if it had not been for the boy!"

Aunt Mag even got a laugh out of this too when they told her about it!

Part Three

Celebrating Life

Using values I learned while growing up from some very special people
in a most special place and time
We can only hope that our children feel likewise
About the people they knew while growing up
And their place and time in their early and formative years
We must try to teach them to never be afraid
To laugh at themselves
If they don't others surely will
Everybody will enjoy laughing together
Not just at someone

The Author

32

Ode to a Flagpole

Or was it a flagpole? Anyway it started out life as a birdhouse pole!

A friend, Bob Fox, who I worked with in Indiana introduced me to woodworking when I lived up there. He bought several old farms and built new houses on them. He would then sell them after the houses were finished and move on to the next property he had bought.

The first thing he would do was build a huge two car garage with a central heat and air conditioner in it. He and his wife, Jackie, would live in the garage until they had finished the house well enough to move into. They would then use the garage as a workshop until the house was completely finished.

Black Walnut grows in that part of Indiana like weeds do everywhere else. Bob would cut enough of it and have it sawn and kiln dried. He and Jackie would then make the cabinets for the house out of black walnut. They did good work and the house was beautiful once they had finished it. They both took courses at IVY Tech, a local trade school, that taught courses in all trades.

I had made a sunroom out of a screened in back porch when Lana and I were trying to sell our house in Indiana and move to Alabama. Bob came over to help me trim it out one Saturday. He brought a small table saw with him.

Bob sent me to the lumber company to buy the trim. He set his saw up while I was gone and was finishing some things inside the room that I had not finished yet. He had a loose fitting shirt on. Well, someway the shirt got caught in the saw blade and started pulling him into the blade, nose first. Bob got a good grip on the sides of the saw and started to try to push himself away will all the force he could muster. The more he pushed, the closer his nose came to the saw blade. His nose was just barely off of the saw blade when the main fuse in the house blew. The lights went off all over the house. Lana ran outside. There was Bob, almost close enough to kiss the saw blade, wet with sweat and trembling.

He had gained his composure well enough by the time that I returned to finish the job. Boy, was that a close one. Bob remembered it well and would not let me forget it either. Our lives crossed paths many times after that and he would remind me of this incident almost every time we met!

Anyway, when Lana and I moved to Alabama and bought our house, it had a two car garage that just begged to have a woodworking shop in it. I bought a table saw and built work tables to go with it. I got several other items like a drill press (cheap one) and a good router.

I was proud of my shop. I used until 1986 when I bought Lana her new red Dodge Daytona Turbo Z. T-Tops and all. She informed me that the woodworking equipment had to go to make a home for her new car.

I sold the saw to a friend in Newport, Arkansas, Nick Singleton, and dismantled the work tables. I put everything else into storage. Lana's new car finally had a home. It moved in to stay. It has now been with us for twenty-two years and shows no signs of leaving. Lana has always liked this car better than any other car she has ever owned. I bought her a new Buick Century in 2003 with the understanding that we would get rid of the Daytona and put the Buick in the garage.

Wrong--big time wrong.

Lana's 1986 Dodge Daytona Turbo Z

The new car still sleeps outside and the Daytona is still in the garage. She drives it every week just enough to keep the battery charged. It has 94,000 miles on it. She likes it so much that she will not even give me a set of keys for it! It is well worth it if this is all that it takes to keep her happy!

Back to the bird house.

My first project was to build a purple martin house. I got the plans from our local library. Boy, was it a nice one! It was a two story job and had sixteen compartments for the birds. Purple martin houses have to be taken down and cleaned each year, or so the directions said. Never mind that my neighbor had all kinds of them nesting in gourds that he never cleaned out! This meant that I had to use screen door latches and hooks to keep the parts together. Both stories and the top were held together with these latches and hooks.

There was a big unforeseen problem that I ran into. All of the wood I had to work with was pine one by fours. This worked well and I was able to finish both stories with no problem. The problem was weight. Each story weighed at least thirty pounds.

I had to stop the project at this point. I could not figure out how to get something that was this heavy into the air high enough to attract the martins.

This stymied me for two or three years. The two stories I had built just sat in a corner of the garage and collected saw dust from other projects.

I finally got tired of tripping over them and decided to finish the project. I built the top and roofed it with shingles to match our house. I painted everything to match the trim on our house as well and even built railings to hold the baby birds up in case they ever wandered out of their nests. Boy was it beautiful. It turned out as well as I had originally hoped.

The entire contraption weighed about a hundred pounds when finished.

Back into the problem of getting it up into the air! This took some planning and a lot of thought. It took me all of one winter to devise a plan.

It was Rube Goldberg plan if ever there was one! It ended up being quite a production!

I bought a sixteen foot close grained four by five pressure treated pine timber for the base. I had to set this pole in three feet of concrete.

Others became involved in this project at that point. My next door neighbor, Harvey Atkinson, was a surveyor and had a motorized auger to drill holes about ten inches in diameter. He volunteered to dig the hole for me. This was accomplished without incident.

The pole then had to be placed into the hole and the concrete poured.

Cindy, my youngest daughter, was in Junior High at the time and was the only daughter I could con into helping me with this task. She is now 34 so you can tell how long ago this was. I don't remember her ever volunteering again to help me with any other outside project! She learned her lesson well with this one!

I dug a shallow trench next to the hole to help guide this heavy timber into place and hold it there while we tried to raise it up enough to slide into the hole.

The first attempt went well until we got the pole up about a third way. We were both trying to push it up with our hands above our heads and walk toward the hole. The heavy pole would not budge after that and started to weave and waver from side to side. I told Cindy to jump out of the way and had to do likewise as the pole came thudding to the ground! Scratch trial one.

The same thing happened on trials 2, 3, 4 and possibly 5! I don't remember just how many times we tried.

We had each almost busted a gut by now and were shaking from exhaustion. Time to rethink the plan! It had to work because it was such a good plan and I had spent all winter making it!

We went inside while I thought of something else. I decided we would try to get it into the hole by tacking an eight foot two by four on each side of it low enough to where we could keep our hands below our waists. I don't remember if it was trial 1, 2, or 3 but the pole finally slid into the hole. We gave each other high fives!

We then tacked on some other two by fours to secure it after we had plumbed it up with a level.

We then mixed and poured the concrete using Sackrete and let everything rest until after the concrete had set up.

Everything else had to be done using scaffolding. I rented two eight foot sections and set them up.

The next step was to attach an eight foot piece of electrical conduit to the top of the birdhouse pole. I had to drop back about three feet below the top of the now upright pole and drill a hole in it to attach the piece of conduit with a bolt to act as a pivot point. I then secured the top of the conduit to the pole using a bolt I could take out and lower everything to the ground. I installed a boat winch to the back of the pole for this purpose and threaded it with medium duty steel cable.

I had the best piece of a pressure treated pine two by four that I could find offset on the back at about a thirty degree angle to give me enough leverage to raise and lower the heavy birdhouse, conduit and all. I had a pulley on the back brace for the steel cable and secured the cable to the end of the conduit with a heavy eye hook. I even added a wooden stop to keep the end of the conduit from reaching the ground when it was fully lowered.

Man, did it look impressive to me when I finally raised it into place and secured everything on top with the bolt. I backed off to take a good look at it. It had the elegant look of a crane used to load and unload ships. Lana said it looked as ugly as a mud fence and something like a drunk hillbilly would design. She was probably pretty close to being correct on all charges! But none of the neighbors complained. In retrospect I don't know why! This is a respectable neighborhood! They were probably all in a state of shock!

The next step was to attach the heavy birdhouse on it and raise everything into place. This had to wait until the following weekend.

I loaded the sections of the birdhouse into my wheelbarrow the next Saturday and wheeled them out.

Then I attached everything to the end of the conduit and started to winch them up into place. Everything went smoothly until the birdhouse was about half raised. At that point I heard a very loud splintering sound and everything dropped to the end of the cable, stopped abruptly, and pieces of birdhouse flew in all directions. My back brace had broken. It would not handle that much weight!

Back to the drawing board.

After discussing my problem with a friend at work, Norman Moore, he had a recommendation. He would go up on Sand Mountain and get a rough sawn oak two by four and we would try again. Norman was an accomplished woodworker and I took his suggestions seriously.

The next Saturday rolled around and Norman brought his oak two by four over. The scaffolding was still up so the job went smoothly. We cut and drilled everything to the appropriate size and mounted the new back brace to the pole with long lag bolts. The cable was again rethread through the pulley and attached to the end of the conduit. The bird house was assembled and we started to winch it into place.

Everything went smoothly and the bird house was soon up in place. None of the neighbors cheered but Norman and I were both happy! The scaffolding could now be taken down and returned to the rental place.

2008 photograph taken during a visit to Tennessee. Left to right: **Fred Thebus, Norman Moore. Al Reid** can be seen standing in the background.

Well, the purple martins ignored their new condo like it carried the plague. The scouts would come by every February but none ever nested there. The directions said that you had to keep the holes covered until after the martins had moved in to keep starlings from taking over. I did not have this problem. The starlings were not interested in it either! The only thing that tried to nest there were a few wrens but they were never too successful.

I guess I had mounted it too high but it was the height the directions said to mount it. It was about twenty feet to the top of the bird house.

The bird house started to deteriorate after several years. The entire pole and assembly would rock gently with the wind. Lana was afraid to walk out in the back yard near where it was for fear it would fall on her head! After listening to her tell me she wanted it down for about two years, I took it down. I had never had to lower it since it had been put up.

I had to rent the scaffolding again because I was too old by that time to climb the shaky ladder to the top bolt to take it out so everything could be lowered.

I got the bird house about half way down but it was so rotten that it just fell apart. It was, as Lana suspected, about to fall on its own in the next high wind! I hauled small pieces of it with my wheelbarrow to the front ditch for the garbage man to pick up.

This is when it became a flagpole! Back to the drawing board for some more redneck engineering! Norman Moore had moved back to Tennessee by now so I had to devise everything on my own.

I added another 8 foot section of electrical conduit capped with a conduit cap. It was not as elegant as the large balls on store bought flagpoles but looked quite elegant to me.

I added a pulley to the top of the conduit to thread a nylon rope through and a boat cleat at the bottom of the pole to secure the rope with. Clips were added to the rope to attach two flags, but I never could find an appropriate Alabama flag.

I only flew the American flag. I once flew a Confederate flag briefly but not for long. I was afraid that the NAACP would picket!

It looked quite elegant to me but it still looked like something you could unload a ship with. Only with a longer boom to handle heavier loads!

It now rose about twenty-five feet and could be seen from blocks away. I gave directions to the house by simply telling people to head for the flag when they got into the neighborhood.

I have only seen one other flagpole similar to mine with a wooden timber at the bottom and conduit on top in all of my travels . It was built later by the person who bought Grandmother Alice's old home place. It was nowhere as elegant as mine since it did not have the boat winch and back brace to make it look like a shipyard crane. I guess there must be something about living in that area that imprinted this design into our genome!

I got the first flag at the Veterans Home. They kept flags for people who wanted them. It was a little larger than the Wal-Mart flags I had to settle for later but they were all nice flags. I think there were four in all. They would get tangled up in the steel cable eventually and a heavy wind would shred them to where they had to be replaced.

The trees finally grew in our neighborhood to the point where my flag was hardly visible except for the houses adjacent to ours.

I really liked the flagpole. I could tell at a glance which way the wind was blowing and how hard it was blowing. I could even tell from the kitchen window without going outside. I could tell if it was raining when the timber was wet. It was used something like a weather rock. I could tell what the weather was like by the condition of the flagpole outside!

It made a nice flapping sound that I could easily hear while sitting out on the patio in the afternoon. This was music to my ears, and besides, it kept the blackbirds at bay.

Strong westerly winds started to bend the conduit on top about three years ago. It was bent so badly last spring that I did not put up the flag anymore. A redneck does have his pride!

I considered lowering it and replacing the bent conduit but Lana convinced me that I should take it down for the sake of the entire neighborhood. I resisted as long as I could but finally decided it had to go. Besides, I was getting so old that I didn't know if I could set up the scaffolding again by myself.

I went out with my bow saw late one afternoon and started to saw it down at ground level. I sawed it so close to the ground that I even skinned my knuckles. I could still smell the pungent aroma of pine pitch as the saw cut into it after all these years. That was one fine piece of wood. I felt a pain in my heart with each stroke of the saw. I really hated to do this.

I took a wedge and a hammer to finish the job after the sawing was almost done. It fell just where I wanted it with a loud thump!

Lana and my oldest granddaughter, Lindsey, clapped and cheered loudly as it thudded to the ground. Lindsey even took the saw and cut the timber up into lengths that could be easily hauled to the ditch for the trash man. I didn't have the heart to do it right then! I took the conduit off the next day to make hauling it easier.

None of the neighbors ever mentioned it was gone. I guess I did my good deed toward community improvement that day though. At least I hope that I did.

I really miss my flagpole. There was a lot of personal history tied up in it.

So long old friend. You are gone, but you will never be forgotten!

33

Gardening in Jackson County

It is October and my garden this year is in a transition from spring and summer crops to fall and winter ones. The last remnant of my spring garden, the last surviving tomato plants, are in a heap in the ditch in front of the house waiting for the garbage man on Monday. I have just enough tomatoes left for one last summer meal and my favorite, chopped tomatoes with cottage cheese. I can hardly wait for next year's crop to get ripe.

The fall and winter garden is coming along nicely. I have cabbage, some already forming heads and others just starting to grow. I have already harvested the broccoli that I planted in August and replanted it. The cauliflower is just starting to show signs of forming a head. The turnips, beets, rutabaga, kale, mustard and other greens that I planted in early September are now ready for thinning and getting the first cooking. This was all completed by the end of the week and was the first picking of greens good. I had enough extra to share with three friends as well.

The only thing that I have left to do this week is to hoe out the random grass and weeds that are trying to grow where I have thinned out certain things.

The only major problems I had this year were rabbits and bugs. Rabbits normally don't bother anything in my garden but they developed a fondness for the plants that I set out in September. They would eat them down past the growth bud. I have replanted these plants 3 different times. I now have more money in plants than I could buy what I have planted if I bought it in the supermarket. I never see the rabbits, they only eat my plants at night, but they are destructive. I have taken out all of the other plants nearby that I suspected they were using for cover. This has slowed them down. They have now only eaten about 8 plants out of the 70 or so that I have planted in this patch. I can live with that! I will have to anyway because it is now too late to replant anything.

October 2008 fall garden green patch.

October 2008 fall garden illustrating rabbit damage. Late season collard, cabbage and broccoli patch.

East End, Curly Leaf Kale and Curly Leaf Mustard Patch.

West end, broad leaf mustard and seven top turnip patch.

October 2008 early season cabbage and broccoli. Collard and cauliflower patch. All broccoli and a lot of cabbage have already been harvested.

Tomato Harvest – Spring 2009

Bugs are always a problem with fall gardens. This has been especially true this year. The bugs got firmly entrenched in what I planted in August and almost destroyed them before I discovered that I had a problem. A systematic spraying over several weeks eliminated them.

It is now time for reflection and to think back to previous gardens and to plan for future ones.

I started gardening in the backyard on a bigger scale three years ago after I retired. I first worked up three different patches that total about Two thousand square feet. I then augmented my basically red clay soil with about 300 forty pound bags of top soil, containing a lot of sand and other organic material, along with the assorted dirt from raised beds that I had prepared for flowers years ago. I also worked in all of the other organic material I could lay my hands on. I work in all of the grass clippings that I get each year as well. I use the grass clippings as mulch first while the plants are growing and till it in after I have taken them out. The result of this over 3 years is that I now have a dark loamy soil that is extremely fertile.

Two thousand square feet probably doesn't sound like much to those who garden on a grand scale like I used to. It is enough to grow everything that I want to eat in the way of fresh vegetables and to supply my closest two friends with all that they want as well. I still have enough extras to share with many other friends. I get two crops off of all of it every year and sometimes three crops from part of it.

One doesn't need a big area if he gardens two thousand square feet intensively.

34

My Original Garden in the Backyard

We moved into our current house in early 1973. I immediately bought a tiller from Sears. It was not a normal small tiller. It was the second largest one that Sears sold at the time. The largest one even had a gearshift lever on it to slow or speed up the tines. Fred Thebus bought one of these. Mine was just as powerful but costs a little less. I even tried to rig up a layoff plow and a rudimentary cultivator that I attached by drilling a hole in the stake in the rear that held it in place so that it would not gallop full speed ahead when you were trying to dig hard dirt.

The layoff plow worked pretty well but I could never get the cultivator to work like I wanted it to.

I am getting ahead of myself. Back to the real test. Using this tiller for the first time.

I pushed it out into the back yard and positioned it in the spot that I intended to dig up. I fired it up and set the stake as deep as it would go. I tried to run it full throttle.

This tiller started to buck and jump like an untrained horse colt that one was trying to ride for the first time. It was impossible to control the tiller and make it dig where I wanted it to dig. If it wanted to dig somewhere, it would just jump there pulling me along with it. Try as I might, I could not control it.

I tried to use it all morning and gave up. I did accomplish digging up some ground but not as I had expected to be able to do. I was stiff, sore and all bruised up the next morning. The bruises came from the handles jumping back and hitting me in the stomach when the tiller had decided to jump back. I had one huge bruise on my left arm. This engine did not have a compression release to start the engine and the pull rope had a habit of pulling out of my right hand when I tried to start it while the engine was hot. That rope had a kick like a mule and would always hit me on the left arm! Come to think of it, I had never seen a mule as stubborn as this tiller was!

Anyway, this experience almost made a Christian out of me. I just knew that if I died and was sent to the bad place, I would surely be condemned to use this unruly tiller through all of eternity! I could think of no worse punishment!

Gardening on Porter Road

Paul Mullaney October 2008.

I had made friends with Red and Johnny Woosley by the time the second gardening season rolled around. This was the couple who had originally owned the farm where our subdivision was built. They had farmed it until they retired and sold it to Leonard Derrick who developed the subdivision. Red and Johnny had kept a portion around their home to leave to their heirs after they passed on. This included a three-quarter acre lot next to their house that stretched all the way to Porter Road. This was not far from the base of July Mountain.

Red and Johnny were a very nice old couple and we became fast friends. They rented me this lot and I started gardening there. I retired my garden spot in the back yard and planted grass over it. My farming operation was moved to this lot.

I had learned not to try to work up new ground with my ornery tiller the previous year. I now had gotten smart enough to have someone with a tractor come in and break this lot and then disk it. This simplified my tiller work and I had also learned by that time that it was not best to always run the tiller at full throttle all of the time.

This tiller was still temperamental and did take spells of jumping and bucking uncontrollably. Red took an active interest in my garden and always had suggestions to keep me from making serious mistakes. He would tell me when things needed worked out and when the bugs needed to be sprayed. He also kept after me to keep the red careless weeds pulled up as well as the Jimson weeds. He did not want them growing on his property. My farming operation was now

216

big enough that I had to take in two garden buddies to share with the expenses and work. My first two were Jim Eiford and Paul Mullaney. They were both from Baltimore originally and had no experience with gardening.

Red and Johnny had a marvelous lawn. They had numerous shade trees everywhere and Johnny had beds of all kinds of flowers scattered around. They had two shade trees out by the well house near the garden. They had a well pump and a spigot there where we would always go for a drink of water while we were working in the garden. They had numerous lawn chairs in this area and we would all sit and talk after we got tired or the day's work was done. It was always cool under the shade trees and any breeze made everything cooler. We had some wonderful visits sitting out there.

I would take a week of vacation about the middle of April each year to get everything ready. I would run the tiller over the whole lot until I got it worked up just right. Jim Eiford was especially fond of ordering a lot of our seeds from Burpee. He always wanted to grow Ford Hook lima beans and Silver Queen sweet corn. They were used to pulling the sweet corn when it was very immature, or rat tooth stage as they called it. It was exceptionally sweet at this stage but did not yield much when cooked.

We grew some exceptionally nice gardens on this lot over the years. We planted 4 rows of potatoes the first year. I was used to growing red potatoes from my gardening experiences as a youth. Red potatoes are especially suited to our climate in north Alabama and yield heavily here. My garden buddies wanted to grow white potatoes--so grow white potatoes we did. We bought 100 pounds of white potatoes from the Jackson County Farmer's Co Op and cut them into quarters for planting. Red Woosley told us that the potato farmers on Sand Mountain always use three pounds of triple 13 fertilizer for every pound of seed potatoes so we put down three hundred pounds of triple 13 and our one hundred pounds of seed potatoes. I worked in the fertilizer in the rows with my tiller pulled layoff plow and we planted everything. I expected the potatoes to rot with all of this fertilizer but they did not. We got a perfect stand and Jim's son, Jay, took an immediate interest in the potatoes. He was attending North East Community College at the time and would be over every evening after class hoeing them with a grubbing hoe. He took exceptionally good care of these potatoes and kept the dirt hilled up around the plants and kept it soft.

It came time to dig the potatoes in early July. Both Jim and Paul brought their entire families over one Saturday Morning and they literally scratched them out by hand. Red had never seen anyone digging potatoes with their bare hands and neither had anyone else. We almost had a traffic jam on Porter Road with everyone slowing down to rubberneck!

The potatoes rolled out of the ground. I calculated we had over two thousand pounds when we finished. Red Woosley was amazed at the yield and so was I.

We planted potatoes again several times but we never got yields like we did the first year. Jay Eiford had moved on by that time and nobody worked the potatoes in subsequent years like he had done.

We had many wonderful gardens over the years from this lot. I eventually bought it from Red and Johnny sometime in the mid 70s. Someone from their family wanted to put a convenience store on it and Red and Johnny did not want it there that close to their house. Selling it to me seemed like their best option at the time.

After everything was planted each year, it became a chore to keep it all worked out and keep the weeds and grass out. I would run the tiller through the garden to keep the middles clean and this took all of the time that I had. We were short of people who knew how to use a hoe once I had tilled everything out. We needed hoers big time! The crabgrass grew like crazy. The entire garden would end up looking like it had a Mohawk haircut in every row. The middles would be clean but the rows had more grass in them than they did plants. Needless to say, our yields suffered.

I should have learned from this that we were working up too much of this lot and the garden was too big for us. No, this never got through my hard head. I was ready when the opportunity came up for additional acreage out on Goosepond Island.

Paul Mullaney withdrew from the garden project after a couple of years and Dr. Ron Jones took his place.

35

Gardening on Goosepond Island

Our Plant Manager, Bud Cannon, decided it would be nice to have a garden on Goosepond Island for the employees of both the Reduction and Rolling Plants. The entire island, except where the plants were, was leased to a farmer. They simply withdrew several acres from the farmer for this garden project.

The acreage was worked up with a tractor, limed and staked off in ¼ to ½ acre plots. They charged us ten dollars per lot the first year but gave everyone more fertilizer than they could buy for ten dollars. Everyone immediately signed up for these lots. Jim Eiford and I got one each. Fred Thebus and Bud Cannon also rented lots close to ours.

It rained between when we signed up for the lots and when it came time to plant. Anyone who knows about the soil on Goosepond Island, knows that it is heavy red clay. It is fine for growing certain things but once it rains on it and the soil dries out, it gets as hard as a brickbat.

Back to my trusty, but unruly tiller. I took my bucking tiller out to work the hard soil up in the two lots prior to planting. I promptly burned out the clutch that engages the tines on the tiller because the soil was so hard. Sears had one in stock but it also promptly burned out as well. It was evident that something else had to be done.

The people who had signed up for the lots decided that we would have someone with a tractor come in and disk up our lots. One person volunteered to have this done for an additional ten dollars a lot. We all agreed for him to do it.

The tractor and driver did not show up on the appointed day. The tractor owner had backed out of the agreement for some reason. I volunteered to find someone else to do it if everyone would pay me what it costs. Everyone agreed.

I found someone and had the lots of my friends and business associates worked up. It did cost ten dollars a lot. I paid the man and tried to collect from those who had agreed to have this done. A few paid me but most did not. Remember, they had already received more than their original ten dollars in fertilizer. I suspected that they had used the fertilizer on their lawns and did not intend to garden. So, I took over their lots and began to plant them in sweet corn. I planted some lots in silver queen and some lots in golden queen.

Norman Moore came to Revere about this time and I had four lots left. He wanted one for a garden and I let him pick out the one he wanted. Norman and I became fast friends and still communicate.

Jim Eiford and I were working out everything for the last time that Memorial Day and planting the skips in butternut and acorn squash. Everything was in excellent shape and there was not a blade of grass or a weed left standing.

Left to right, **Fred Thebus** and **Norman Moore** during an August 2008 visit to Tennessee. The back of **Bob Bridges'** head is also shown.

We decided to plant one of the extra lots in late sweet corn. I had tilled up everything and was using my tiller powered layoff plow to work in fertilizer in the few remaining rows. We had already planted about two-thirds of it.

Jim Eiford looked up over Sand Mountain and saw a big black cloud brewing. He said "Jerry, you had better stop and let's get out of here." I replied "Just three more rows Jim. Just three more rows!"

Norman Moore had seen this cloud as well and had loaded his tiller up in his car and was heading out. It was starting to sprinkle by now and there was an unbanked curve leading out of the garden spot up a slight incline, near where my car was parked. A big gust of wind hit Norman's car just as he got in the middle of the curve and blew him into the ditch. Jim Eiford had already headed for his car.

I decided it was time to go about this time and shut the tiller off and was ready to leave. The rain came down in buckets and immediately saturated me, the ground around me and everything. I don't know if any of you have ever tried to walk on wet red clay or not. It is impossible to do. I slipped and hit the ground. I got up and tried to walk again. Hello ground again. I made a big splash this time. The wet red clay was as slick as trying to walk on glass that had been coated with grease. I couldn't stand up and walk!

I ended up having to crawl to my car on my hands and knees. I was literally coated from head to foot in red, clinging clay.

The story does not end here. About the time I finally made it to my car and made it inside, Norman Moore crawled in on the passenger side. He was soaked and muddy as well. I had my toolbox on the passenger side floorboard and Norman had to put his feet up on it. I can still see his footprints on the top of my toolbox some thirty-four years later.

We sat there and watched it rain. Both thoroughly soaked and muddy. We were more than a little dazed!

I tried to move my car and it would not budge. It was stuck in the wet red clay. Jim Eiford could not move his car either and Norman's car was in the ditch.

We may have still been there to this day if it were not for someone in a pickup truck who had mud grip tires on the back. He let the tailgate down and Jim, Norman and I sat down on the tailgate. This gave him enough traction to pull out of there.

He dropped us off at what is now the Village Shopping Center. There was a pay phone outside of Clements Jewelry at the time. We all called home for someone to pick us up.

I had on boots that day. I literally took off my boots and dumped the water out on the pavement while we were waiting. I also had to take off my socks to wring the water out of them by hand!

It had finally dried up enough three days later to where we could get Brian Maze to pull us out with his pickup truck and a towing strap.

Man, that was an experience I will remember to my dying day.

Little did we know, mud would be the least of our worries that year.

The farmer had used herbicide to keep the grass and cockleburs under control. We did not know this. We went back when the corn should have been ready. The first lot that I checked, near to where Norman had been blown into the ditch, was unbelievable. I could not see the corn for everything else growing in it. There was grass everywhere and the cockleburs were taller than I was. Man that red clay soil really grew cockleburs. These cockleburs rivaled those that I described in the Rabbit Hunt story in a previous section.

I kept stepping on something on the ground in this lot. I parted the weeds and grass to where I could see what I was stepping on. It was acorn squash. We took them out of this lot by the bushel baskets full.

Fortunately, not all of the lots were that overgrown. We had more sweet corn that year than we could pick or possibly use. We charged the people who did not pay to have their own lots disked up fifty cents a dozen to go in and pick their own. I recovered most of my money.

Sweet corn will keep for about two weeks in the field before it gets too hard to use. It just gets more mature and milkier each day. The birds love it after it gets too mature for humans to use. They will strip the husk back and peck at the corn on the cob. The birds got a lot of sweet corn to feast on that year.

We were still gardening on the lot by Red and Johnny Woosley that year. We had a total of over two acres in garden, possibly two and one-half acres. We had so much stuff that we could not possibly pick all of it. A lot of what we grew that year was wasted. Norman Moore came over and helped us garden the lot by the Woosley's. He had a motor scooter that he rode a lot back then. We were all sitting out under the trees once we had finished one afternoon. Norman was with us. A garter snake had somehow gotten up in the tree that Norman was under. It fell out into his lap. Man, he did a dance to get rid of that snake. The snake was more afraid from the fall and all of the commotion than Norman was. It hastily beat a retreat by slithering into the nearby grass. Norman didn't say a word after he had regained his composure. He just got on his motor scooter and went home. It was a while before he came over again.

A story that Norman insisted that I include, when I told him recently that I planned to write this story, was Jim Eiford taking some produce from the garden back to his folks in Baltimore to share with them. Red Woosley was telling me about what Jim had picked to take back and was chuckling when he told me. Everyone knows that bigger is better when it comes to something that you have grown, right. Well, this doesn't hold true for okra. Okra needs to be picked every day so that it doesn't get so big that it gets hard. Jim picked some okra to take back and picked the largest pods he could find. I knew it was inedible from what Red told me that Jim had picked.

Jim didn't have a word to say about the produce when he got back. I asked him about the okra. All he had to say was they didn't like it very much. I can just imagine everyone's surprise in Baltimore when they bit down into the okra! I know they didn't like it and probably couldn't eat it. I had forgotten this story until Norman reminded me about it.

The Bucking Tiller Takes One Bounce Too Many

The ornery tiller finally took one bounce too many. There was a metal bracket welded to the back of the gas tank that firmly attached it to the engine. The tiller finally bounced and bucked so much that the metal bracket broke from metal fatigue. The gas tank was just flopping around on top of the engine.

I took the gas tank off and took it to work to see if John Green, who ran the tractor repair shop, could have it repaired. He did not want to do it. He told me of all the safety precautions he would have to take to be sure that he did not blow up the tank and get someone injured. He finally relented and had a new bracket welded on.

This repair lasted for a year or two but the metal bracket broke again. I decided that this ornery tiller had bucked its last time in my garden.

A young guy at work, Jim Campbell, wanted to start gardening so I gave it to him. I explained to him the problem with the gas tank but he wanted it anyway. He told me later that he would have his wife sit on top of the gas tank when he wanted to use the tiller. I would have liked to have seen this. I think that I could have sold tickets to people wanting to watch this spectacle!

Garden Tractor

I later bought a garden tractor. It was made like a mini road grader and was it ugly. It did a good job though and was patterned after an old model G Allis Chalmers.

Jim Eiford 3rd from left at First Methodist Church ground breaking.

It had a breaking plow, disk, grader blade and cultivator. Man, I thought I was in the "big league" now.

We gardened the original lot plus we had several lots on Goosepond Island. We planted the lots on Goosepond in sweet corn again. The garden was looking very good early on but we had an extremely dry year. Everything withered. There was a little corn but someone stole what little we had.

This was the straw that broke the camel's back for me and gardening. I was getting too busy at work with new responsibilities to spend much time gardening. I sold my garden tractor and equipment and sold the lot back to the Woosleys. I washed my hands of gardening.

Then I took a job in sales and traveled extensively. It was only in later years that I bought another tiller and started over again in the backyard. This was on a small scale in an area next to the fence. I did this for about two years but work and travel started taking too much time. I parked the tiller in the garage for a year or so and gave it to my next door neighbor who wanted to start gardening. He gave it back to me when he moved. My other neighbor, Harvey Atkinson, needed a good tiller so I gave it to him. He still uses it.

I still wanted to garden but just didn't have the time. It was only after I retired that I got into it again.

Harvey Atkinson in front of my 2008 fall green patch

36

Twenty Dozen Fruit Jars

I have always been naïve. Some, including my wife, claim that I still don't have a clue about domestic matters! They are probably correct.

There was no excuse for any of my actions in this incident. Lana and I married in 1970 and I should have been housebroken by the time this story took place.

I had started gardening big time by then. The garden produce began to flow in at a copious and alarming rate. We could not possibly use everything. We could not even pick everything when it needed picking.

I could not understand Lana's attitude. She would not freeze anything for use in the winter! Mother would freeze and can everything she could get from dad's garden and would get mad if dad gave anything away while I was growing up! Dad gardened over two acres. I thought all women and mothers should be the same way. This worried me for the longest time.

I finally decided that my wife didn't like frozen vegetables because she grew up before home freezers. I thought she would probably use a pressure cooker and can everything that way as her mother had surely done while she was growing up.

I put my plan into action the Christmas a year before the fruit jar incident. I ordered her the biggest pressure cooker that Sears had in their catalog for Christmas that year. I waited in anticipation until she opened her gift. She looked over the big box wrapped in Christmas wrap for the longest time. Surely such a big box held something nice I'm sure she thought. I eagerly watched her expression as she started to unwrap it. Instead of joy, her face fell in disappointment!

She relegated the unopened box into an obscure corner of the kitchen. It remained unopened. I am now sure that she stored it in plain sight so that she could look at it every day and get mad at me all over again!

I was again bothered by her lack of interest in preserving the bountiful garden harvest that poured in the following spring, when I had time to pick something. I still could not understand her attitude.

This bothered me all spring of that year. The pressure cooker remained unopened.

The solution finally hit me like a bolt out of the blue! I said "I'll bet she would use the pressure cooker if she had jars to can something in." I had completely forgotten one of the important links in the canning process. I decided that I would take care of this omission in my thinking process for Mother's Day that year.

Warehouse groceries was new in town then and was where Piggly Wiggly is now. We had a Ford Grand Torino station wagon by then so that Mother's Day I let all of the back seats down to prepare to haul her booty home. This gave me an area of about four by eight feet to fill up with her present.

I then head down to Warehouse Groceries and started filling up the back of the station wagon with boxes of quart fruit jars. I got twenty dozen jars in there before I ran out of room. Man was I proud of myself for getting her such a wonderful present. I congratulated myself all of the way home. Surely she would be overjoyed!

I pulled the station wagon up into the driveway and rang the doorbell so I could show her the wonderful gift and let her know how much I cared. She took one look at the piles of fruit jars in the back of the station wagon and her face fell further than it did the Christmas I gave her the pressure cooker. I am sure that she had a few choice words to say on this occasion but I don't remember exactly what they were. It is probably best that I don't remember them. She finally said something that can be repeated and it was "I was raised on a farm and got all of that out of my system a long time ago." She walked back into the house sadly shaking her head!

I was still puzzled by her reaction. I asked my garden buddies for their advice.

Jim Eiford laughed so hard he almost rolled in the floor. He finally composed himself and said "That woman is going to kill you. You will wake up one morning dead!"

I don't remember what Paul Mullaney said, but I remember him shaking his head in disbelief.

Anyway, this story soon spread all over the plant. Everyone was laughing at me everywhere I went. Those still alive I think may still be laughing. I am not sure of the ones who have passed on.

Anyway, that was the last Mother's Day I ever got to buy a present for Lana. She bought a funky statue to put in the foyer of the house at a yard sale well before Mother's Day the next year. At least I thought it was funky. She told me that she bought it before I could buy her anything as she did not trust my judgment. She informed me the next year that she was not my mother and never to get her anything else for Mothers Day. She told me to buy something for my mother from now on if I wanted to buy something for someone on Mother's Day.

The twenty dozen fruit jars were stored on special shelves I had made in the garage for canned goods. Few of the jars were ever used. The shelves are still there but are filled with junk such as partially used paint cans, motor oil and half empty pesticide jars. Some of the stuff I don't even remember what I originally bought it for. My wife reminds me every year that all of this junk needs to be thrown away. I am afraid to do this though because I still might get the urge again to can something. Heaven forbid!

My next door neighbor, Harvey Atkinson, took all of the fruit jars off of my hands several years later. Most of the boxes had never been opened. He and his wife quit gardening and preserving a few years ago. He has been trying to give them back to me. He reminds me that they are clean and there about twenty dozen of them. I politely turn him down and recommend that he list them on "You Tell It, We sell It." He has not done this yet.

I don't even want to see these fruit jars. I don't intend to go there again!

Does anyone want twenty dozen clean quart fruit jars that date back to the mid '70s and have a storied history behind them?

I could also be influenced to throw in a slightly used and very large pressure cooker!

37

My Experience with Ladders

I hate ladders and always will. This is for good reason.

I have not always hated ladders. There was an old ladder built into the side of the barn on the old home place that I did not hate. It led up into the hayloft. The hayloft was full of old things. There were the old saddles and horse gear up there, an old grain cradle and briar blade, some old furniture, and miscellaneous things that people has stored up there from time to time. There was a big box of photographs and letters that Uncle Walter had left up there from World War II and the occupation afterward. I was especially intrigued by the pictures of the Dutch people in their native clothing and wearing wooden shoes. I never did understand how wooden shoes could be comfortable and imagined the sound they made when people walked around in them.

Reading those old letters was an education for a young boy in itself. I never knew that things like that happened and that grownups talked about them.

Grandma Alice and Grandpa Nathan never did and certainly not Mom and Dad. I would read them in wide-eyed wonderment!

One letter was particularly interesting. It was from Uncle Walter's wife. In it she relayed that the next door lady had come down with the crabs right after his last visit home. She informed him in no uncertain terms that she thought he had given the neighbor lady crabs. I didn't know what the crabs were. I had never heard about them. It didn't seem to have hurt Uncle Walter's health any. If joining the army meant that I would get to go to all of the places and see all of the things that he had, I was ready to go. I didn't care if it meant that I had to catch the crabs! Sign me up!

There was always a big pile of hay for a young person to jump around in. The hay loft was a fun place, especially on a rainy day. The tin roof made it very hot up there unless it was a cloudy day.

The rungs on the ladder were worn down from the countless steps of all of my ancestors. It was comforting to know that generations of my ancestors, people I had not known and would never know, had made the same trip up into the hay loft as I was doing.

My first experience with modern ladders came after we moved into our current house. The house is built on a sloping lot and the north side of the house is a lot higher up than the south side. The outside of our house is brick with painted wooden trim. The wooden trim started to mildew after two or three years and looked dirty. Lana also did not like the color and wanted it changed. I bought the tallest step ladder and a long, shaky, aluminum extension ladder that I had ever seen. I had never been up on an extension ladder. I never trusted it.

I rented a pressure washer to clean the outside of the house and Lana went to Sherwin Williams and chose a color and bought the paint. I bought the necessary brushes and buckets and started to work. I started on the south end of the house first. Everything went smoothly but I did not enjoy painting the north side of the house high up on that shaky aluminum ladder. I finished and was proud of the way the job turned out.

The house was mildewed again in two or three years and I had to repeat the process. I had to do this every three years or so afterward. The long aluminum extension ladder seemed to get shakier and shakier each time I had to paint.

After about fifteen years, I decided that enough was enough. I had the wooden trim covered with vinyl siding and the rest was trimmed in painted aluminum formed to cover where they could not put vinyl siding. I thought the painting chore was over and hung my ladders up on the fence behind the storage shed. I was glad to retire that shaky aluminum extension ladder.

Things went well for another ten years or so. No painting was needed. The new aluminum gutters leaked a little here and there but I was able to stop most of this without having to get out the shaky ladder. I did notice that the gutters were pulling away from the side of the house but I was able to pull them back in place and secure them with a gutter nail or two.

I did not realize that we had simply covered up a structural flaw with the vinyl siding. The shingles did not overlap over the edges enough and there was no flashing on the edges of the roof decking. This allowed rain to run back up under the roof and onto the soffit and fascia. This kept the wood soaked since there was not enough ventilation because of the vinyl siding to let everything dry out. The wood was rotting and I did not know it.

This problem was brought to light when a portion of trim covered with the formed painted aluminum fell on the front porch. I had a contractor come out to repair this which he did. He told me that I had a bigger problem. A lot of the fascia and other trim was rotted and needed replacing. He could not even give me a quote until he got into the job to see just how much needed to be replaced. Anyway, he did not have time to do the job right then and would get back with me when he did have time.

I decided not to wait. I started taking down the gutters and the formed aluminum trim on front, carefully so that I could reuse the aluminum trim. I also had to take down the vinyl siding covering the soffit. It was a mess underneath.

All of the fascia boards (the boards of front where the gutters are attached) were rotted and had to be replaced. The soffit (the underneath of the overhang) was rotted and fell onto the ground when the vinyl trim was removed.

I started taking the trim off all around the house with the same results. All of the fascia boards were rotted and the soffit fell.

I broke out the ladders and went to work. I did not have to replace the soffit because the vinyl trim was not attached to it. It was part of the problem anyway because it did not have enough vents in it to provide for proper ventilation. The fascia boards were standard size 1x6 and I used pressure treated lumber where needed.

229

I contracted with someone to replace the roof with painted steel roofing with ridge ventilation, more overhang and new gutters when I was finished. This person originally did not want to replace the fascia boards. I was to put back the vinyl trim.

I started with the back of the house. Everything went smoothly. Too smoothly. Another variable was introduced at this time.

I fell out on my patio one Saturday afternoon and put a big gash in my head. A trip to the emergency room! They found my blood pressure was high. My original doctor, Louis Letson, had retired years before so I had to get a new one. They also decided I was diabetic as well and put me on both blood pressure and sugar medication.

I did not adjust to these medicines easily. I would get a dizzy spell without any warning. This is bothersome, especially when one is on top of a ladder. This is when they always seemed to want to strike.

I took one tumble off the top of a ladder. Nothing broke so I climbed back up. Another tumble and nothing broke again either, but I called it a day.

I had finished about half of the front but things slowed down. If I got the faintest hint of dizziness, I would not climb up the ladder.

I finally finished the back, south side, front and about half of the north side. I was on the long shaky aluminum ladder when a dizzy spell got me and I tumbled off again for the third time. I hurt myself this time and quit. I said to heck with this. I had nasty bruises for two weeks.

The roofing and gutter contractor finally came over and finished what was left on the north side so that he could finish what I had contracted him to do.

I paid him when he had finished and insisted that he take all of my ladders with him as a gift. I told him I was through with ladders for good and did not even want one on the place to tempt me. He was happy to get my ladders and left smiling. I don't know if it was because of my gift of about two hundred dollars worth of ladders or the spectacle he could imagine that I had made when falling off of the ladders.

We were both happy the job was done! Tin roof and all.

Lana is from Indiana. She insists that only rednecks live in a house with a tin roof. They put tin roofs on their barns in Indiana but not their houses! I won't rise to this one. I just agree with her. Many houses in our neighborhood now have painted steel "tin" roofs!

Storage Shed Roof Starts Leaking

The storage shed roof started leaking a few years after all of this happened. I called my roofing guy to have a matching painted steel roof put on it. He measured it and promised to do the job in a few weeks. A month came and went. Then two. Still no roofing guy!

I bought a new long step ladder and another extension ladder. They were made of fiber glass this time and that is a little more rigid than aluminum.

I bought several gallons of roof sealer and hired my grandson to put it on. He was light enough to not harm the roof on the shed and I held the ladder for him.

This repair lasted until recently but the roof is leaking again. I have given the extension ladder to my son in law but still have the step ladder.

I have had two roofing contractors come out to measure and give me quotes which I accepted. There is still not a new roof on the storage shed. It looks like I will have to put the sealer on myself this time.

What the heck. The roof only leaks when it rains. It has not rained much in the past few years.

I may be forced to buy another extension ladder and do this job myself. But again, I may just put a bucket under the leak like Grandmother Alice and Grandpa Nathan did at the old log house!

Roofing Man

My leaky storage shed roof is finally replaced. It is now weatherproof and watertight after over three years of failed attempts at having it repaired. It is slightly swaybacked however. So much so that it looks as if I could put a saddle on it and ride off into the sunset. Especially after a few beers!

This is a June of 2009 happening:

We had an intense storm called a gravity wave that did a vast amount of damage both to trees and roofs in Jackson County over the Easter weekend in April. It is almost impossible to get any roofer to schedule immediate repairs to roofs or even to replace them in our area right now.

There was a roofer in early June doing a metal roof replacement across the street from where I live. He had about completed the job by Wednesday of that week so I stopped over to see if he would give me a quote on my storage shed. All he could do was say no or so I thought. As it turned out he had a big job set to start on Monday of the next week and he had the balance of the week to do a small job like my storage shed roof. He would work through the weekend to complete the job if he had to. I was surprised when he said yes!

I will simply call him the Roofing Man and not mention his name.

The Roofing Man had come down from Tennessee to our area to do roofing work some time before the April storm. He was working alone and had no helpers as it turned out. He had initially brought his wife and six children with him and they were living in motel rooms. He had been working around the Chattanooga, Tennessee area and they were living there but for some reason he had migrated on down to our area.

If there ever was a man who was walking around with a dark cloud over his head, it was the Roofing Man. If anything bad ever happened to anyone, it seemed like the Roofing Man received a double dose. I didn't know any of this before he started my job but I soon learned.

The Roofing Man came over and gave me a quote that Wednesday afternoon. If I would buy all of the materials and would pay him in cash, he would do my job for four hundred dollars. I had seen that he did good work from the house he had done across the street. We made the deal and he would start the job sometime on Thursday when he completed his job across the street. This seemed reasonable to me so we struck a deal and shook hands on it. He had his fourteen year old daughter as a helper that day.

He did not get an early start across the street on Thursday and finished up in mid afternoon. He promised he would be over to my house early on Friday to start my job and gave me a list of materials to buy. I arranged for my grandson Blake Hancock to be his helper for two days. All was set--or so I thought. I withdrew the required money from the bank. The Roofing Man took his daughter swimming that afternoon instead of starting my job. He also moved to a nicer but much more expensive motel; it had a pool for his daughter. It was becoming evident that his plans were changing on a daily basis.

Blake showed up at the appointed time on Friday but no Roofing Man. I didn't know if he was coming or not but he finally called and said he was at the dump and would be over as soon as he had finished there. Blake immediately set to removing the sheet metal screws that held the metal roof in place. We waited until the Roofing Man showed up to start removing the sheet metal roofing. Blake had all of the sheet metal screws removed by then and only had to remove a few so that the roofing would slide right off. The Roofing Man made his appearance about 11:00 AM.

Blake took a break for his grandmother to fix him something to eat and the Roofing Man and I went to buy the materials. We got everything loaded and home and most of it unloaded. The Roofing Man received a call from his daughter about that time. She was getting bored at the motel room and wanted him to come and get her something to eat. I wanted to keep the Roofing Man on the job as long as I could and did not know if he would return after taking a break. I volunteered to go pick her up and bring her over to the house and get them both something to eat at Burger King. The Roofing Man agreed and off I went as he prepared to get started. He and Blake were removing the last of the sheet metal screws as I left. I still didn't know what his family situation was but it was becoming evident that something was wrong. Blake had to go home by then to clean up and report to his normal summer job.

Daughter and food arrived back home and the Roofing Man took a break to cool off and eat. We then got started in earnest.

We first carefully removed all of the painted metal trim all around the storage shed. We had to reuse most of it. We then removed the metal roofing from the shed. It slid off in pieces and we piled it up some distance away from where we were working for a neighbor to haul away. This neighbor collects scrap aluminum wherever he can find it for his son to do something with. It was then inspection time to determine what we had to do before the decking went on. There was more damage than we anticipated but the roof had been leaking for over three years. A good number of rafters had rotted and would have to be replaced as well as other structural members that we found as we progressed.

Back to the lumber yard for more supplies. One of several trips required.

The Roofing Man prepaid for minutes on his cell phone. He received several calls that did not come through that Friday as he was out of minutes. He said it was his wife in Tennessee. It seemed to upset him every time that he received them, but he soon recovered. I still did not know the story.

I did not want anybody to get dehydrated working on my roof. This was the first hot spell that we had in 2009 and none of us were used to the hot humid weather that we had to work in. I kept my refrigerator in the garage well stocked with whatever anybody wanted to drink. Many trips to replenish my stock of drinks were required during this job. Over breaks to cool off and drink something, the Roofing Man began to tell me his story.

Sometime during the roofing job across the street his wife had a relative come from Tennessee and take her and five of his six children back there. She only left the fourteen year old girl. He was trying to work and take care of her at the same time. It seems that the wife has no sooner gotten back to Tennessee than she started calling wanting him to come and pick her and the children up and bring them back. He had told her that she had someone take her to Tennessee and he had to work. She could find her own way back if she wanted to come back. He did not really want it this way from the reaction to her calls that he could not answer.

Anyway we did not get much accomplished that Friday. We had only removed the roof and identified what had to be done. We decided that we would get started as early on Saturday as we could. My granddaughter, Shelby Hancock, agreed to come over Saturday to be with the daughter. Shelby was two years older than the daughter but they got along well. Blake had other plans that interfered with his working that day.

Storage shed repairs in progress Saturday

The Roofing Man had bought minutes for his cell phone overnight and did talk with his wife several times on Saturday. I had never seen a man hammering away with a cell phone cocked on his shoulder holding a conversation at the same time and never missing a beat with either. I didn't even know it could be done until then.

It soon became evident on Saturday that the Roofing Man only had a few tools to work with. He told me the story of several people attacking him in Chattanooga and stealing all of his money and most of his tools. One of his attackers had a sword and cut him badly enough that he required emergency room treatment. Up went his shirt and he showed me the scars. Other tools he had lost at the dump on Thursday. Fortunately I had more than what was needed and let him borrow them. I had enough tools to do the job but I lacked the experience and was also too old to climb on top of the roof. I did keep close watch over my tools and accounted for them each night.

It soon also became evident that the Roofing Man may be a good roofer but he lacked experience as a carpenter. It took him a long time to figure out exactly how to proceed with the reconstruction before we could start with the decking and roofing. He did get the job done tough.

All the help he required from me was to hand him material and tools as he needed them. He remained on top of the roof as much as he could. I had brought some lawn chairs out to the shade of a large Foster holly tree near the shed early on. I would move the chairs from the West side to the East side in the afternoon.

The Roofing Man was very talkative on Sunday. He would take any opportunity that he could to tell me stories, mostly about his family situation and what led up to it. He said that he hoped that I didn't mind his chatter because it was like therapy for him. He also told me that he normally drove nails with a hatchet because it was more balanced than a hammer. He said that he had lost his hatchet. I could just imagine a disturbed roofing man driving nails with a hatchet while talking on his cell phone. I did not ask him if he had lost his hatchet in the head of a previous employer. He might have thought that would have been therapy also. I had a hatchet in my tool cabinet but I did not let him borrow it or tell him about it. I quietly moved my observation post from the Foster holly tree to the patio. I didn't think he could throw a hammer at me with any accuracy at that distance!

I should have remained by the Foster holly I now realize. The poor tortured soul was simply trying to talk his way through his family situation toward a solution. I wasn't much help to him and I don't know if I could have been.

By mid afternoon the last of the rotted wood had been replaced and the decking was ready to be put up. Neither the Roofing Man nor I, with our sun baked brains and addled and tortured states of mind, thought to run a chalk line across the replaced rafters to see if they were all level. We could have then shimmed up any rafter that was lower than the others. We just started putting up the decking without doing this. The swayback portion of the roof resulted but did not become evident until the shingles were in place.

Most of the reconstruction was finished on Sunday. The majority of the decking, all of the tar paper felt as roofers call it and several shingles were in place by the end of Sunday. The storage shed was blacked in and would not leak if it did rain. The Roofing Man would not be here on

Monday as he had business that he had to take care of in Chattanooga that day. No work was scheduled for Monday. It was apparent to me by then that the Roofing Man was desperately struggling to deal with a family problem that he did not know how to cope with on his own. He was about to the end of his wits. I expected him to bring his family back with him on Monday but for some reason he did not.

I had discussed with the Roofing Man on Sunday that my covered patio had leaked in certain spots ever since it was installed and the contractor had never been able to solve this problem. He inspected it and described some special flashing he could get in Chattanooga that should solve this problem. I told him to buy it for me on Monday if at all possible.

The Roofing Man returned on Tuesday with the special flashing for the patio and immediately started to work putting on shingles. Most of the shingles were in place Tuesday afternoon. The Roofing Man worked until dark.

I thought that we could finish the job in about 2 hours on Wednesday but it took much longer than that. We were finished about noon. The painted aluminum trim took a long time to put back on correctly. The woman whose roof the Roofing Man had supposed to start on Monday was putting a lot of pressure on him to get started. The Roofing Man was getting ants in his pants to get on his next job before all of the trim was back in place but he kept on until everything was completed. I gave the Roofing Man an extra hundred dollars for the job as there was much more reconstruction required on my storage shed than either of us thought would be required before we started. I also gave him two pairs of saw horses that I intended to throw away anyway. He did not have any and I did not need them.

The Roofing Man was on his way to his new job at a house on the other side of our subdivision and we were both extremely happy that this weekend job that ended up taking almost an entire week was finished.

But this is not the end of the story.

The Roofing Man did not have time to put up the special flashing on my patio cover and there was not enough room on his truck for him to carry all of his tools to the next job with him. He had his air compressor with him on the back of the truck on Wednesday and it took up a lot of room. We had been using my air compressor up until then to run the Roofing Man's compressed air roofing nail gun. He left a large plastic tool chest at my house for a few days until he could pick it up. He would then put up the special flashing, take the trash from my construction job to the dump and pick up the tools he left over here.

Things did not work out as planned.

I kept track of his progress because I wanted him to pick up his tools and complete my job.

The Roofing Man reported to his new job and still did not have a helper. He managed to carry all of the shingles up a ladder to the roof. This was a lot of shingles as it was a fairly large split level house. All he had to do was nail the new shingles over the existing ones. But he could not get his air compressor started. He worked all of the balance of Wednesday trying to get it started.

The woman fired him on Thursday and got someone else to finish the job.

I did not hear from the Roofing Man for about two weeks. I put the trash out to the end of my driveway and the garbage people picked it up during one of their normal runs. I called and left the Roofing Man a message that I still needed the flashing put up.

He returned my call from the Chattanooga, Tennessee area.

He had gone back to Chattanooga after being fired from the job I described and was robbed again and all of what few tools that the poor man still had were stolen. About all he had left were his air compressor that did not start, air powered roofing nail gun, a skill saw and an electric drill. All of the other tools that he had left were in the tool box at my house. He was staying with a relative who was letting him use his phone to try to line up work. He only had enough gas to get down here but not enough to get back to Chattanooga.

The Roofing Man said that he took a tire iron to one of his robbers and did some damage. The cops were called and the Roofing Man was arrested and had to face a judge.

The Roofing man said there were warrants out for all three robbers, two men and a woman, but the policemen did not know it at the time. One of the men had fled before the policemen arrived and the woman and injured man swore that the Roofing Man had started the ruckus. They did not show up for the trial so the charges against the Roofing Man were dropped. He still lost his tools.

I told the Roofing Man that I would give him one hundred dollars to come down and finish my job and pick up his tools. This was not much but it was all that I could do and perhaps it would help him get a new start.

He came down after his trial was over and brought a helper with him this time and finished the job. I paid him and he picked up his tools. I wished him well and sent him on his way.

Finished storage shed swayback and all. The Shingles have since lay
down flat and the job looks much better

236

After all of this confusion, aggravation and learning there is someone with more problems than me was over I was able to finish the job for a little less than the last guy quoted me. And this guy never showed up for such a small job even after I had agreed with his quote.

The storage shed is weather tight and leak proof finally. I think the job looks nice, swayback and all. It will serve as a constant reminder of this experience for as long as I am still around.

Lana asked me the other day what I thought the Roofing Man was doing now. I told her I didn't know but I hoped he was doing better than when we knew him. His stories made an impression on both of us.

But he was just a poor unfortunate man trying to deal with the harshness his life confronted him with and trying to do the best that he could to cope with it all. I sure hope that the dark cloud is not still riding over his head and that he is happy no matter where he is!

38

My Two Careers as a Lumberjack

Or was it three? I lost count somewhere along the way!

There were two large trees and one small one in the front yard when we moved in. There was a large red oak, a good-sized scaly bark hickory, and a small elm.

They must have moved dirt too close to the trees when they built the house because the oak and hickory died shortly after we moved in. The power board came and cut them down and up into sizes small enough to split for firewood. A fellow who worked with me, Ike Roberts, and his dad came over and split them up and hauled them away. Ike's dad burned wood in his fireplace. This probably doesn't count as a lumberjacking career.

My next experience with trees came after I had planted six apple trees in the backyard. They were supposed to be dwarf trees but they really grew. Soon they were taking over the backyard. I bought a chain saw and got a neighbor boy to come over and help me cut them down and remove the stumps. This took a lot of time but went smoothly. This was a large enough project to count as a lumberjack career since it involved cutting down trees and buying a saw.

Two elm trees came up by the fence after I cut the apple trees down. They grew fast and were soon large trees. I was busy gardening and didn't have time to cut them down while they were small, or didn't take the time. They had soon grown so large that they were touching the fence. They both died one winter. I suspected Dutch Elm disease.

I sat on the patio and looked at the dead trees all spring. I decided that I could cut them down. I had not been able to find anybody that cuts trees for a living that could work them in right away. This was also an expensive proposition, I thought, and decided to do the job myself.

As I normally do, I had planned everything down to the smallest detail.

I pulled my truck into the backyard and backed it up to the most northern tree. I climbed as high up in the tree as I could, using my shaky aluminum extension ladder, and tied a rope around it. I tied the other end to the trailer hitch on my truck and pulled forward to put as much pressure as I could on the tree in the direction that I intended for it to fall. So far, so good. Everything was going as per the plan. The neighbor boy who had helped me take out the apple trees arrived to watch.

I checked everything out. The wind was calm, the rope was taunt and the tree was bending slightly in the direction that I wanted it to fall.

I had to cut the tree above the fence since it had to start growing into it. I notched it in the direction that I wanted it to fall and checked everything out again. I pulled the truck forward a little more to try to put more tension in the rope.

It was just me and the neighbor boy out in the backyard. Nobody else seemed to be paying attention.

I fired the saw up again and started to make my cut. I stopped a couple of times to be sure that things were going according to the plan. I then started to cut deeper and the tree made a cracking noise and started to fall in the direction that I intended. We then had a big gust of wind just at the wrong time. Instead of falling where I had planned, the wind was blowing it toward me!

Needless to say, I dropped the saw and started running. The neighbor boy backed up. I tripped and fell!

I then crawled on my hand and knees as fast as I could. Don't believe it if anyone ever tells you that a fat man can't move fast.

I didn't quite make it. The tree top came crashing down right behind me and the uppermost limbs gave me a good whack across the back.

The saw had been revved up when I dropped it and was still revved up. It was running along the ground like a puppy dog straight for me.

The neighbor boy calmly walked up to the saw and turned the switch off.

Neighbors from all around ran out into their backyards to see if I was alright. Bob Stubblefield, who lives on the other side of the fence where the tree was growing, actually jumped over it and was in my backyard by the time I had crawled out. Other neighbors were standing by the fence and looking at me bug eyed and with their mouths open.

I was alright, though a bit shaken. I brushed myself off and thanked everyone for their concern. I then slunk off to the house. I left everything in place. Tree, saw, rope, truck and all. I didn't want to see any more of that tree that day.

I later cleaned everything up and hauled the tree to the ditch.

I decided at that point to wait on the professional to take out the other tree and pay him anything he wanted!

My third lumberjack career had a similar theme and ending.

I planted a Bradford Pear tree on the north side of the house in a low spot in the yard. It grew quickly and made a beautiful tree. It had beautiful blooms on it in the spring and nicely colored foliage in the fall. It got quite large, but not as large as the ill fated elm tree. We thoroughly enjoyed the Bradford Pear tree for several years.

This came to an end one spring night when the wind from a thunderstorm blew half of the top out of it. Fortunately it did not fall on anything.

I cut out what I could but the tree was now malformed. I decided to take the entire tree out because it would never be pretty again.

Again, I called the professionals. They would not touch it due to the weather. They said that the wind gusts were too high.

Later one Saturday morning, I decided that the wind was calm enough for me to tackle the pear tree.

I used a similar strategy as I did on the elm tree except I would have to take it down from the top since it was located in a bad position and would likely fall on something.

So, I got my truck and rope out and climbed the pear tree with my shaky aluminum extension ladder. I tied the rope as high up as I could and pulled the truck forward to put tension on the rope, like before.

I then fired up my chainsaw and started the cut as high up in the tree as I would trust my ladder.

Again, a sudden gust of wind. It did not cause the problems that it did with the elm tree. It only blew the top back and pinched my chainsaw. It would not cut and I could not get the saw out. It was wedged in too tight.

Time to make a new plan.

I had to go buy a new chainsaw to cut my old one out of the tree!

Well, I got the new saw up in the tree and made my cut lower in the tree than my first attempt. I was determined this tree was going down. Nothing was going to get in my way!

The sawing went smoothly this time with one exception. The top did not fall exactly where I had planned.

It sort of wobbled around a bit before it fell. It wiped out my gutter on the North side of the house and then fell and bent the top rail of the fence. Mrs. Atkinson was out by her garage door putting some garbage into her garbage can and saw what was happening and beat a hasty retreat into her garage. She thought the tree top was going to fall on her, and it may well have. It almost hit my truck on the way down.

Nothing seriously was injured except my pride and I quickly recovered.

I had people come out and repair all of the damages. It would have been much less expensive for me to have waited on the seasoned lumberjack!

I decided then and there that my days as a lumberjack were over. This was largely at Lana's insistence.

I took all of the gas out of my chainsaws and put them into the garage. I gave the old one away because I got tired of it being in my way all of the time. I gave the new one to my son-in-law when he needed something to saw up a tree that the wind had blown down in his yard.

I now have just a bow saw. This is all that I had when I started on my lumberjack careers. It is enough for small jobs around the house, such as pruning and cutting down small stuff. I shouldn't be able to get into too much trouble with this saw!

I am now officially retired as a lumberjack.

39

The Oil Tanker

Norman Grede

This story took place in the mid 1970s. While I remember most of the story vividly because it included me in a most awkward situation, I will have to rely on the memory of a friend, Norman Grede, to help me remember some of the details. Norman was the plant Safety Manager at the time this episode took place and was an observer. I was the most active participant and may not remember all of the pertinent details. What I am trying to say is that I have probably blotted some of the pertinent details out of my memory since I was pretty embarrassed by this incident. It is only funny to me in retrospect. The foolish things one will become involved with in youth!

I was plant Laboratory Supervisor at the time. We worked at the Revere Copper and Brass Company's aluminum rolling plant in Scottsboro, Alabama. I was responsible for monitoring all of the rolling coolants at the plant at the time.

What is a rolling coolant? These are fluids that provide for cooling the steel rolls used in the rolling process.

I will try to give a brief layman's description of the process. I know that very few people have ever seen an operation like this and probably never will have the opportunity to. A good bit of metal rolling has been moved overseas to places like China. Basically, the rolling operation is

242

similar to a wringer on an old type clothes washing machine. A steel, aluminum, or some other metal strip is passed through the "wringer" instead of clothes. Pressure is put on the wringer to make the metal thinner each time it is put through the process. This generates a tremendous amount of heat due to friction and other factors that turn the energy from the electric motors that drive the "wringer" into the work of making the metal strip thinner. The function of the rolling coolant is to remove this heat as well as to provide the required amount of lubrication needed to keep the metal being made thinner from welding to the steel rolls used as the "wringer."

This story is about trying to reclaim the rolling coolants used on the cold mills. This is where the strip is passed through the mill at room temperature. A mixture of something like kerosene is used to remove the heat that has been mixed with a waxy material to keep the aluminum strip from welding to the steel "wringer" rolls.

It was thought at the time that water was a thing to avoid letting build up in the cold rolling coolants. This was to avoid a white defect on the aluminum that is called water stains. These cause all kinds of problems in later trying to do anything with the finished product from the cold rolling operation. Remember this was in the mid 1970s. It is now in the early 2000s. Some people now directly inject a controlled amount of water into the coolants in the cold rolling operation to improve cooling and to get thinner aluminum strips from the same amount of electricity used to turn the "wringer" rolls.

Water could contaminate these coolant systems from roof leaks, fire sprinkler discharges or any number of other ways. We constantly tried to keep our guard up and keep the water out.

Well, we had a large amount of water contaminating one of our large kerosene based coolant systems. Times were tough and we were trying to save as much money as we could. It was an expensive proposition to discard 25,000 gallons if the kerosene based coolant and make up with new materials. Kerosene costs about thirty cents a gallon back then. We discarded our used coolant by selling it to a waste oil dealer in Birmingham and thought we were lucky to get ten cents per gallon for it. Never mind that he would sometimes just send in a trucking firm that he had sold our waste coolants to as diesel fuel. The bills of lading were clearly marked as "diesel fuel" when he sent the trucks to pick it up our waste coolant.

I decided to try to put the spent coolant into 5,000 gallon tanker trailers. We did not have any such tankers but got Decatur Chemical Haulers to send in the desired number of them. These tankers had about five individual compartments in each tanker. They were spotted at our plant. We had an old beat up truck to move them around.

Each individual tank had a cone shaped bottom. Everyone knows that oil and water don't mix. Water is heavier than oil, right, and will settle to the bottom of a tank. In this case, this was the cone shaped section of the bottom. We would simply pump the spent coolant into the tanker on Saturday, allow it to sit and settle until Monday, and then simply draw the water off of the bottom and discard it.

At least this was the plan. I have always tried to make plans for everything starting at an early age. When I was in college, I had to work a forty hour or more workweek while taking all of the college courses I could. I had to take a minimum of twelve semester hours in college to keep a draft deferment. This is what I always did. Remember Vietnam was heating up back then and they were drafting everybody with a warm body!

To state it simply, I was either in class, studying, working or trying to catch a few winks of sleep. To complicate matters, I worked what was called a "grasshopper" shift. I worked the four to twelve shift of Monday and Tuesday. I was off on Wednesday and Thursday and the twelve to eight shift on Friday and Saturday, and the day shift on Sunday. This was not a bad shift once I became numb! I had to plan my time closely to accomplish all of this. There was no room for any deviation. I could not even date except occasionally for a few hours on Saturday night and during the summer if I did not attend summer school.

Well, I thought that I had this tanker business planned down to the smallest detail.

Wrong.

Norman Grede was working on something else that Saturday when this episode unfolded. He saw all of the oil tankers parked out front and asked me what was going on. I explained to him what we were trying to do and he wanted to stay and watch it.

At the appointed time, we pulled the first tanker into place and started hooking up the hose to load it up. The tractor had been removed from the tanker and the front end was only supported by the small "dolly" wheels in front that are part of every eighteen wheeler trailer.

I climbed the ladder on the back of the tanker and open all of the hatches to the individual tank compartments. It was my plan to stay on top to tell Buddy Hastings, the fellow who was doing all of the work, when the tank was full so he could stop pumping into that tank and move to another one. Buddy was filling the truck from the valves on the bottom of the cone shaped section.

So far, so good.

My plan did not include one very important part that soon became evident. We had not decided which tank to fill first.

Buddy hooked everything up to the front tank and started filling it. I thought it was nice when a plan started to come together, and it did for awhile. I was watching the tank level, Buddy was standing by the switch to turn off the pump and Norman was standing by to be sure everything went safely.

I suddenly started to get an uneasy feeling when the tank got about two-thirds full. This was probably because the back wheels started bouncing up and down. I hollered for Buddy to shut off the oil flow, but it was too late. The front of the tanker hit the pavement with a dull thud. The back wheels were up in the air for what seemed like a height of twenty or more feet. I had moved to the back of the tanker at that point to see what was wrong with the back wheels.

The tanker was balanced on the dolly wheels, nose to the ground and tail high in the air.

The dolly wheels dug into the pavement.

It has long been my method to make a plan and work it. If it became evident that there was something wrong with the plan, make a new one and work it. We had to make a new plan quickly to get me off of the top of the tanker before one of the dolly wheels collapsed and sent the tanker falling onto its side.

Buddy and Norman were shouting for me to jump. This did not seem like a good option to me, perched high on top of the tanker.

Buddy then went to get a fork lift and tried to get me to climb onto the forks. The forks were greasy and there was nothing to hold on to. Scratch option two!

We finally realized that the tanker was perched like a giant see-saw. Perhaps it would settle back down if we just filled up the back tank.

Buddy hooked everything up to the back tank. I climb back up to the back tank to watch the level. Norman was standing at a safe distance with a worried look on his face. We started pumping. The tanker started to settle back down ever so slowly. Man, it is still nice when a plan starts to come together, or so I thought for a brief moment. We had overlooked another very important thing.

The tanker settled back down to the pavement with a shuddering jolt. There I was with my head over the back tank watching closely. When the tanker hit bottom on the pavement, a huge cascade of spent coolant came gushing toward me. Shocked and in disbelief, I was standing there wet clear past my underwear! I must have looked like a drowned rat.

I climbed back down the back ladder and tried to shake the oil off, sort of like a wet dog shakes off water! Norman, or was it Buddy, gave me a shop rag to wipe my eyes out with. I was becoming more embarrassed by the minute.

I staggered toward my car to go home, take a shower and clean up. The only instructions I remember giving Buddy as I left was to be sure to fill the back tank first on the rest of them.

40

Lana, The Grubbing Hoe, Japanese Quince and Me!

I won't say which tactics and strategy that Lana uses to motivate me. I will just say that they are most effective!

I didn't even know what tactics and strategy were until our company got rid of a bunch of people in the lab that developed new products. They used the money they saved to teach all of the sales force how to sell. It didn't matter if we didn't have anything to sell, we knew how to do it with tactics and strategy. My sales took a nose dive and never recovered! Our customers were not interested in buying tactics and strategy.

Enough of that.

Lana convinced me to take out two bushes and trim out the dead wood in another. I expected one of them to give me trouble, one to be a piece of cake and one to require a medium amount of energy. As normal, I got it all backwards!

I started taking out the Japanese Quince that I thought was a piece of cake. I just had to cut it down to ground level with my loppers so that I could mow over the top of it. Wrong! I couldn't trim it close enough. I then decided to dig it up and got my grubbing hoe out of the storage shed. You have to see this grubbing hoe to understand how formidable it looks. It is no ordinary grubbing hoe! I had a normal one that I used to try to dig out another bush years ago and broke the handle out of it. This gave me an excuse to take a two week break and drink beer while I decided what to do next. I ended up going to the Jackson County Farmers Co-op and buying one. It was over twice as big as the old one but didn't have a handle in it. Not to worry, they had a handle that would almost fit it even though it a little too big. It was big enough that I could have used it to addle an ox or anything else that I could hit on the head with it! The handle is big enough around to use as an axle for a wagon wheel! The whole thing, grubbing hoe handle and all, weighs five or six pounds! I hired my grandson to take out the original bush and never used the impressive grubbing hoe. It intimidated me!

Well, I started hitting the bush base with this grubbing hoe and it bounced back! That was not right I didn't think and tried to decide what was wrong. I hit it with a vengeance for about five minutes and had to take a fifteen minute break to catch my breath. I did this for about an hour with plenty of breaks and two diet Mountain Dews. It took me a little time, but I realized that that it had sent down a tap root almost all of the way to Japan. It was trying to go home! It had thirty-five years to do so as that was how long it had been planted! It was a maze of tangled roots underground and was tough digging.

I decided pretty quickly that neither I nor the grubbing hoe was any threat to this bush! It was in no danger of being dug up! It didn't seem a bit worried and just sat there unmoving! It is frustrating to have to admit to being defeated by a puny bush! I then did the other chores thinking about the Japanese Quince all of the time. The bush I thought would be a problem was a piece of cake. I didn't have any problems with trimming out the dead wood in the other bush.

I then had to re-think my strategy and tactics for the Japanese Quince. It is hard to realize when you are up to your butt in alligators that your original intent was to just drain the swamp.

I realized that all I really wanted to do was to get it down to where I could mow over the top of it without puncturing a tire or ruining a lawnmower blade. I didn't have to dig it completely up after all!

A grubbing hoe has two cutting blades. It has a flat blade in front to dig with and a small blade in back that is perpendicular to the handle for using like an axe, sort of. I had already dug down about six to eight inches and decided to just chop the top out.

Easier said than done!

I started at one edge of it and fussed and cussed between blowing breaks and diet Mountain Dews. I made slow but steady progress. When I finished, I picked up wood chips out of the grass twelve feet away!

It took me two more hours and I was wringing wet with sweat when I finished. I got it all out four to six inches below the ground. I put a generous handful of high nitrogen fertilizer all over it to rot the rest out and covered it back up.

I was feeling pretty good and wiping the sweat out of my eyes in celebration!

Lana came out then, looked everything over, and asked-- "What Have You Been Doing All Day?"

Some days you can't win for losing!

God bless women. None of us would be here without them! Love them, cherish them, be good to them and give them all the love that you can! Even take out a Japanese Quince for them occasionally!

<u>*41*</u>

Rotten Window Sill and Other Home Repairs

I try to find a little humor in everything that I do. It is hard to find humor in home repairs. This is especially true in small towns across America such as the one that I live in.

Lana and I have lived in this house for almost thirty-five years and things are starting to need attention. Some things need a lot of attention.

The glazing on all of the windows was getting into a sad state. It was cracking, peeling and outright falling out in areas. I thought it needed to be repaired.

Lana did not have to motivate me on this one. I did this all on my own!

When will I ever learn to leave well enough alone? Never, I guess.

I started trying to address the problem over six months ago during a plumbing repair. What does plumbing have to do with window repair? Read on.

A local plumber came over years ago and fixed something that I had screwed up big time and got me out of my dilemma one Mother's Day at my daughter's house no less. She insisted that I had to do all of her plumbing work before this but will hardly let me in the house since. This is another story. It is funny to me but not to her! Big time mess in the middle of the night! One half of the house flooded! Where was the water cut-off valve? No one knew!

I made a vow with this plumber to retire my plumbing tools as long as he would never compete with me in selling the products that I sold. He and I made a pact that he had the right to do all of my plumbing work. He said that this was a safe bet for both of us since he had never heard of the products that I was selling!

This worked until a little over six months ago. There are subdivisions springing up in our little town like Johnson grass. They are going up everywhere. I don't know who will buy these new houses but this does not seem to slow anything down . They are on a building frenzy! Build them and they will come seems to be the motto! My plumber got caught up in all of this. He had a contract to do the plumbing work on a number of new houses and didn't have time for small jobs like mine. These small jobs were what kept food on his table before this.

So, I un-retired my plumbing tools six or seven months ago. The icemaker in the refrigerator would not work anymore. Lana insisted that it be fixed. I took pipes apart to isolate the problem. It turned out to be the only galvanized fitting in the entire house. The rest of the plumbing is copper. The zinc had corroded off of the ice maker cut off valve over the years and corrosion had completely stopped it up. The problem was that it was next to the cabinet wall and I couldn't get any of my tools on the copper fitting well enough to get the galvanized valve loose without twisting the copper pipe in the wall and causing a major problem. I did this years ago in Indiana and shut all of the water off in the house for 3 days over a weekend. It was Monday late before it was repaired. My wife still brings this up when I make her mad. Three days without a bathroom leaves an impression I guess. I had outside privileges after dark so I got by!

Back to the rotten window sill. I had almost given up in frustration by late in the afternoon. I decided I need a new tool but did not know what it was. I went down to Marvin's, a local big box store, to look at tools. I found something that looked like it might work and was in the checkout line talking about my problem to the guy behind me when the guy in front of me perked up. He said that he was in the home repair business and would follow me over to look at everything.

He crawled into the cabinet, took a quick look and went out to his truck. He came back with two of the biggest channel lock pliers that I had ever seen. He slid back in and had everything taken apart in less than a minute. Man, was I impressed. He put the new brass valve that I had bought in and had everything working in about five minutes. He had water to the ice maker! I had slid in and out of that cabinet for so many hours that day that my back was already starting to get sore. It finally developed into a horrible bruised area that lasted for two weeks!

I was so happy at that point that I decided to let him look at the glazing project on my windows and give me a quote. He took a quick look and punched a few buttons on his calculator and gave me a most reasonable price. He would take down the storm windows, do the glazing, paint the windows, clean them all and put the storms back up for a price that I would not have even tackled the job myself. Needless to say, I agreed and he wrote me up a contract. **The only problem was that I had to pay him half of it up front!** This did not seem to be a big deal to me. My back was getting more sore by the minute. I wrote him a check. I was very happy at that point!

This guy came over once to take down two storm windows and try to remove the loose glazing on two windows. He only made headway on 1 of them. He tried to glaze this window with his fingers and no tools. He made a big mess! This was before the check cleared the bank! I never saw him after that!

After numerous phone calls to him, he had all kinds of excuses. His father was in the hospital dying for two months. He was in grieving for two more months and was not doing anything. He kept promising to do the job for awhile. He finally offered to pay me back my partial payment but I never received any money. This guy is a professional on preying on older people!

Or, in the spirit of charity, he quoted me on something that he did not know how to do! Anyway, I was taken advantage of. The money involved is not enough to start legal action. It would cost more than I could recover. On the bright side, everything worthwhile cost money. I got a valuable lesson on what not to do in any case. I would gladly have paid this guy the $250 to never set foot on my property again when I finally realized what a mess he had made!

So, I hired professionals. The first stage of the process was glazing the windows and was completed as promised. It cost me more money than the original "Jack Of All Trades" guy quoted but it was completed in two working days to my satisfaction. The second stage was caulking and painting everything. It took me a month to get the painting crew over but this was also completed as scheduled. This also costs me more than the guy quoted originally. I had spent 2 ½ times the original quote by now but the job was being done properly!

The third step was new storm windows. The old ones were put up when the house was new about thirty-five years ago. Some of them tried to fall apart when I took them down to clean the windows! I didn't do this very often, not often enough! I had the people that glazed the windows making the new storms. This is considerably more money. I had ended up spending about four times the original quote from the shady guy by now!

At least this was the plan. Hang on! The expenses kept snowballing!

The first lesson from all of this is to avoid cheap quotes from people you don't know, especially people who want half of the quote as a down payment!!!

The second lesson is: don't get carried away with the project.

The glazers found a rotten window sill on the north side of the house. I decided I could do this myself, no problem I thought!

Wrong!

Window sills are not standard sized lumber and I could not find anybody that sold them locally. The guy who contracted to paint the windows said that he would replace it for $150 when he had his people over doing the painting. We cut a deal. In the meantime, I started thinking about having new vinyl windows put in on the north side of the house! This opened up another area where I soon found out that big time scam artist work.

The first guy came out and gave me a quote on windows that he swore would do everything but put me to bed at night, kiss me good morning and cook my breakfast. The only problem was he wanted $1000 per window. I immediately knew something was wrong here since Home Depot had these windows for $140 apiece, but I would have had to install them myself. This was beyond my capabilities I soon decided.

I ended up having Home Depot come out and do it, rotten window sill and all. Five windows and $2300 later, the job was completed, new storms and all. A job well done! I had to celebrate a little bit.

A family member was over last Saturday and said, "Man did you get ripped off. I do this for a living. I can get better windows for $180 apiece and do the job for $300/window and make all kinds of money. I can do your whole house in a day. It takes me about twenty minutes per window."

Fortunately, I had already contracted with Home Depot. This family member had helped me replace an outside steel door on the garage last year and I have seen him work. It took him all day, he finally got the door in but it is not plumb. It leans to the outside on top.

This is another story. Anyway, I can just imagine his twenty minute window replacements.

The Home Depot guys came out and three of them spent four hours to do five windows. They did it right though and did a beautiful job.

My original $500 project ended up costing me $4000 but the job is well done. I doubt that the windows will need any major repair for another thirty-five years or at least as long as I am around.

My home improvements for this year are done and I am happy. I can spend the rest of the year dreaming up what needs to be done next year!

I will read this account again several times in the meantime and try not to get carried away next year. I may have to read it often to keep my plans in check! Maybe Lana will hit me in the head with a hammer if I get too carried away!

42

Cataract Surgery

I went directly from my window project to cataract surgery. I finished with the windows one Thursday and had cataract surgery the following Monday.

The first surgery was in my right eye. I was apparently born with a good bit of this cataract and it progressively got worse over the years. I could never remember seeing much out of this eye. I could not even see the big E on the eye chart for several years before surgery.

My eye doctor wanted me to have the surgery because the cataract was so dense that he could not see my retina. He said that he knew that I could not see out of this eye if he could not see into it! The doctor wanted to keep a watch over the condition of my retina so that he could guard against eye problems that can come with old age. The goal was never to restore sight in this eye as they did not know if they could or not. It was thought that I would gain some vision but nobody could predict how much. He just wanted to see my retina.

I had never had any operation before so I remember this surgery vividly!

This surgery is routine and normally takes ten minutes or so. This was not routine surgery for the following two reasons:

1. Since I was born with part of this cataract and had the rest of it so long, the entire thing was as hard as stone. The surgeon knew this to be the case up front though and expected it. She said that she would have fun doing this eye!

2. I had been taking a drug called Flomax. There were no problems associated with cataract surgery known when I started taking this drug. The advertising for this drug now states that "An Inoperative Floppy Iris" condition may result during cataract surgery if this drug has been taken. Whoa! What does this mean?

The surgeon described the effects that she could not dilate the eye completely if this drug had been taken. She said that it didn't matter if I had stopped taking this drug five weeks before, which I had done, or five years before the surgery. It would still cause this problem. The eye has to be completely dilated before the surgery so the surgeon can see how to do the surgery properly. She said there were precautions that she could take that would normally overcome this. She did not explain. I found out after surgery what these precautions were.

They have a device called "Iris Hooks" which they use. They make extra incisions during surgery so that they can insert these hooks into the eye and pull the iris out of the way to allow them to see how to do the surgery. I'm glad I didn't know this before surgery.

The surgery itself is really an experience. They use as little pain killer and anesthesia as possible so that there is not a lengthy recovery period before the patient can be released. This is outpatient surgery and they work patients in and out about as fast as getting a haircut! From the time they take a patient back until the time they are released can be as little as 1 ½ hours.

The first thing they do is check the patient's vital signs and start an IV with feel good juice in it to relax the patient. They then put drops and gel in the eye and instruct the patient to keep the eye closed for ten minutes. Guess what? This jell sets up and immobilizes the eye for surgery.

The patient is seated in a recliner before all of this starts and stays in the recliner until after surgery. After the patient is feeling good and glued tight, they wheel the recliner into the operating room and start them on oxygen, why I didn't know at first. They lower the recliner all the way back until the head is much lower than the rest of the body and put a paper hood over everything except the eye that they will operate on. They then tape the patient securely to the recliner, hood and all! The patient can't move their head or even get up and run out of there if they wanted to!

My surgery took about thirty minutes instead of the usual ten minutes or so. My painkiller drops were running out by the time they had finished. I told the surgeon about it but she just kept on working. I just had to clench up my fist and make the most awful ugly face under the hood imaginable. It felt like they were scraping the inside of my eye with a putty knife. Come to think of it, they may have had to do something like that to get all of the hard cataract out!

I had much more than normal swelling and pressure after the surgery than is routine because of the iris hooks and the extra difficulty they had in getting the cataract out. Normally, three types of eye drops three times per day are required for two to three weeks for everything to completely heal. At different times I had several regiments of four different kinds of eye drops for about five weeks. I had to put drops in every two hours for a good part of this time. This eye became slightly infected before everything healed up.

I had originally decided to have the cataracts from both eyes removed. I had about decided that the other eye was not nearly as bad as I originally thought before everything was over with the right eye.

Anyway, the vision in the right eye did improve. I now have more vision in this eye than I ever remember having and more than I had hoped to recover.

The bad news is that I have so much vision in this eye now that I have a bad case of double vision. My eyes had never had to work together before but now I am having to learn how to track the same thing with both eyes. This condition is almost gone.

I had surgery on the other eye recently. Everything was routine and went according to plan. The swelling was a little more than normal due to the iris hooks but has stabilized.

I can now see things out of my left eye that I don't even remember being able to see. I am sure that I could see things this clearly years ago but just don't remember it.

I guess that a cataract is sort of like a glamour photograph if it is not too dense and doesn't block out too much light. A glamour photograph is slightly out of focus and hides all of the imperfections in the haze just like a cataract.

I am now seeing like I am supposed to out of my left eye. I looked in the mirror this morning and could see just how old and ugly I really am. At least I can now see just how lovely Lana truly is!

43

Very Happy Birds

I started feeding the birds in the backyard this winter when it started getting cold and nasty. My original goal was to just help them survive the winter.

I did not intend to be a bad influence on them and introduce them to bad habits. I may have inadvertently done just this.

I started with a feeder to feed mixed seeds. It is a nice one and looks like an old time country church, steeple and all. It took the birds about two days to find it.

I then got another one to feed black oil sunflower seeds. It is also a nice one and looks like a country cottage. Birds of all sizes like black oil sunflower seeds.

I then got a large thistle seed feeder for the finches and other small birds and moved a suet feeder to the area where I was feeding the birds.

I read in a bird book that some small birds will only eat on the ground. I started sprinkling mixed seeds on the ground for them under the pine tree where I hung all of the feeders. I have lost a lot of bird food in the past years by hanging the feeders over grass. The birds would not eat food that spilled from their feeders if it fell into the grass. I do not have this problem under the pine tree as there is no grass growing under it. One kind of bird or another will eat everything that hits the ground under this pine tree.

Lana complained about the expense at first but soon quit doing this. She would sit for hours by the kitchen window and watch the birds eat. She would tell me when the feeders were empty and needed refilling.

We have counted as many as twenty male cardinals feeding at once as well as numerous finches and other small birds. We even have several mourning doves feeding there. All of the birds feed peacefully since there is something there for all different kinds of birds. There is even one woodpecker feeding with the other birds. He eats some of the smaller seeds as well as feeds on the suet.

I soon found that cracked corn was the best food to sprinkle on the ground. There are all sizes of corn pieces in it and some bird or another will eat everything. It is also relatively inexpensive and the birds just love it.

I was soon feeding the birds twenty pounds of various seeds and cracked corn a week. Then the blackbirds found the feeders. There were just a few redwing blackbirds at first. They soon brought all of their friends and the starlings. The blackbirds soon started trying to run everything else off and devour everything in the feeders. They pretty much accomplished this except for a squirrel who had developed a fondness for black oil sunflower seeds. He raided the sunflower feeder regularly.

I had to feed everything else early in the morning and late in the evening.

I soon had to start buying fifty pounds of bird food a week. I would buy 1 bag of cracked corn and a bag of either mixed seeds or black oil sunflower seeds each week.

My neighbor who lives behind me has five fairly large Bradford pear trees planted along the fence. These trees are about 150 feet from where I am feeding the birds.

The blackbirds would accumulate in these trees and watch the feeders. They would just sit quietly and stare at the feeders. The reminded me of the Alfred Hitchcock movie "The Birds" by the way they acted.

They would start to come back as soon as I put something in the feeders. I rationalized this behavior as they are God's creatures too and have to eat! I do wish they would spread their affection around to others but I think that I must be the only person in the neighborhood feeding birds regularly this year.

This went on for several weeks and I kept up my weekly trips to the Jackson County Farmer's Co-op to buy a sack of cracked corn and some other food that I was about out of.

I made my weekly trip about three weeks ago to get cracked corn and a sack of mixed seeds.

I usually unload the truck as soon as I get back home and move everything into the garage. Lana wanted me to do something else this day as soon as I returned home. I forgot the bird food in the back of the truck. It rained that night.

I did not remember my bird food still being in the back of the truck until the next morning. I went out with dread to move it into the garage.

The mixed seeds were in a heavy plastic bag and the rain had not bothered it. The paper bag of cracked corn was another story.

I gave it a gentle nudge and the top of the wet paper bag almost came off spilling a large amount of cracked corn into the truck bed. I had a leftover large cardboard box in the garage from another project. I put this box under the tailgate to where I could slide the wet bag off into it. I was able to salvage about 80% or more of the cracked corn in this way and moved it into the garage. I spread the wet cracked corn around as evenly in the box as I could to allow it to dry.

I swept as much of the cracked corn from the truck bed onto the concrete driveway as I could but I could not get all of it. Wet cracked corn does not sweep very well. I decided that the birds could get their corn ration from the driveway until they ate it all up.

Wrong. The birds would not look for the cracked corn there and kept waiting for me to feed them in the regular place. Lana swept this corn into the grass alongside the driveway in about three days.

Well back to spreading about three quarts of cracked corn under the pine tree early every morning and evening.

I spread the cracked corn around every day in the cardboard box to try to help it dry. It soon began to develop a strange, slightly sweet smell. This smell got stronger each day.

I had about two large feedings of it left that Saturday morning. I decided to feed it all to the birds at one time and let them eat it all. I took the box out and spread it all out under the tree as well as I could. It had a particularly rank odor by now! I then went to buy a new bag.

I came back and unloaded the new bag of corn and put it in the garage. I went in to see what was on TV but there was nothing particularly interesting on. It was a fairly warm sunny afternoon and I decided to go sit on the patio as I usually do on nice afternoons.

There was an unexpected commotion going on in the Bradford pear trees behind the fence. The blackbirds were sitting pretty close together and wildly flapping their wings in what seemed to me a display of very joyous behavior! They normally just sat there very still and very quiet just staring at the feeders waiting for me to put something in them.

They were also singing a loud rancorous melody that only another blackbird could enjoy!

Blackbirds have never been known for their pleasant songs.

All of this reminded me of the way everybody would behave when my Grandmother Alice made me go with her to a revival at the local country Methodist church. Everyone would get down and into the spirit after a rousing song service and the old ladies would just sit there, with sweat running down their faces using their hand fans with the funeral home advertisement on the back and some religious picture on the front, shouting "Amen" every time the preacher made a point in his sermon. This was a marvelous sight for a youngster to behold!

Well, the blackbirds in the Bradford pear trees were having a similar moment, or it seemed to an old man who had not quite figured out what had happened yet.

It all became a little clearer when I went to fill up the feeders. All the birds at the feeders normally flew away as soon as I came out of the back garage door to feed then. Not this day!

There was a small finch with some red on its head sitting on the back rim of the sunflower seed feeder. I expected it to fly away as I approached the feeder but it did not. I lifted the feeder off of the wire hook that held it in place and the finch still did not fly away. I then set the feeder down gently on the ground and the finch then fluttered away unsteadily and did not fly far. I was amazed.

I went back to the house and got some mixed seeds. There was another small finch sitting on the front lip of this feeder. I walked all of the way up to the feeder and the finch just sat there! I then lifted my finger up toward the finch. It showed no fear and just sat there looking at me. I almost touched it before it fluttered unsteadily onto the ground and just sat there. The blackbirds were still singing their bawdy songs in the Bradford pear trees and flapping their wings as if in applause.

It then dawned on me! I had some drunken birds on my hands!

A few of the blackbirds in the Bradford pear trees were sober enough to come to the feeders. The rest of them just kept up with their flapping and singing.

Remember, I did not set out to lead any birds astray.

I do not know if birds have hangovers or not. All that I do know is that there were not very many birds eating heavily the next day!

Marijuana Plants

I went to the Limrock Nursery yesterday to buy some cabbage, broccoli, cauliflower and collard plants for my fall garden. I immediately saw some beautiful soft stemmed hibiscus plants as I pulled up into the parking lot. I have been looking for such plants for many years. They will survive our winters and come back each year.

I bought my garden plants and discussed the hibiscus plants with the owner. He has some lobed leaf hibiscus with dinner plate sized blooms. I bought 2 of these plants.

He also had a different kind of hibiscus with feathery leaves. He said they looked like marijuana but were hibiscus plants. He showed me some that were blooming and they had beautiful large red flowers. I bought two of them.

We loaded all of the plants in the back of my truck and I drove back to Scottsboro at 30 MPH so as not to tear up the hibiscus plants.

My wife, Lana, is from Indiana. The government introduced American hemp to Indiana sometime around one of the World Wars to make rope from. These plants now grow wild and are in all of the ditches along the roadways. They are of such low grade that the government drug enforcement people just ignore them.

I got back and unloaded the plants by the covered patio in back of the house. Lana wanted to know why I had brought home some marijuana plants. I explained to her that they were hibiscus plants and not marijuana. She would have none of this. She looked up hibiscus plants in our garden book and showed me that there were none listed in the book that looked like marijuana and none by the name of "Texas Red." The plants that I bought have no blooms yet, only flower buds forming.

I decided to try to have some fun with these plants.

My next door neighbor, Harvey Atkinson, loves tomatoes and wants a lot of the extra ones that I might have from my garden. He was coming over today to get some tomatoes and I expected him to clean my ripening table off. This is always fine with me as I don't know what I would do with my extra tomatoes if it were not for him. I am always happy to see him come over wanting tomatoes.

He arrived using a walking cane and hobbled his way to the garage door. I explained to him that I might be growing marijuana but didn't think so. I showed him my hibiscus plants.

Harvey only took one small bag of tomatoes. He looked at my hibiscus plants and told me that my other next door neighbor, a policeman, might be interested in them. He told me to watch out for helicopters flying around because, "Those people are not out for a joy ride, they are looking for plants."

Marijuana or Hibiscus?

I then told Harvey that I intended to plant them along the fence separating our property and asked if he would report me. He said, "It just depends on how large of a reward they offer."

Harvey then left with his small bag of tomatoes and moved much faster going home than he did when he came over. He took one final glance at my plants as he left! He forgot and left his walking cane on my covered patio.

My next visitor was Fred Thebus. Fred gets most all of my garden surplus that Harvey does not want.

Fred brought over a special six pack of beer that he wanted me to try. Over a beer sitting on the patio, I explained my dilemma with the hibiscus plants. He looked at the two regular leaved plants and said "Now those are hibiscus plants." He said he didn't know what the other two were but they looked suspicious.

It came up a thunderstorm about that time and blew my plants over. I told Fred, "I had better bring in my marijuana plants!"

I told Fred that I wouldn't know what they really were until they bloomed. I told him that if they were hibiscus plants they would have large red blooms on them. If they didn't have hibiscus blooms on them, I would place plastic bags over the seed heads to keep them from pollinating. I had seen a special on TV years ago where they did this and got the most potent kind of marijuana. I think they called it Sesimilla. Anyway it brought about $2,000 a seed head way back then!

The rain had slacked up by then and Fred decided he had to go. He didn't want any more of his beer. He just gathered up a small sack of zucchini squash, some egg plants, a few tomatoes and left. He did not even wait for me to pick him some cucumbers, which his family loves. He waited until he got home to call me and ask me a question about something that he had initially came over to find out!

Well anyway, I enjoyed Fred's beer after he left.

I intend to call both Harvey and Fred and invite them to come over to see my hibiscus plants when they start blooming.

But, as always, the joke may be on me. They may not have hibiscus blooms on them. The laugh will then be on me. I don't know exactly how I will explain my way out of that one. I may even have to tell my story to the police!

Marijauana? Next to the sunflower and normal hibiscus

45

Mistaken Loyalty

(Written for Lindsey when she was thinking about dropping out of school.)

When I was about 15 or 16, I had a very trying crossroads to face. You have to understand where I came from to appreciate this story.

My great grandfather, Richard T. Tidwell, fought in the Civil War. Things were very tough back when he started his family. He bought a rough scrabble farm and built a log house on it.

With his first wife, he had four daughters which he loved dearly. His first wife died at an early age.

With his second wife, he had four sons. He considered them as field hands and used them like they were in servitude, as most farmers did back then. My great grandfather was very successful as a farmer in later years due to his sons and a steady income from his crops. Some say he turned this corn into corn liquor or white lightning. A lot of farmers did this back then and in times before. The truth rests with their long dead memories. Nobody in modern times ever knew if this was true or not. I don't doubt it as the signs were there still when I was growing up. Barrels sunk into springs and other signs that could be of a bootlegger. Nobody ever knew this for sure but family stories substantiated this. Remember, times were tough back then!

His sons were poor dirt farmers like him but they never did accumulate the business knowledge attributed to him.

My grandfather approved of lying about my father's age to let him join the Civilian Conservation Corps when he was 15 or 16. My dad grew up in Oregon and later Florida where he met my mother.

Dad's first station was in Scottsboro, Alabama, where he received his first training. He and I looked for the site of this old camp once when he was visiting. We never did find it. I later located this camp from details from an old man who had delivered milk from his family farm to the camp. He made keys at Word Lumber Company until he retired.

When dad visited, I had just made some booths for a carnival at Caldwell School. I set them up and the local press came out to take pictures. Dad didn't want to be in any of them but they got him anyway. He thought some of the local women might recognize him and cause problems. The older Tidwells always did have a way with women! I think this has been lost, or at least, I hope my grandsons don't inherit it!

Most of dad's salary from the CCC corps was sent directly to his parents. They used this money to keep the family farm from ending up in foreclosure and taken away from them. Grandpa later gave my dad five acres from the family farm for this service. I remember Grandfather Nathan telling everyone that the property line would run from the elm tree on the road to the cherry tree way back on the hill and then back to the road. The elm tree is still there, but my mother hit it head on and totaled a car. The scar is still visible. The cherry tree is long gone and replaced by a railroad tie set into the ground. Dad finally got this land when Grandmother Alice sold the family farm.

When I was 15 or 16, dad and his first cousin, William Tidwell, found a farm in Tennessee. They thought they wanted it but decided they couldn't afford the payments. Neither one of them had much money.

Anyway, I went with them to look at the farm. I volunteered to drop out of school to work the farm. There was a small crib in the corner of the barn where I told them I could make my bed. It was small and I would probably have frozen to death during the winter. It was just a couple of one by tens tacked into a corner.

I believe they would have taken me up if they could have afforded it!

Well, they didn't get the farm.

I finished high school and college. This is the basis of my later success in life.

This is why I have stressed to my children and grandchildren that they get a good education!

Children of 15 or 16 have a funny sense of family loyalty. They are willing to make the mistaken sacrifices they think are necessary for the family.

These sacrifices are not really needed anymore and do more harm to the children than they realize at the time.

It will demote them to a lifestyle of servitude for the rest of their lives.

Lindsey, this was written just for you. I don't want you to end up in servitude to your family!

There is no need for this. You will realize soon that you have your own life to live.

I and Grandma don't want you to end up with no education, a low paying job and no way out of your predicament!

Grandpa

Even Roses Have Thorns

Lindsey's Story

Lindsey Brooke Hancock, my granddaughter, was born Lindsey Brooke Wininger on March 2, 1992 at the Jackson County hospital in Alabama. She says it was at 7:17 PM. I don't remember the time but I was certainly there.

Lindsey has faced enough trials and tribulations in her 16 short years to try even the soul of the strongest adult and make them want to throw up their hands and give up trying. She has remained remarkably upbeat through all of this and faces each challenge that life throws her way with the grace one would expect from a much older person. Lindsey's grandma and I are extremely proud of her accomplishments.

Lindsey's mom married her father when both of them had just finished high school at Scottsboro High. They have two surviving children. This was a case of children trying to raise children. Her parents divorced soon after Lindsey was born and I doubt that she has any memories of living with her biological dad. It was years later before Lindsey's mom would allow any contact between Lindsey and her older brother and their other grandparents.

Lindsey's mom married again to a Hancock soon after the divorce and they all moved to Kentucky. Lindsey had a stable or semi-stable home life for a while in Kentucky. Her mom's second husband adopted the two oldest children so that they would all have the same last name. This marriage dissolved soon afterward and the separation was messy. Lindsey's mom showed up on our front porch one day with four children in tow.

The schools in Kentucky were not up to par with ours in Scottsboro. They moved Lindsey back one grade and she had to take a special class for slow readers when she enrolled in Nelson Elementary. She was in this program for two years.

We helped all of them in any manner that we could, but they were soon in a place of their own. The separation and divorce became messier and messier. Lindsey's stepdad would come over to our house, or theirs, hyped up on something, we suspected Meth, to slash tires and break windows. We called the police over numerous times. They would chase him down and haul him off. He would shortly be out of jail and back to his destructive ways. He later was convicted of burglary and sent to prison for several years.

All of this took a heavy toll on the emotional stability of the children.

As a single mom, Lindsey's mom had to get a job to support the children. She had to work night shifts and leave the children while she worked. We kept them at first but as Lindsey and her brother grew older, their mom would leave the younger ones at home under the older children's care.

Lindsey's mom worked hard and it was all she could do to provide food, clothing and shelter for them. Neither of her ex-husbands contributed anything financially to the family. Lindsey's mom is to be commended for her heroic effort to keep everyone's body and soul together.

The children soon became independent and resented taking any direction from us or anyone else. They visited us less and less.

We were there to offer understanding, support, love and what semblance of a stable family life we could.

I cannot say that the children had a dysfunctional family. They had little normal family life at all. They became just a group of people living in the same house and having to share the same fate.

Lindsey joined the school band in junior high and in high school. Being a member of this group acted as a substitute for family life for her. She soon had a circle of friends and they got her interested in church. Lindsey began to lose interest in keeping up her grades about this time. There was no one at home to make sure she did her homework. Her friends and activities soon began to dominate her life. Especially band!

Lindsey's first major disappointment came in junior high school. Lindsey's mom could not keep up with the payments on her Clarinet. The people who provided the band instruments came and took her Clarinet one day in front of the entire class. Lindsey was humiliated as well as very embarrassed by this happening in front of all of her friends. Her mom had not warned Lindsey that this might happen.

We had an old Clarinet refurbished that one of Lindsey's aunts had used in school and gave it to her so she could stay in band. Lindsey was on top of the world again! We bought her a new one when the old one literally fell apart.

Again Lindsey remained generally upbeat and faced the challenges of life as they came her way. She started going through adolescence about this time and it dealt with her pretty hard. As with most girls of this age, she would be on top of the world one minute and be in a deep moody blue funk the next hour. She would then be back on top of the world in a little while.

Lindsey realized that her grades were not good enough to stay in band sometime about the middle of 9th grade in 2008. She decided that her best option was to drop out of school and get her GED later. She would not discuss her reasons with anyone. She had made her mind up and that was that!

I cannot say enough good things about Mr. Hancock, the Scottsboro High School Principal and Mrs. Petty and Mrs. Kirby, the counselors at Scottsboro High. They are all dedicated professionals and went out of their way for Lindsey. I am sure they do the same thing for any student in a difficult predicament. They tried to do everything they could to persuade Lindsey to stay in school, but Lindsey had made her mind up. Lindsey did drop out of school for about a month before she decided she would go back. She told me that she was looking at her band uniform in the closet one day and realized that she could never wear it again. This is what changed her mind.

Lindsey's dream was to remain in band and to do whatever it took to be able to do so.

Lindsey called Mrs. Kirby, as I understand it, to see if she could still pass if she came back to school. Mrs. Kirby persuaded Lindsey to give it another try.

Lindsey did fail Algebra and History but Mr. Hancock, Scottsboro High School Principal and Mrs. Kirby offered her a way around it. She would have to go to summer school but could take only Algebra. Mrs. Petty arranged for Lindsey to take her History class through a correspondence course from the University of Alabama. Mrs. Petty did not gloss anything over and told us that this would be a most demanding and difficult challenge. She told Lindsey that high school students usually do not do very well in this course. I promised to help tutor Lindsey. Three chapters had to be completed and mailed in each week.

Lindsey said she would do whatever she had to so she could stay in band. Mrs. Petty explained to Lindsey that she had to make a B or better in each course to pull up her other grades enough. Lindsey was more determined about this than I have ever seen her about anything else. She would do it or "bust a gut" trying in my opinion!

So started the summer of "Boot Camp Purgatory" for both Lindsey, me and grandma. Grandma had to put up with us. I don't recommend this to anyone as a fun way to spend the summer.

I would pick Lindsey up from home at 9:30 to 10:00 every morning. We would study History until she had to go to her four hour Algebra class at 1:00 PM each day. It was back home to study History from 5:00 PM until whatever time it took to complete that lesson. There were several 10 hour and longer days. Lindsey did finish her assignments in time each Friday so she could take the week end off.

The homework consisted of one or more chapters in a textbook that we had to order from the University of Alabama. True - false, multiple choice questions and essays were required on most lessons. The homework for some lessons was nothing but essay questions. The homework questions were sent in a spiral bound book from the University of Alabama and the questions were tricky. Some could be answered in several ways.

What I am particularly proud of was that Lindsey lost no points on any essay question. We would discuss the question and I would tell her what had to be included. The rest was up to her. I did not even read her essays sometimes. She completely amazed me with those that I did read. You should see the one about Louis XV! She wrote all of them in ink except for the first few lessons. The submitted lessons had to be in ink and she only wanted to do it once!

I think that Lindsey must have inherited something about writing from her grandpa!

She made a 96% average on her homework!

Lindsey did start band camp during the last three weeks of summer vacation and has been fitted for her new band uniform. She has completed everything in her History course except taking the Final Exam. That will happen on Monday in late July.

I was at the High School this Monday to set up a date and time for Lindsey's final exam. Mrs. Kirby told me about her conversations with Lindsey when she wanted to drop out of school. I am sure that the only reason that Lindsey did remain in school was because of Mrs. Kirby's positive attitude!

Mrs. Kirby said that she was so proud of Lindsey. She said that she was so proud of how hard Lindsey had tried to achieve her goal and that it was good that Lindsey had a dream. She added that Lindsey had a bunch of lemons but had made lemonade out of them.

My wife, Lana and Lindsey's grandma, summed everything up much closer to the point for me. We were discussing the situation the other day and the home life that the children have. We would both like to do more for them but can only do something when one of the children make their desires known to us. Anything more from us would be perceived as meddling. We can't tell anyone what they should do, we can only offer suggestions. I made the comment of "Life never guaranteed anyone a bed of roses." Lana said "Jerry, remember even roses have thorns!"

I am so proud of Lindsey for having the dream to stay in school and be in the band and to make whatever sacrifice she had to so that she could make her dream come true. She has made tremendous improvements in other area this summer as well. Her vocabulary, reading skills, attention span and study habits have all shown remarkable improvements. Lindsey and I have been able to bond this summer as never before. She is becoming less of a girl and more of a woman every day. I picked her up from home during her lunch break from band camp this Wednesday. She wanted to go to Burger King, her favorite eating establishment, and eat inside. I had been working in the garden all day and had not cleaned up. I was hot, sweaty, dirty and in the rags I wear in the garden. I looked like a bum. There were a lot of her friends from band camp there as well. She spoke to everyone. I apologized to her for embarrassing her in front of her friends and for looking like a smelly tramp. She looked at me and said, "You can never embarrass me, you are my grandpa." My heart grew two sizes larger with pride that day as Dr. Seuss would have said!

I now know that she will make a fine well adjusted young woman. She already is in my book.

Pink Hair

The Continuation of Lindsey's Story

I was rooked into this one! I am very naive about these kinds of things! Especially when it comes to women or soon to become women!

What could I do against the conniving mind of a soon to be woman? Nothing!

This story all started off innocently enough. Lindsey mentioned that she had her mother's approval to change her hair color. This was just after we had been up to the Scottsboro High School to check on the availability of summer school.

Well, I stopped at Wal-Mart and gave her some money. I did not go in with Lindsey as I know nothing about hair coloring. She had change left but I told her to keep it! I didn't know that the dye she wanted was fluorescent pink!

Lindsey had beautiful blond hair. Not from a bottle, just naturally!

When I picked her up again to check on summer school. She had slightly pink highlights in her hair. I didn't know it at the time but she had a pact with her friends to do something radical with their hair this summer. I understand now that her closest friend had decided to highlight her hair with florescent green! Grandpas are sometimes slow on the learning curve!

I think that Lindsey and her friends, while they are good kids, are mutually self-destructive! They reinforce each other in the wrong way when they are together.

I picked Lindsey up to take her to the school to finalize the plans for summer school. She had definite pink highlights in front and in her bangs. She looked like she was trying to be a punk star!

I mentioned this to Mrs. Petty, one of the school councilors, but she ignored it. She was just interested into getting Lindsey into summer school and the University Of Alabama correspondence course!

Lindsey did get into the programs. She made a C in algebra and a B in the correspondence course.

But in the meantime, her hair got pinker and pinker. I didn't know what to do!

As it turned out, the school system solved my problem. They told everyone with these radical hair colors that they had to dye their hair darker and the same color or they could not come back to school!

Lindsey tried to dye her hair a darker blond but the pink turned out to be purple. Her friends thought this was "cool." Grandpa didn't agree though!

The word finally came down from the school authorities that Lindsey had to change her hair color to the same or she could not come back to school! Her grandmother mentioned parting it on the other side and covering everything up. Lindsey would not listen to this because she has her hair layered and she didn't think it would look right. Young girls are not practical!

We got down to the last day. Lindsey called me in hysterics. I told her I would come over.

I told her she had several options. First she could part her hair on the other side. She would not even consider this.

I then told her she could borrow one of her grandmother's wigs. She became more agitated with this idea. An old woman's wig - Never!

I then told her we could go to a professional beautician and have her hair dyed. The only place open at that time was Wal-Mart. She flatly told me that she was not going up there and let them mess her hair up!

We compromised by her going to the Wal-Mart beauty shop and getting their recommendation. We would then get the color of dye that they recommended and she could dye it on her own.

I thought this was a reasonable plan. We walked into the beauty shop at Wal-Mart and Lindsey did not even want to ask for suggestions. She just did this because I insisted on it. Then the beautician turned around. She had jet black hair that was obviously dyed and fluorescent flamingo red highlights. Lindsey was immediately captivated! I explained the situation to the beautician and asked when she might work Lindsey in. She said right now! That was luck. Lindsey had to go back to school the next day.

Lindsey sat right down in the chair and the woman went to work. The color she chose was a medium brown. Lindsey and this woman became friends during the hour and a half time this process took. They were both going to communicate with each other on "My Space." Imagine, both had fluorescent highlights in their hair!

Lindsey's hair turned out beautifully. There were blond and lighter highlights in her hair. There was even a natural looking sheen!

Lindsey said this was her most desired color for her hair. She did look much better than with "glow in the dark" pinkish purple highlights!

Lindsey was very happy. I am sure the school officials were pleased as well.

Lindsey has not called me since. I am sure that things went well at school. She only calls me when she needs something.

The downside to all of this was I spent about ten dollars for the original dye packet that I didn't even know what I had bought and seventy dollars for the final dye job!

She did look beautiful with the new color but not as good as I thought she did as a blonde.

Well, what do grandpas know anyway?

Grandpa does know this. There is a lot of girl in this young woman yet! She will grow into a spicy woman like her grandma. I just hope that she can find a young man that will love and appreciate her and hopefully just be able to keep up with her!

46

The Last White Pine Tree Falls

We originally had four white pine trees in our yard, two in the front yard and two in the back.

The first one was a live Christmas tree that we planted after the holiday season. It made a particularly lovely tree. Lana liked it so much that we had the other three planted about thirty years ago.

The first one started to die about twenty years after it was planted. No amount of watering or spraying it with chemicals helped it much. It had sentimental attachments for Lana because she and our oldest daughter, Sonya, had planted it. Lana gave me strict orders--I had to save it if I could. We even had Cook's Pest Control to come out to spray it twice.

Nothing we did helped it much. I had the Jackson County Forester come out and give me his opinion. He said there was nothing we could do. White pine trees were native to our area a hundred years or so ago but a fungus had wiped them all out. He said that about as long as you could get them to live here now was twenty years.

It took the tree a couple of more years to completely die and it got scraggier and scraggier looking each year. I had someone come out to take it down and haul it to the ditch when it finally passed on.

Pine beetles got two of the others over the years and I took them down with my bow saw.

This left the sole survivor in the back yard. This was the one that I had hung my bird feeders from. I particularly loved sitting out under its shade on a hot spring or summer day. It made a very dense shade and you could catch the breezes that came from any direction. It always seemed cooler under there than anywhere else in the yard.

This sole surviving tree had begun to show signs of distress for the previous three years. Some of the needles on the lower branches had started to turn brown and I had started watering it regularly. This always perked it up and I decided the problem was caused by the dry summers we had had for the past few years.

About two weeks after I had bought my hibiscus (marijuana?) plants, Lana and I could still not agree on where I should plant them. I wanted to plant them along the fence but she didn't want them there. She even started calling them my marijuana plants all of the time. She would tell me when the wind had blown my marijuana over, or when my marijuana plants needed water. They still had not bloomed and I still didn't know exactly what they were.

As things turned out the way they did, it is a good thing that we disagreed on where they should be planted.

I had cut the grass one day and it was particularly hot and dry. I did little but raise a cloud of dust with my lawn mower and it all seemed to collect on me and the lawn mower. I pulled the mower out near the pine tree and hosed it off. I came into the house to check on the weather as they had forecasts thunder storms for that afternoon.

I saw a big red line of storms coming our way from the north. I knew I had to get the lawn mower back into the garage right away!

I was a little too late. The wind had started to blow from the north as soon as I got up on the mower. It blew so hard that it blew my campaign hat back and the strap caught around my neck. I was trying to get the hat back on which caused me to look at the pine tree.

Suddenly an even bigger gust hit the pine tree, blew my hat back again and the pine tree started to move, directly toward me or so it seemed. The pine tree was between thirty to thirty-five feet tall by then I guessed by stepping it off after it fell and was a good 14 inches in diameter.

There I was, perched in the seat of my lawn mower with no place to move. I just watched the tree getting closer and closer. It hit the ground about three feet from the lawn mower with a swishing whomp! There I sat, bug-eyed, dumbfounded, and very glad that I had not washed the lawn mower any closer to the tree!

Lana came home about an hour later and noticed that the tree was down immediately. We went out and looked it over. She said that the last place she would have looked for me was buried under the pine tree!

The entire root system of the pine tree had started to rot and decay. There was very little left to anchor it to the ground. It was just waiting for a wind to blow it over. Fortunately the wind came from exactly the right direction and the tree missed everything in the back yard when it fell, me and the lawn mower included.

This ended most of the bird feeding though. The birds were disoriented, as were the three squirrels who fed there. The birds were used to hiding in its cover and flitting down to eat from the feeders when they were hungry.

The birds came back and sought cover in the downed pine tree and starting looking for their feeders. The squirrels came to investigate and ran up and down the tree trunk, trying to figure out what had happened. The bird feeders were buried under all of the pine tree limbs.

The birds and squirrels were still trying to find food in the vacant area three weeks after the pine tree had been cleaned up.

The birds were still eating about twenty pounds of various kinds of food a week when the pine tree went down. I dug the feeders out from under all of the rubble and they were unharmed. I hung them along the fence on shepherd's crooks the next day. I still wanted to feed the birds because we had a pair of golden finches that had stayed here all summer. They usually just migrate through in early spring and fall. They nest in northern climates. I was trying to get them established in this area.

271

The birds don't like to eat from the feeders by the fence. There is very little cover for them and we have a number of hawks flying around from July Mountain. The golden finches are still here as well as a number of other finches.

I was sitting on the patio the afternoon that the pine tree had hit the ground so spectacularly and was trying to come up with a plan to get it cut up and out of the backyard.

I got my trusty bow saw out and began to saw the limbs off. This was slow going but I had removed about two or three when a neighbor came over and volunteered to help. He said that he had been a forester most of his life and had a friend who had some chainsaws and experience as a forester as well. He asked if I needed any help. I was really glad to see him.

He and his friend, as well as another neighbor, came over and made short work of cutting it up and hauled it to the ditch in less than forty-five minutes. I asked what I owed them and they didn't want any money at first, but then mentioned an absurdly low price. They had even cut the stump out and pulled it to the ditch with their truck. I paid them twice what they had wanted and was happy to find out that I had such wonderful neighbors. They seemed to be happy as well.

I guess that one might say that this was my last career as a lumberjack, even though I only cut off three small branches!

I then surveyed the hole left in the ground by the pine tree. It still left a sizable hole, even though most of the roots had rotted. This was about the proper size and would be the perfect spot to plant my hibiscus (marijuana?) plants. They still had not bloomed.

I headed to Wal-Mart to get some bags of topsoil and potting soil. I first had to dig down where I was going to set out the plants to get up all of the roots so that I could plant them as deep as they needed to be planted. This took some doing and I broke my towing strap trying to pull out a stubborn root and had to go buy another one.

I planted everything mulched it good with shredded pine bark and watered it.

The hibiscus rewarded me about two weeks later with the loveliest, largest red and other color hibiscus blooms that I have ever seen. Mostly red ones but there were a few pink and burgundy ones as well. They seem to love their new home and have put on a lot of new growth. They bloom only on the new growth. I still have dozens of buds forming and they dazzle everyone with their show of color that gets to see them. Lana stills calls them my marijuana plants occasionally but not as often as she did. She will even occasionally admit they are funny looking marijuana blooms, even though neither of us ever remembers seeing a marijuana bloom.

The seasons of this year have cycled through spring, summer and autumn is almost here. The cold chilling winds of winter will surely not be far behind.

This causes me to reflect and to especially compare the cycling of natural seasons with the cycles of my life. I have described some of my experiences and the people that I knew while growing up, which would be my spring. I have also described some of my adventures and misadventures and the people that I have known in adulthood, which would be my summer.

The autumn of my life is now on me with winter sure to follow. This is the natural order of things.

It has taken me sixty-six years to experiences the things that I have tried to share. I have shared some of them but not nearly all of them.

I am sure there will be stories from the next sixty-six years but I will not be an active part of them. I can only participate now pretty much from the sidelines. I will probably be so decrepit and have arthritic joints by then that I will be unable to type them anyway. Especially if I get my hand caught in a table saw again and mangle any more fingers.

Perhaps some of my grandchildren or great-grandchildren will write them for me. I hope so. Some of my grandchildren are already budding writers.

48

Family Memorials

Richard T. Tidwell is buried in the Tidwell cemetery near Killen, Alabama.

The inscription on his grave marker reads:
R. T. Tidwell
April 1 1845
Oct 4 1917
A tender father and
A faithful friend

Richard T. Tidwell's First Family.

The grave marker for **Rebecca McGee Tidwell**, first wife, has not been found. I believe that she is probably buried in the Tidwell cemetery, along with son William, but without formal grave markers. Facing Richard T. Tidwell's grave marker from the foot of the grave there is an adult sized grave to the immediate left of Richard T.'s grave. It is marked by a large flat triangular stone at the head and a smaller sized stone at the foot. The head stone was covered with leaves and I tripped over it. This is identical to the early grave markers that I found in the old part of the Harrison cemetery near Killen, the oldest cemetery that I visited. Her children and their families are given as follows:

Grave marker for **Derinda Naomi Oma Tidwell Peck.** Peck cemetery, Killen, Alabama.

Grave marker for **Mattie B. Tidwell Phillips .** The old Lexington cemetery in Lexington, Alabama.

Grave marker for **Florence Alabama "Bama" Hale**. The old Killen cemetery, Killen, Alabama.

It is not known where **Fannie Tidwell Brewer** died. Her grave marker has not been located. From Uncle Albert's note her children lived in Colorado and she could be buried there.

Derinda Naomi Oma Tidwell Peck's Family.

All grave markers are in the Peck cemetery, Killen, Alabama, except for Percy D. Peck.

Derinda Naomi Oma Tidwell Peck is buried next to her first husband **Andrew Peck.**

John Samuel Peck was Oma's second husband and is the father of her children.

Percy D. Peck died elsewhere. His burial site is unknown.

Granville Alison Peck

Dalma Bama Susan Peck.

Bessie M. Peck Martindale

Lucian Peck

Hiarm Peck

278

Lucile Lucy Peck Covington

Fred T. Peck

Albert Peck

279

Walter Lee Peck

Emma Mattie Peck Covington

The grave marker of **Mattie B. Tidwell Phillips** in the old Lexington, Alabama cemetery.

Grave marker of **Andrew Lee Phillips**, Mattie's husband, in the old Lexington, Alabama cemetery, as are most of their children.

The location of **Ora C. Phillips Taylor's** grave marker is not known. She died in Florence, Alabama, in the late 1970s.

Pete Phillips

Edward A. "Polly" Phillips

Mary Phillips died in Florida according to Virgiline Tidwell Hale. The location of her grave marker is not known. Ancestry.com lists her full name as Mary Elizabeth Phillips born May 15, 1906 in Lexington, Alabama. She died about 1993 in Mobile, Alabama, and her husband is listed as H. L. Worral.

Martha Isabell Phillips White.

Rebecca "Becky" Phillips Houf.

Uncle Albert's Note

Typed as written by Albert Henry Tidwell before 1951 if the family stories are true about him having to reconstruct his family history in order to join Social Security since he did not have a birth certificate. Uncle Albert's social security number was issued before 1951 according to the Social Security Death Index.

I was able to obtain the original handwritten note from Ollie Tidwell and typed it for a crude family history that I was doing in 1997. Uncle Albert had written down the 1/2 heirs of Richard T. Tidwell and listed only their husband's initials.

I have retyped it for this work.

Our father Richard Tidwell married three times.

1) The first wife was Rebecca McGee who was the mother of these ½ heirs.

   a) Mrs. L. L. Phillips

   b) Mrs. W. A. Hale

   c) Mrs. J. S. Peck

   d) Mrs. T. W. Brewer

2) The second marriage was to Nannie Urban and their children were:

   a) Jesse (Jesse) Tidwell

   b) Albert H. Tidwell

   c) Edward Tidwell

   d) Nathan Jerry Tidwell

3) The third marriage was to Mrs. L. C. Denison who had no children by our father.

   The heirs of Mrs. J. S. Peck were:

   a) Percy Peck Address unknown - Somewhere in Texas

   b) Bernie Peck - Address unknown - Somewhere in Texas

   c) Walter Peck - Address unknown - Somewhere in Texas

   d) Lutie Mobley - Address unknown - Somewhere in Alabama

   e) Granville Peck - Florence, Alabama

   f) Bama Peck - Address unknown

   g) Bessie Martindale - Killen, Alabama., Rt 1

   h) Lucile Covington - Killen, Alabama

   i) Mattie Covington - Rogersville, Alabama

   j) Albert Peck - Killen, Alabama

   The heirs of Mrs. T. W. Brewer were.

a) Willie Brewer - Lived in Colorado - Address unknown

b) Kathleen Brewer - Lived in Colorado - Address unknown

c) Thomas Brewer - Pueblo, Colorado

d) Elizabeth Lewis - Pueblo, Colorado

Richard T. Tidwell's Second Family

Nancy C. Erbin, second wife is buried in the Tidwell cemetery near Killen, Alabama.

Her grave marker inscription reads:

Nannie Tidwell
1863
Dec 18 1896
A tender mother and
A faithful friend

All of Nannie and Richard T. Tidwell's sons and a lot of their descendents are buried in the Cox cemetery near Killen, Alabama.

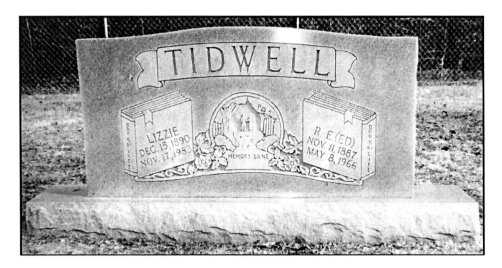

<u>Richard Edward Tidwell</u> (Cox cemetery)

<u>Albert Henry Tidwell</u> (Cox cemetery)

Jesse F. Tidwell (Cox cemetery)

Nathan J. Tidwell and **Alice Genova Reid Tidwell** (Cox cemetery)

Richard Edward Tidwell Family

The burial site of **Robert Tidwell** is not known.

The burial site of **Annie Mae Tidwell Wallace** is not known.

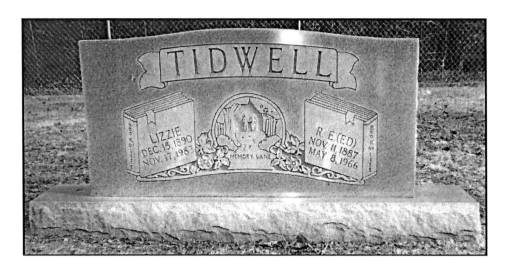

Uncle Ed and Aunt Lizzie (Cox cemetery)

Lou Edna Tidwell (Cox cemetery)

Albert Henry Tidwell Family.

Albert Henry Tidwell (Cox cemetery)

Wife Cleavie Lee Haygod Tidwell (Cox cemetery)

Daughter Vernon Tidwell (Cox Cemetery)

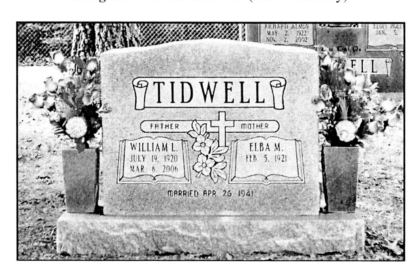

Son William Tidwell (Cox cemetery)

Ethel Tidwell Hendrix is the only surviving child of **Albert H. and Cleavie L. Tidwell.** The burial sites of the other children are not known to the author.

Jesse F. Tidwell Family

Jesse F. Tidwell never married and had no family. (Cox cemetery)

Nathan Jerry Tidwell's Family

Nathan Jerry and Alice Genova Tidwell (Cox cemetery)

Walter Glen Tidwell died in Mobile, Alabama, and is buried there. A photograph of his grave marker is not currently available.

Richard Almon and Elois Holloway Tidwell (Cox Cemetery)

Russell Almon Sr. and Debra Kay Snoddy Tidwell (Cox cemetery)

Reba Jane Tidwell and husband **Oscar Finney Gray** (Cox cemetery)

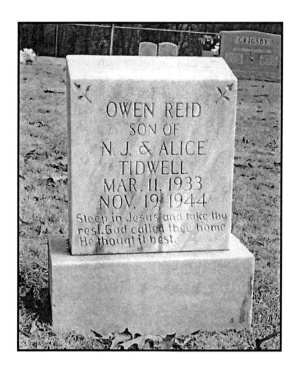

Owen Reid Tidwell (Cox cemetery)

Lucinda Tidwell (wife number three) is buried in the Tidwell cemetery near Killen, Alabama.

Her grave stone inscription reads

Lucinda Tidwell
Died
Sept 16 1916
We will meet again
293

John Dee Tidwell Family

John Dee and Derendia Tidwell (Cox cemetery)

Emma Tidwell Cox and Guy Cox (Cox cemetery)

Beulah Tidwell Grigsby and Irskine Grigsby (Cox cemetery)

Doc and Maggie Tidwell (Cox Cemetery)

Mattie "Matt" Tidwell Myrick and John Myrick (Old Killen cemetery)

Ella Tidwell Cox and Ray Cox (Harrison cemetery)

Richard McBride Tidwell is buried in the Tri-Cities Memorial Garden in Florence, Alabama.

Ann Laura Tidwell Stutts and **Alan Stutts** (Old Killen Cemetery)

296

Doxie Oliver and Maggie Tidwell Family

Uncle Doc and Aunt Mag (Cox cemetery)

Earl E. Tidwell (Cox Cemetery)

Where **Virgiline Tidwell Hale** will be buried. J. T. Is already there. Hale Cemetery near Killen, Alabama.

Floyd Arvel (Bud) Tidwell is buried in the Cox cemetery near Killen, Alabama, but no grave marker has been erected yet.

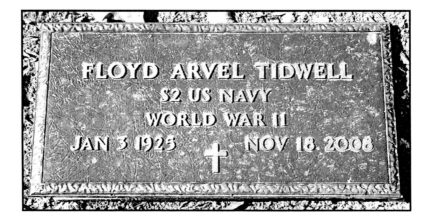

Floyd Arvel (Bud) Tidwell's foot marker commemorating his service in World War II

Marguerite Tidwell and **Gilbert Trousdale** (Antioch cemetery near Killen, Alabama)

Christopher Columbus Everett Reid

Confederate Monument marking the common grave of prisoners who died at The Federal Civil War Prison at Alton Illinois.

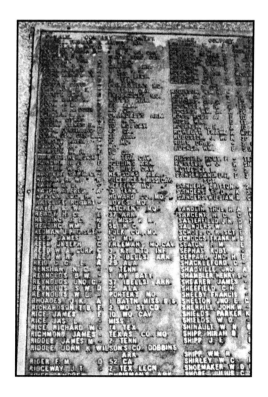

Listing of all the known names of men buried in a common grave placed on the Confederate Monument.

Different Views of the Confederate Monument marking the common grave at the site of the Federal Civil War Prison at Alton, Illinois. Top clockwise bronze plaque listing the known names of men buried there, another bronze plaque on the monument, a view of the monument at nightfall, a view of the monument during the day.

John Wesley and Emma Jane Owen Reid

Richard McBride Tidwell Family

Richard Kenneth Tidwell (Tri-Cities Memorial Garden, Florence, Alabama)

Marjorie Thompson Tidwell (Tri-Cities Memorial Garden, Florence, Alabama)

Charles Allen Tidwell (Tri-Cities Memorial Garden, Florence, Alabama)

49

Tiki Lanterns

I have been looking at Tiki lanterns now for several years. My thought was to ring my covered patio with them.

I buy most of my Diet Mountain Dews and a few other things normally from the Dollar General store near where I live. They had Tiki lanterns for two dollars each during one of my last visits. I looked at them closely but could not tell from the way they were wrapped if they had candles with large wicks or a metal reservoir. I decided that since they only cost two dollars each it must be candles. I bought four to give them a try.

When I arrived home, I took them out of the back of my truck and carried them to the patio. Lana ask why I had bought such an item but settled down when I told her the low price. She walked away shaking her head thinking that for sure I was getting senile or even worse was losing it completely. I don't know for a fact but she probably started looking in the yellow pages for old folks homes!

I eagerly unwrapped the first one and it had a metal canister for lamp oil. I didn't have any lamp oil and it took me two days to find some in our small town. I filled the metal reservoirs and stuck the bamboo poles in the ground around the patio. It was dry in early July of this year and I had to soak the spots where I would place them with water before I could get them into the ground.

We had had no rain in over a week and everything in my garden was wilting for lack of moisture. I have three garden patches and I was in the process of watering them that day. I would run the water for four hours on one patch and then move the sprinkler. Watering from overhead like I was doing can only be done in late afternoon or after dark in the above 95 degree temperature we were experiencing.

I had to turn off the water off at 9 p.m. that night for the patch I was watering. I was tired that afternoon and took a nap but set the alarm clock to wake me to turn the water off.

The temperature had cooled into the low 70's by the time I went out to turn the water off. The katydids and other insects in the trees in the surrounding yards were making the same pleasing night sounds that instantly took me back to having to sit out on the front porch for the house to cool down at the old log house of my childhood. I could never sit out on the patio for long before this late at night or the ruthless bites of mosquitoes would make it so uncomfortable that anyone sitting outside with me, would follow my lead in swatting their way back into the house.

But tonight I lit the Tiki lanterns. The lanterns immediately flared up and the flames quickly established themselves at six to eight inches tall with flashes upward of ten inches and began to emit a copious amount of smoke. This did not concern me as we had a slight breeze from the north that quickly carried it away. The lamp oil was scented with a citrus odor and the smoke did not smell like lamp oil smoke. It had a slight odor that was not unpleasant to smell at all.

303

Insects were immediately captivated by the flames. They would circle the flames once or perhaps twice, mostly in a clockwise direction, but no more. I don't know if they were incinerated by the flame or the smoke and heat drove them away. There were large insects, some moths and many small insects that I thought must have been mosquitoes.

No bugs or insects of any kind on the patio tonight.

I quickly went in and turned off all the lights on the back side of the house and navigated my way back to the patio by touch. The entire patio was lit in a rich golden glow. It reminded me of the familiar golden glow the old kerosene lamps gave off at the old log house. This carried me back in time to a simpler place that I remember only with warm thoughts and feelings. In the distance, I could hear people engaged in loud conversation. Closing my eyes, I could almost believe it was a conversation between Uncle Doc, Aunt Mag and Grandmother Alice discussing religion out on the front porch of the old log house.

That started my trip down memory lane. The details of my book were fresh on my mind and I began to reflect on the stories that I have included in it. I learned a good deal from the research that was required for it and I documented for posterity what I witnessed firsthand before these stories were lost in the deep, dark and endless bog of time. From conception to writing and then publishing it has been a journey of some two years and was preceded by a brief work that I did some ten years ago. I used this work as an outline.

The only thing missing from this night was the ever present animal smells from the barnyard on the old farm. Animals of all kind must leave droppings and we didn't keep the barn as clean as our ancestors probably did. There was the musty smell from the horses, mules and cows. Then there was the sharp acrid smell from the hog pen. Hogs will always root out any depression in the hog pen and quickly make a mud hole out of it. They would wallow in this mud hole and leave their waste there, both solid and liquid. The sun would soon heat it and it would sit there and fester and smell more rank and ripe every day. The hogs seemed to like it more and more the smellier it became and would spend most of the day in it. Any small breeze in any direction would make the smells drift day and night and it was always present. One did not have to ask what animals a farmer was tending. His nose would tell him well in advance. Also the ever present smells from the outhouse where we left our own offerings on a daily basis were unmistakable. The old farm was a smelly place.

We used the same hog pen that Richard T. Tidwell had used, Grandpa Nathan used it and we did well up into the 1960s. Many generations of hogs had left their imprint on it and it smelled particularly bad, even after we had killed the hogs in the late fall. I did not miss this part of the old farm this magical night.

Then there were the stories that I did not include. My original goal in this book was to tell what I witnessed firsthand while growing up. I did not write directly about the controversial subjects of sex, religion or politics. I did dance around these subjects and got pretty close to them but I took pains not to address them directly. These stories would have added much color but it would do nobody any good to discuss them. Neither the living nor the dead. Some things are better left in the black and fuzzy bog of time.

Then there were the stories that I did not tell that I never witnessed first hand or heard of before. There was the story about the original name of the Brush Creek community that Virgiline Tidwell Hale and her nephew Donnie Tidwell told me. Donnie bought the only surviving print that the author is aware of featuring John Dee Tidwell taken in front of the old L. D. Holloway Store. The photograph is mounted on an old piece of wrapping paper and is imprinted with L. D. Holloway Store. Virgiline Tidwell Hale said that Hiram Cox worked here. This photograph was obtained by Donnie during the auction of Marguerite Tidwell Trousdale's estate and is framed. I have never seen it and it is apparently too faded to copy. The money raised by the auction was donated, according to Marguerite and Gilbert Trousdale's will, to the Lauderdale County Christian Nursing Home.

Holloway Town, where Mack Riggs had his original general store business, was named for its original owner L. D. Holloway. There were also four rental houses on the property and a water powered grist mill at one time. Donnie also said the original complex contained a barber shop. This I had never heard of before. Anyway, The building from the original grist mill was still standing when I came along but the barber shop was long gone.

John Dabney, owner of Dabney Wholesale Grocery in Florence, Alabama, later bought the property and he established a summer house there. He smoked cigars and the ever present cigar smoke could be smelled from the road. Dad said that John Dabney always paid the local boys to whitewash the numerous tree trunks in front of the house before he took up residence in the summer. Dad also said that the cigar smoke smelled so good that Uncle Walter traded some of his work whitewashing tree trunks one summer for one of those cigars. It apparently smelled better than it tasted when being smoked according to Dad.

John Dabney also built the first swimming pool we were ever aware of. It was a spring fed underground concrete structure that was still standing in my youth. The spring water was too cold to swim in as I remember. The rest of us had to contend with skinny dipping in Brush Creek. It was also very cold water but not as cold as spring water always was.

John Dabney also owned several horses which he would let the children from the neighborhood ride during the summer. This was a treat for all of us as none of us had horses of our own. He would also load up the children sometimes in his Willis station wagon and take us to Killen and treat us to ice cream. This was a special treat for all of us as well.

At some point John Dabney decided to sell his summer home and property. He offered it to dad at a very low price and offered to finance it for him. Dad was a very cautious man and could not see his way clear to buy it. Almon McGee, a friend of dad's and fellow electrician, then approached dad to buy it on the halves but dad could not see that this was a good investment. After John Dabney's death the summer house was sold to a man named Hensley who owned a construction company that built homes in Florence. Almon McGee bought a good portion of the property and perhaps all of it. I don't remember just how much.

This was the same property that Richard T. Tidwell had owned at one time.

Then there was the story that Virgiline Tidwell Hale told me about J. T. Hale having bought and paid for the property where they lived before their marriage. Virgiline had saved an equal amount of money from working at the J. T. Flagg knitting mill in East Florence, Alabama. They used Virgiline's money to build their house. They were short nine hundred and fifty dollars of having enough money to complete the house. Marguerite loaned them the needed money at no interest. Virgiline said they paid back the loan in three months. She also said this is the only money they ever borrowed.

The house was heavily damaged by a storm after J. T. Hale's death. Virgiline built it back in its original configuration using anything that was salvageable and still lives there.

Then there was the story from Joanne Tidwell Forsythe's work about John Dee Tidwell buying his homestead from Mary Ann Urbin(Erbin), mother of Nancy (Nannie) C. Urbin (Erbin), the second wife of Richard T. Tidwell and the mother of all of Richard T's boys. I had never heard this story before.

I was transported back in time and thoroughly enjoyed it. Mesmerized by the setting and sounds--and especially the golden glow of the Tiki lanterns. I was lost in thoughts of long ago. I lost track of time. I sat outside unmolested by the insects for about two hours before the flames of the Tiki lanterns began to burn low and I was forced back to reality.

It was time to blow out the Tiki lanterns and go back inside. So long old memories-- for now. I will light the Tiki lanterns often and return to you. But for now it is off to bed to dream of the dear folks from the special place where I grew up. They will be sweet and most pleasant dreams!

Index

Pruitt, Maurice, 6

R

S

T

U

W

Wallace, Annie Mae Tidwell, 34, 288
Wallace, Selma C. Tidwell, 34
Walter Glen Tidwell, 64, 66, 67, 68, 69
Ward, Trina, 86
Warren, Polly C., 6
Warsop, Thomas, 183
Westmoreland, William, 8
Wheeler, Joseph, 20
White, Carmichael, 29
White, Martha Isabell Phillips, 283
White, William J., 17
Williams, Scott K., 19
Willliams, Scott, 21
Wilson, Alexander, 184

Wilson, Margaret, 184
Wilson, Mary Reid, 184
Wininger, Lindsey Brooke, 263
Woosley, Johnny, 216, 217, 222
Woosley, Red, 216, 217, 222
Worral, H. L., 282

Y

Young, Alsie Carr, 197
Young, Lelia Maud Reid, 196
Young, Loran Richardson, 197
Young, Maud Reid, iii, 199
Young, Orion Owen, 197
Young, Robert Henry, 196
Young, Thomas Jerome, 197

Bluewater Publications is a multi-faceted publishing company capable of meeting all of your reading and publishing needs. Our two-fold aim is to:

1) Provide the market with educationally enlightening and inspiring research and reading materials.

2) Make the opportunity of being published available to any author and or researcher who desires to be published.

We are passionate about preserving history; whether through the re-publishing of an out-of-print classic, or by publishing the research of historians and genealogists. Bluewater Publications is the *Peoples' Choice Publisher*.

For company information or information about how you can be published through Bluewater Publications, please visit:

www.BluewaterPublications.com

Also check Amazon.com to purchase any of the books that we publish.

Confidently Preserving Our Past,
Bluewater Publications.com
Formerly known as Heart of Dixie Publishing

LaVergne, TN USA
26 February 2010

174428LV00001B/1/P